Beginning Programming

Beginning Programming

Adrian and Kathie Kingsley-Hughes

Wiley Publishing, Inc.

Beginning Programming

Published by
Wiley Publishing, Inc.
10475 Crosspoint Boulevard
Indianapolis, IN 46256
www.wiley.com

Copyright © 2005 by Wiley Publishing, Inc., Indianapolis, Indiana

Published simultaneously in Canada

ISBN-13: 978-0-7645-8406-0

ISBN-10: 0-7645-8406-5

Manufactured in the United States of America

10 9 8 7 6 5 4 3 2 1

1MA/SU/QT/QV/IN

About the Authors

Adrian and Kathie Kingsley-Hughes have worked in the PC and programming arena for over 10 years, first using their skills to solve real-world problems for industry before later moving on to teaching others to become programmers. In recent years they have had opportunities to teach programming to thousands of aspiring programmers through online classes. There they discovered the joys of teaching programming to people from all walks of life that had no previous background or experience in programming.

Adrian and Kathie live in beautiful North Wales, UK, and divide their time between the hi-tech world and outdoor leisure activities.

Credits

Acquisitions Editor
Katie Mohr

Senior Development Editor
Kevin Kent

Development Editor
Howard A. Jones

Production Editor
Felicia Robinson

Technical Editor
Wiley-Dreamtech India Pvt Ltd

Copy Editor
Foxxe Editorial Services

Editorial Manager
Mary Beth Wakefield

Vice President & Executive Group Publisher
Richard Swadley

Vice President and Publisher
Joseph B. Wikert

Project Coordinator
Erin Smith

Graphics and Production Specialists
April Farling
Lauren Goddard
Denny Hager
Clint Lahnen
Lynsey Osborn
Rashell Smith
Ron Terry

Quality Control Technicians
Amanda Briggs
John Greenough
Joe Niesen
Carl William Pierce
Brian H. Walls

Proofreading and Indexing
TECHBOOKS Production Services

Contents

Contents

Contents

Contents

Contents

Contents

Contents

Contents

Introduction

With so many computers in general circulation, at work, in homes, and at libraries and schools, it was inevitable that people who were before happy to be "users" would want to take the next step and learn how to make the computer work for them in new ways. They quickly realize that what they need to do is learn the art of becoming a programmer, and one of the first steps is picking up a book like this.

The problem with most programming books is that they assume that the reader either:

❑ Is so enthusiastic that he or she has read loads of material about programming before coming to the book.

❑ Has some background with computers that has exposed him or her to programming before.

We don't assume anything-what we do is to look at programming right from the beginning.

Who This Book Is For

Most computer programming books are aimed at people who are really already on the road to becoming programmers and who want to delve into a particular programming avenue. These people know the difference between a function and an array and know that all good programmers declare variables and use comments.

This book is different-this book is aimed at those who want to learn to be programmers but who haven't had a background that has exposed them to programming or programmers-teachers, pupils, nurses, lawyers, lorry drivers, pilots. People who see the ability to get a computer to work for them as an advantage that they want to have access to.

Before, programming books concentrated on people who wanted to become career programmers. This book is for everyone else!

We're also excited if you've picked this book up because you aspire to be a professional programmer. This book will give you the firm grounding that you need to be able to narrow your field of study and concentrate on the task of specializing in particular programming languages or tasks. In these pages, you won't find any "how to become a work expert programmer in 5 minutes" or "how to write world-beating applications," but what you will find is solid information that will enable you to take your skills in the direction they need to go.

What This Book Covers

The purpose of this book is to allow those who are interested in programming to gather the skills and experience they need to fulfill their goals. The primary focus of this book is, therefore, the skills that are at the core of being a programmer. It shows you the theory of programming and takes a look at this theory in action in real code. I use a variety of languages throughout the book to help demonstrate and explain these concepts.

The languages that you will be looking at include:

❑   C++

❑   Java

❑   VBScript

❑   JavaScript

This book shows numerous examples of these languages in action as well as providing opportunities to use a variety of programming tools and compilers.

How This Book Is Structured

The book has been structured to guide you through the steps you need to take to become proficient in the skills that go to making a good computer programmer. I recommend that you begin with Chapter 1 and work your way through the book, chapter by chapter.

❑   **Chapter 1: What Is Programming?** This chapter looks at what programming actually is and what it means to be a programmer.

❑   **Chapter 2: Why Learn to Program?** This chapter looks at the myriad reasons that people have to want to learn to program and the different routes that individuals can take to become programmers.

❑   **Chapter 3: How Computers "Read" Code.** This chapter examines how computers store and process code. This is intended to give the reader insight into what goes on behind the scenes in a computer.

❑   **Chapter 4: From Concepts to Code-The Language of Code.** This chapter examines the basics of computer languages and how text and numbers are represented in the digital world. Here you'll take a detailed look at how binary and hexadecimal number systems form a key part of code and how ASCII allows alphanumeric characters to be represented as binary.

❑   **Chapter 5: The Tools for Programming.** This chapter looks at the tools that you need to work with source code and become an effective programmer. You'll find out about text editors, compilers, and other utilities that make the whole process of coding a lot easier and less stressful.

❑   **Chapter 6: The Simple Coding.** In this chapter you're taken through the process of writing code that actually works and that actually carries out a task. You'll be introduced to a number of key concepts in programming that are consistent among programming languages.

❑   **Chapter 7: The Structure of Coding.** This chapter delves into how to take code from being just lines of code to giving it structure that enables it to carry out tasks based on various inputs and to allow certain code statements to be run based on the testing of conditions.

❑   **Chapter 8: Problem Solving.** Writing code is all about solving problems, and in this chapter you'll see how best to work through the problem-solving process. This chapter looks at how to break the coding process down into a sequence of smaller, easier-to-manage steps.

- ❑ **Chapter 9: Debugging.** Any time that you write code there is a chance your code is going to contain problems. This chapter looks at the variety of errors that can creep into code and how to spot them and eliminate them.

- ❑ **Chapter 10: Interface.** While you've been creating code you also should have been keeping an eye on how your program is going to look to the end user. This chapter provides hints, tips, and useful practical advice about how to make your applications easy to use.

- ❑ **Chapter 11: Putting It All Together.** So far you've looked at the individual stages of programming. In this chapter, I bring it all together and you go through a programming project from conception to finishing the product. This gives you an opportunity to bring all your skills together to experience the programming process from beginning to end.

- ❑ **Chapter 12: Interacting with Files.** This chapter gives you experience working with the file system and shows you how to create, modify, and delete files and folders.

- ❑ **Chapter 13: The Windows Registry.** The Windows registry is the key storage area for settings applications, and this chapter provides you with experience navigating the registry and looks at how you can write code that accesses, reads, and modifies the registry.

- ❑ **Chapter 14: Organizing, Planning, and Version Control.** Keeping track of your project and the code that goes into it is important if you are not going to find the coding process stressful and hard work. This chapter is concerned with how to keep control over your source code and how to handle the files that you will be creating.

- ❑ **Chapter 15: Compiling Code and Alternatives to Compiling.** This chapter shows you the code compiling process and looks at the benefits that compiling code brings to the programmer.

- ❑ **Chapter 16: Distributing Your Project.** In this, the final chapter, you examine ways that you can distribute your code or applications to your end users. You'll see a variety of schemes you can use to get your code to those who want to use it.

What You Need to Use This Book

All the tools and materials you need to work with this book are easily available on the Internet or already installed on your computer.

Mainly you will be using a text editor for creating code. Windows Notepad is ideal for this, but if you want something with a lot more power you can use a variety of alternatives, some free, some commercial.

The tool that I will be using is called UltraEdit, a powerful commercial package that you can download from www.ultraedit.com. This is the best text-editing tool that I have come across for programmers. It's not free but it certainly gets the job done. If you don't want to use this, you are free to use a free alternative.

You will also need access to compilers. The main compiler that I will be using is the free Borland C++ compiler. You can download this compiler from www.borland.com/products/downloads/download_cbuilder.html.

Other tools that you will need will be introduced as they are needed.

Conventions

To help you get the most from the text and keep track of what's happening, I've used a number of conventions throughout the book.

> **Boxes like this one hold important, not-to-be forgotten information that is directly relevant to the surrounding text.**

Tips, hints, tricks, and asides to the current discussion are offset and placed in italics like this.

As for styles in the text:

❑   I *italicize* important words when I introduce them.

❑   I show keyboard strokes like this: Ctrl+A.

❑   I show filenames, URLs, and code within the text like this: persistence.properties.

❑   I present code in two different ways:

```
In code examples we highlight new and important code with a gray background.
```

```
The gray highlighting is not used for code that's less important in the present
context or that has been shown before.
```

Source Code

As you work through the examples in this book, you may choose either to type in all the code manually or to use the source code files that accompany the book. All of the source code used in this book is available for downloading at www.wrox.com. Once at the site, simply locate the book's title (either by using the Search box or by using one of the title lists) and click the Download Code link on the book's detail page to obtain all the source code for the book.

Because many books have similar titles, you may find it easiest to search by ISBN; for this book the ISBN is 0-7645-8406-5.

Once you download the code, just decompress it with your favorite compression tool. Alternately you can go to the main Wrox code download page at www.wrox.com/dynamic/books/download.aspx to see the code available for this book and all other Wrox books.

Errata

We make every effort to ensure that there are no errors in the text or in the code. However, no one is perfect, and mistakes do occur. If you find an error in one of our books, such as a spelling mistake or faulty piece of code, we would be very grateful for your feedback. By sending in errata you may save another reader hours of frustration and at the same time you will be helping us provide even higher-quality information.

To find the errata page for this book, go to www.wrox.com and locate the title using the Search box or one of the title lists. Then, on the book details page, click the Book Errata link. On this page, you can view all errata that has been submitted for this book and posted by Wrox editors. A complete book list including links to each book's errata is also available at www.wrox.com/misc-pages/booklist.shtml.

If you don't spot "your" error on the Book Errata page, go to www.wrox.com/contact/techsupport.shtml and complete the form there to send us the error you have found. We'll check the information and, if appropriate, post a message to the book's errata page and fix the problem in subsequent editions of the book.

p2p.wrox.com

For author and peer discussion, join the P2P forums at p2p.wrox.com. The forums are a Web-based system for you to post messages relating to Wrox books and related technologies and interact with other readers and technology users. The forums offer a subscription feature to e-mail you topics of interest of your choosing when new posts are made to the forums. Wrox authors, editors, other industry experts, and your fellow readers are present on these forums.

At http://p2p.wrox.com you will find a number of different forums that will help you not only as you read this book, but also as you develop your own applications. To join the forums, just follow these steps:

1. Go to p2p.wrox.com and click the Register link.
2. Read the terms of use and click Agree.
3. Complete the required information to join as well as any optional information you wish to provide and click Submit.
4. You will receive an e-mail with information describing how to verify your account and complete the joining process.

You can read messages in the forums without joining P2P; but in order to post your own messages, you must join.

Once you join, you can post new messages and respond to messages that other users post. You can read messages at any time on the Web. If you would like to have new messages from a particular forum e-mailed to you, click the Subscribe to this Forum icon by the forum name in the forum listing.

For more information about how to use the Wrox P2P, be sure to read the P2P FAQs for answers to questions about how the forum software works as well as many common questions specific to P2P and Wrox books. To read the FAQs, click the FAQ link on any P2P page.

What Is Programming?

If you've picked up a book on programming, you must have a pretty good idea what programming is. After all, why would you want to learn something if you don't know what it is? However, many students who are new to the wonderful world of programming, or even practitioners of the art who have learned a little programming to do a particular job and built on their experience from there, might benefit from a quick rundown of the history of programming, what programming is, and where it's at right now.

The History of Programming

The history of programming spans more years than most people would imagine. Many people think programming is an invention of the late twentieth century. In fact, the history of modern programming and programming languages dates back nearly 60 years to the mid-1940s.

However, before we pick up the story in the 1940s, we need to go still farther back in time, all the way back to 1822 and Charles Babbage. While he was studying at Cambridge University in Britain, Babbage came upon the realization that many of the calculating devices of the time, such as astronomical tables, tidal charts, and navigational charts, all contained critical errors and omissions. These errors caused the loss of many ships at sea, along with lives and cargo. Because he considered human error to be the source of these inaccuracies, his idea was to take the guesswork out of creating and maintaining such tables and charts by using steam-powered machines. One such machine, dubbed the Difference Engine, was to occupy much of Babbage's time for the rest of his life. He even approached the British government for financial assistance — the first (but by no means last) request for a government grant to fund computer science research.

After 10 years of working on the Difference Engine, Babbage realized that it was a single-purpose machine that could ultimately only carry out one operation. He realized that this was a major limitation and, for a time, abandoned it in favor of the more versatile Analytical Engine. This engine would contain the basic components of a modern computer and led to Babbage's being called the "father of the computer." The Analytical Engine did not gain wide acceptance because Babbage suffered from an affliction that has plagued programmers and computer scientists across the centuries: an inability to clearly document and convey his ideas!

Work on the Analytical Engine continued until 1842, when the British government, tired of the lack of progress and results, abandoned the idea and withdrew its funding. However, Babbage still continued to work on it until 1847 when he returned to work on the Difference Engine, and between then and 1849 he completed 21 detailed drawings for the construction of the second version of the engine. However, Babbage never got around to actually completing either of the devices. In fact, it wasn't until after Babbage's death in 1871 that his son, Henry Prevost, built several copies of the simple arithmetic unit of the Difference Engine and sent them to various institutions around the world, including Harvard University, to ensure their preservation.

Progress continued throughout the 1800s, and in 1854 Charles Boole described the symbolic logic system that bears his name (Boolean logic) which is still in use today (and is covered later in this book). This system took logic terms such as greater than, less than, equal to, and not equal to and created a symbolic system to represent them.

It's said that necessity is the mother of invention, and necessity came to a head in 1890 when the U.S. Congress wanted to add more questions to the census. The increasing U.S. population meant that processing this data took longer and longer, and it was estimated that the census data for 1890 would not be processed before the 1900 census unless something could be done to improve and speed up the process.

So, a competition was created to drum up interest in computing and to deliver data processing equipment to the government. This contest was won by Herman Hollerith, and after successfully proving the technology, he went on to process census information in other countries and later founded a company called Hollerith Tabulating Co. (This company eventually became one of three that joined together in 1914 to create CTR, the Calculating Tabulating Recording Company. That name might not be familiar to you, but 10 years later the company was renamed International Business Machines, or IBM — a name you will undoubtedly have heard of!)

Hollerith also has another first to his name — his machines were the first ever to appear on a magazine cover!

Progress then seemed to slow down a little and by the mid-1920s digital computing tools were rarely used in business, industry, or engineering. In fact, the tool most commonly used was the humble analog slide rule. Things began to change in 1925, however, when, while at MIT, Vannevar Bush built a large-scale differential analyzer that incorporated integration and differentiation capability. This massive creation was funded by the Rockefeller Foundation and was the largest "computer" in the world in 1930.

The next major player in this story is a German scientist by the name of Konrad Zuse. In 1935, Zuse developed his Z-1 computer. What was more remarkable than the fact that he built this computer in his parents' living room was that this was the first computer to make use of relays and to be based on the binary system of counting. It was the first of its kind and heralded the modern age of computers.

Zuse continued his work and developed the Z-2 in 1938 with the help of Helmut Schreyer. He applied for financial assistance from the German government in developing and constructing his machines, but he was turned down because the project would take longer to complete than the war was expected to last. Zuse eventually fled to Hinterstein when the war came to an end, later making his way to Switzerland where he rebuilt his Z-4 machine at the University of Zurich.

It is Zuse who also gave birth to modern programming in 1946 when he developed the world's first programming language, called Plankalkül. He even went as far as writing code for the Z-3 to play chess against him. This language was groundbreaking and contained much of what is seen in modern languages, such as tables and data structures.

Zuse later went on to found a computer company that was eventually integrated into the Siemens Corporation.

The year 1945 saw another important development in computing, the introduction of the one word that we are all pretty sick of hearing — bug! In 1945, Grace Murray Hopper (later Admiral Hopper) was working on the Harvard University Mark II Aiken Relay Calculator. Machines in those days experienced continuous problems, and during one of these incidents on September 9, 1945, an investigation by a technician revealed that there was a moth trapped in between the circuitry (the record shows that it was in the points of Relay #70, on Panel F). The technician removed the moth and affixed it to the logbook that documented the computer's use and problems. The entry in the logbook reads: "First actual case of bug being found." The phrase that was born from this was that the machine had been "debugged" and the terms "debugging a computer" and later "debugging a computer program" were born.

History does show that although Grace Hopper was always careful to admit that she was not there when it actually happened, it was one of her favorite stories that she recounted often.

Things now begin to speed up. The year 1949 saw the development of a language called *Short Code*. This code had to be made into machine-readable code by hand (a process known as *compiling*), so there was very little about it that was "short."

In 1954, IBM began developing a language called FORTRAN (which stands for *FORmula TRANslator*). FORTRAN was published in 1959 and became an immediate success because of its easy-to-use input and output system and because the code was short and easy to follow (and is still in use in some places today). FORTRAN also was the first commercial high-level programming language, meaning that the code was easier for a human to read because it follows the familiar rules of syntax, grammar, and structure.

In 1958, FORTRAN II and ALGOL were published, as well as work being carried out on LISP, while in 1959 another popular and long-lived language called COBOL (Common Business Oriented Language) was created at the Data Systems and Languages conference (CODASYL). COBOL is a commercial institutional language used primarily on large machines and is still used in many companies today.

Things continued at breakneck speed with many new languages and variants on existing languages developed and released. During 1968, work started on a language called *Pascal*. Pascal was released in 1970 and is still used extensively for educational purposes. The year 1970 also saw the publication of two other languages that revolutionized computing. These are Smalltalk and B-language. Smalltalk was important because it was a language based completely on objects (don't worry about this just yet), and B-language was important because of what it led to.

What did B-language lead on to? Well, in 1972 Dennis Ritchie created a language based on B-language which he eventually called C (after calling it NB for a while). C brought with it simplicity, efficiency, and flexibility and heralded a new age in programming in which it was possible to do a lot more with less code, more quickly and easily than before.

The year 1975 saw the release of TinyBASIC by Dr Wong. TinyBASIC took only 2 KB of memory and was loaded onto the computer via paper tape. It was groundbreaking too because it was the first known freeware (that is, it was free to use and did not need to be purchased) program.

The text strings "All Wrongs Reserved" and "Copyleft" were found within this program.

Coincidently, 1975 was also the year that a young Bill Gates and Paul Allen wrote and sold to MIT their own version of the BASIC language.

Things continued at breakneck speed throughout the 1970s, 1980s, and 1990s, with more and more developments that lead us to where we are now: with a myriad of different programming languages that each has its own strengths and weaknesses. We've also seen the appearance of the Internet, which has bought with it a whole host of languages. The other huge advantage of the Internet is that it is now easy to share information and programs with others, meaning that the interest in programming and programming languages has grown and grown, fueled by the free exchange of information, ideas, and applications.

We've taken a brief trip through the history of programming, highlighting some of the main events that bought us to where we are now. With that done, it's time to take a look at what programming actually is.

What Is Programming?

There is no single answer to this question. Programming means different things to different people. However, there is a definition I've come up with that I'm quite happy with:

Programming is the ability to talk to the computer in a language it can understand and using grammar and syntax that it can follow to get it to perform useful tasks for you.

Put into its simplest terms, that's all that programming is! You write code and the computer interprets your request and does something.

Doing something is a vital part of programming. You always program the computer to do something (even if that is waiting for another instruction!). Programming is all about doing something and moving forward. Whenever you are programming, no matter how simple or complicated your task, you are always giving the computer an instruction. Usually these instructions are given one at a time. Even though sometimes it can seem as if you're asking your computer to do a lot of different things "all at once," you are in fact giving it step-by-step instructions as to what to do.

The code also has to be correct and unambiguous. It can't contain any mistakes, errors or ambiguity. Any of these cause the code to fail and errors to occur. There is no capacity for the computer to make guesses about what you meant or to correct your code as it goes along.

Another thing you will notice as you begin to program is that rarely will you write code that does only one thing and one thing only. Even the simplest of projects usually consists of several steps, for example:

1. Program is executed.
2. Initial parameters are checked.
3. Parameters are changed.
4. Clear up after running.
5. Program exits.

Why So Many Programming Languages?

But if you are giving the computer instructions in a form that it can understand, how come there are so many different programming languages? Surely you write in code that the computer understands?

Well, while it's true that different types of computer understand different types of code (so a PC is fundamentally different from a Macintosh), each type of computer really only understands one language, and that's not the language you write code in. The code you type in is not the code that the computer then goes on to understand. A program (either an interpreter or a compiler) is required to convert the code from text into a binary language that the computer can decipher. This is the great part about computer language.

A computer operates by reading instructions in binary, which you might be familiar with. It is a number system but it differs from our usual base 10 system by only having two digits — 0 and 1. Figure 1-1 shows the decimal numbers 0 to 9 represented as binary.

Decimal digits: 0, 1, 2, 3, 4, 5, 6, 7, 8, 9
Binary bits: 0, 1

Decimal	Binary
0	0
1	1
2	10
3	11
4	100
5	101
6	110
7	111
8	1000
9	1001

Figure 1-1

Now take a close look at Figure 1-2.

```
0100001001101001101101110011000010111001001111001001000000110100101110011001 10010000
0011101000110010101100100011010010110111101110101011100011001000000110000101 101110
0110010000100000011010010110011000100000001110111011001010010000001101000011 00
0000110100101101110001000000011000100110100101101110011000010111001001111001 00100
0000011101110110100101110100011010000001000001101111011101101011001000100000 011
0001101101111011011010111000001110101011101000110010101110010011100110010000 0111
0101011100110110100101101110011001110000011010010111010000010000001100001011
0100011011000010000001110100011010000110010100100000011101000011010010110110101
10010100100000011101000110100001101001011011100110011101111001001000000111011101
1011110111010101011011000010010000010000001100111011001010111010000010000001110110 01
1000101011001001110010010000000110001101101111011010101110000011011000110100 1011
0001101100001011101000110010101100100000010000001101001011011100110010001100 10101
1001010110010000010000000101000011000010110110001110100011010000011011110111 01010
11001110110100000010000001101111011101010111010000010000001101011011001010111 100101
10001001101111011000010111001001100100001110011001000000011101110110101111011 1101011
0110001100100001000000011000100110010100100000001100001001000000011011000110 11111
01110100001000000111001101101001001101101011100000110110001100101011100100000 10000
1001010010010110
```

Figure 1-2

Binary is tedious and if we had to work in binary with our computers using it all the time things would get very complicated indeed (although our keyboards would be a lot simpler!).

Wondering what Figure 1-2 means? That's the last paragraph written out with binary used to represent the letters using a system called ASCII (American Standard Code for Information Interchange). Don't worry just yet about what all that means (later on you will be able to come back to that and read it if you want), for now, just be thankful that programming will not mean writing out endless streams of zeros and ones!

When you are programming, or, more specifically, writing code, what you are actually doing is writing code that another program can understand to translate that code into something that the computer can understand, hence the name *interpreter*. So, when you are writing code, it is not the rules of the computer you have to follow, but rather the rules of the interpreter (or, similarly, the compiler) which will translate that code into something the computer understands.

Figure 1-3 shows a simplified diagram showing the code-writing process:

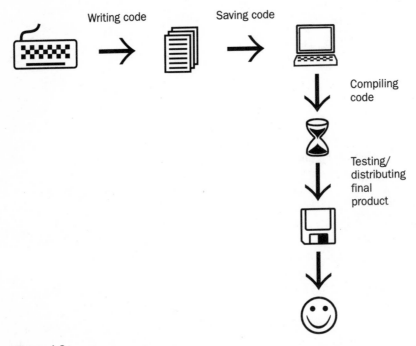

Figure 1-3

Different Code, Same Results

Just to show you how different code can achieve the same results, take a look at the following code in different languages, some of which you may have heard of.

BASIC

```
10 print "Hello World!"
20 goto 10
```

Atari BASIC

```
10 REM HELLO.BAS
20 POKE 764,255
30 PRINT "Hello World"
40 IF PEEK(764)=255 THEN GOTO 30
```

C

```
#include <stdio.h>

main()
{
for(;;)
{
printf ("Hello World!\n");
}
}
```

C++

Old version of C++ code:

```
#include <iostream.h>

main()
{
for(;;)
{
cout << "Hello World! ";
}}
```

Newer version of the code:

```
#include <iostream>

int main()
{
std::cout << "Hello, World!\n";
}
```

COBOL

```
000100 IDENTIFICATION DIVISION.
000200 PROGRAM-ID. HELLOWORLD.
000300 DATE-WRITTEN. 02/09/04 17:24.
000400* AUTHOR FRED F
000500 ENVIRONMENT DIVISION.
000600 CONFIGURATION SECTION.
000700 SOURCE-COMPUTER. RM-COBOL.
000800 OBJECT-COMPUTER. RM-COBOL.
000900
001000 DATA DIVISION.
001100 FILE SECTION.
001200
100000 PROCEDURE DIVISION.
100100
100200 MAIN-LOGIC SECTION.
100300 BEGIN.
100400 DISPLAY " " LINE 1 POSITION 1 ERASE EOS.
100500 DISPLAY "HELLO, WORLD." LINE 15 POSITION 10.
100600 STOP RUN.
100700 MAIN-LOGIC-EXIT.
100800 EXIT.
```

FORTRAN

```
c
c Hello, world.
c
Program Hello

implicit none
logical DONE

DO while (.NOT. DONE)
write(*,10)
END DO
10 format('Hello, World.')
END
```

Java

```
class HelloWorld {
public static void main (String args[]) {
for (;;) {
System.out.print("Hello World ");
}
}
}
```

JavaScript

```
<title>
Hello World in JavaScript
</title>
<script>
alert("Hello, World!")
</script>
```

Mathematica

```
While[True, Print["Hello, World!"]]
```

Pascal

```
Program Hello (Input, Output);

Begin
Writeln ('Hello World!');
End.
```

Perl

```
print "Hello, World!\n" while (1);
```

Python

```
while (1) :
print "Hello World";
```

QBASIC

```
begin:
print "Hello World!"
goto begin
```

Smalltalk

```
Transcript show:'Hello World';cr
```

Visual Basic

```
Private Sub Form_Load()
Static I
I = 1
for I = 1 to 10
msgbox "Hello, World!"
Next I
end sub
```

VRML

```
#VRML V1.0 ascii

AsciiText {
string "Hello, World!"
justification LEFT
}
```

All of this code written in a variety of languages does one thing: it shows the words Hello, World! on the screen in one form or another.

Figure 1-4 shows an example of what it looks like in C++:

Figure 1-4

Figure 1-5 shows what is displayed by JavaScript:

Figure 1-5

Why "Hello, World!"?

Why is it that "Hello, World!" is used in so many programming examples? The origin and history behind this statement is heavily laden with urban legend and myth. However, it does seem that the first tutorial that contained a reference to Hello, World! was for the B-language that predates C.

It seems that before that it was used as a simple way to determine that everything was set up right and the language worked. So, who am I to break with tradition?!

Programs Needed to Create Programs

So, can you create programs from scratch? Well, you could, and the people who trail-blazed before you needed to do this, but after creating the first languages one of the first things that computer scientists started creating were programs to make writing other programs easier. Once this happened it became easier and quicker to write code in a particular language. Soon one language was used to create tools to work with a completely different (or new) language. This enabled newer languages to have greater complexity and sophistication, which means that they end up being able to do more.

There are two kinds of program that help you write code and make programs:

❑   A development environment

❑   A compiler

The interpreter mentioned before is not needed to write code, only to run it.

Development Environment

A development environment is a program that you use to type the code into. Some languages need a specific development environment (for example, Visual Basic), while others need only a simple text editor (JavaScript is an example of a language you can work with using nothing more than a text editor). There is also a huge array of languages where you have a choice as to what development environment to use (C++ is one such language).

Development environments are discussed in more detail later, for now, just knowing that they exist is enough!

Compilers

A compiler is a program that changes the code you type into code that the computer can understand. This process is known as *compilation*.

The compiler reads the code that you type, checking it for errors and making sure that it follows all the rules and makes sense. If problems with your code are found, the compiler should (if it's a good compiler) tell you about it and halt the process. If no problems are found, the compiler outputs a file that you can run (or execute) on its own, and it should carry out the instructions as laid out in your code. On a PC this file is typically called an executable file and has a file extension *.exe*, as shown in Figure 1-6.

Figure 1-6

Summary

In this chapter, we've looked at what programming really is. Now I'm not expecting that after this chapter you should have any idea how to write a program, but you should have gotten a sense (albeit brief!) of the following:

- ❑ The history of programming
- ❑ An introduction to some programming languages
- ❑ A sneak peek at some code
- ❑ An overview of the programming process, from code to executable
- ❑ An exposure to some important programming terminology

In the next chapter, we'll look at why you *really do* need to learn how to program!

Why Learn to Program?

Why learn to program? A very good question! Learning to program isn't something you can do in 5 minutes, and there are so many avenues that you can take and options for you to choose from that even getting into programming can seem complicated.

And once you're learning to program, when do you stop? How many languages? Which of the new avenues will you pursue?

In this chapter, I'll help you to answer a few simple questions so you can plan your programming path early on. A little bit of planning at the early stages will not only help you make the right choices at the start, saving you time and energy and allowing you to concentrate on what you want to do rather than what you think you need to do, but will also let you see what doors programming can open that will be of interest to you later in your career.

> I say "programming career" often. When I say this I don't mean that you should make a career out of programming in the traditional sense where you use it to make money (although there's nothing wrong with that). What I mean is that learning to program is a mini-career in itself. You'll begin by learning a little, and then for a while you'll concentrate on applying that skill. In the meantime, you'll learn more. The more you program the more you'll learn. Along the way, you'll make some decisions (such as what languages to learn and what avenues to follow), which will mold your future programming career even more.
>
> Not to mention the fact that learning to program can be a lifelong study . . . all the more reason to call it a career!

So, before we get stuck in some code, let's look at the reasons behind learning to program!

Why Program?

Even if you've already decided that you want to learn to program, it's not a bad idea to think about the reasons behind your desire to herd the 0s and 1s!

I find that there are several categories of people who want to learn to program. Here are some of the broader of the categories:

The "Career" Programmer

Unsurprisingly, the number one reason that people want to learn to program is so that they can make a career move. Anyone with a computer or that surfs the Web cannot help but notice that there are programs and Web pages everywhere. All of these programs, Web pages, and graphics have been written by someone, as has all the software that controls everything behind the scenes that you don't see. Learning to program is seen as the key that will unlock the door to all this, making a myriad of new opportunities available.

And all of this is perfectly true.

If you are in a job you don't want to be in and think that programming will provide you with the keys to help open new doors, you are absolutely correct. Learning to program will do that and also gives you options. You could take the traditional route and look for work within the established industry. The demand for programmers swells and collapses with economic health and prosperity, but even during hard times the programmer has always fared well because programming is seen as a specialist skill, and in a software company the programmers are the craftsmen and -women at the frontline actually making products. So, while belts may be tightened in some parts of the company, the programmer's job can often be quite safe.

Another option open to you is to take a gamble and become a freelance programmer and work for yourself. This way you can pick and choose the companies and jobs that interest you.

Many freelance programmers also enjoy flexibility, so if you like changing scenery often and meeting and working with new people you can look for and take jobs that move you about, whereas if you dislike that you can look for opportunities that allow you to work from home, working your own hours. Typical programming contracts can vary in length from a few weeks to months to several years.

> *If self-employment is an option that interests you, make sure that along with learning to program you also bone up on setting up companies, bookkeeping, corporate law, and contracts.*
>
> *Don't leave these things to chance!*

Another option open to you is to use your programming skills to unleash your creative and inventive side and create, develop, and release your own software applications. To do this successfully, generally you need to find a niche where there is a need, then create software that fulfills that need. If there is already software serving that niche you need to make yours different in some way. Here are a few ways that small software makers have given the big boys a run for their money:

❑ **Cheaper software.** Because you are much smaller than the big boys, you will be able to serve the market more cheaply. Being cheaper means that your software is accessible to more people too, thus increasing your sales.

❑ **Market knowledge.** Do you know what people want? Can you see a need? Do you know how much people would pay? These are important questions, and if you've got answers to these questions you are in a strong position to take advantage of this fact!

❑   **More specific features.** So much commercial software is heavily influenced by marketing departments that insist on features in software that they think the user will want. The problem is that these marketing people aren't usually the people who will be using the software in the long term. If you already work in a field that is being served by software you think could be improved upon, then you have a massive advantage!

❑   **Better support.** Because you know the software you've created intimately, you are in a good position to be able to provide excellent support for it.

❑   **Lower distribution costs.** It costs a lot of money to release commercial software — creating CDs, boxes, and promotional material; getting it to the stores; and so on. Then, once the software is at the store, the store will want a cut of the price too, adding to the cost to the end user. You, on the other hand, could release the software on the Internet at a low cost. You can pass this saving on to your customers.

❑   **Small, fast, focused.** Because you're not going to have to please marketing people by making your software flashy, you can concentrate on getting it to do its job and do it well. It's a well-known fact that some of the most robust, bug-free software available comes in the form of shareware from small companies or individuals.

Even when there is already free software filling a need, there is always room for improvement. Take text editors. As far back as the Windows operating system goes, it has always come loaded with a text editor — Windows Notepad (see Figure 2-1).

```
form validation.TXT - Notepad
File  Edit  Format  View  Help
<SCRIPT LANGUAGE="JavaScript">
<!--
function validate(frm) {
    //
    // Check the Email field to see if any characters were entered
    //
    if (frm.title1.value.length == 0)
    {
        alert("Please enter a title for the photo.")
        frm.title1.focus()
        return false
    }
        if (frm.desc1.value.length == 0)
    {
        alert("Please enter a description for the photo.")
        frm.desc1.focus()
        return false
    }
        if (frm.key1.value.length == 0)
    {
        alert("Please enter keywords for the photo.")
        frm.key1.focus()
        return false
    }
}
//-->
</SCRIPT>
```

Figure 2-1

You would think from this that there would be no need whatsoever for another text editor and that the market (at least the Windows market) would have been well and truly stitched up. Not so. One of my favorite shareware programs is in fact a text editor called UltraEdit (www.ultraedit.com), shown in Figure 2-2.

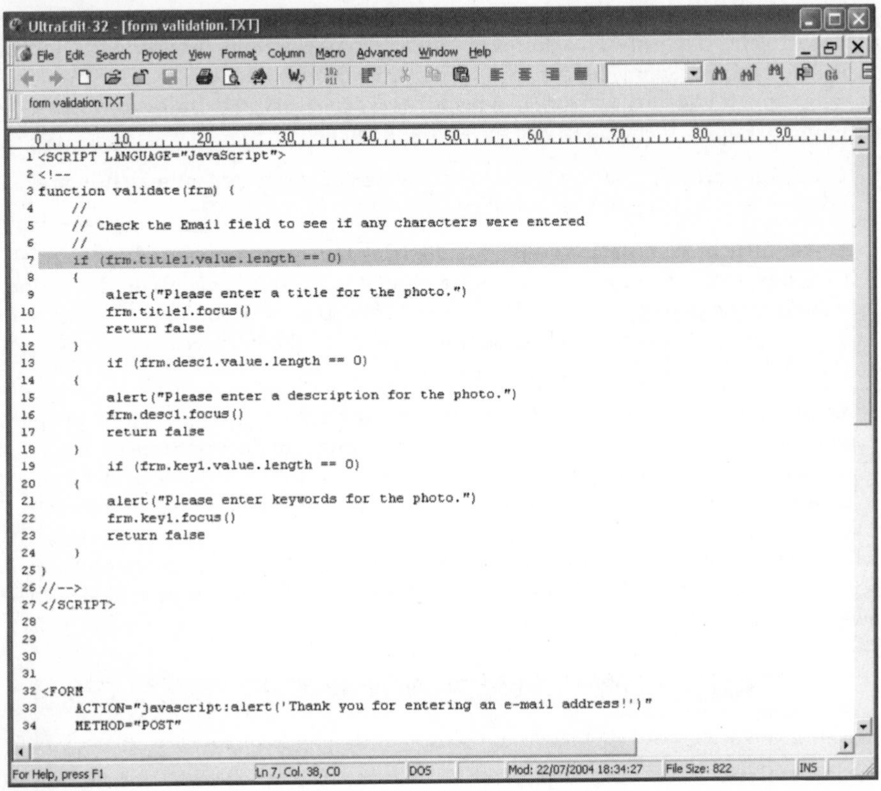

Figure 2-2

This amazing software application has been around since 1994 and continues to grow in success and is the creation of one man — Ian Mead. He took the idea of developing a text editor that did what people wanted and ended up creating the award-winning UltraEdit.

> UltraEdit is fantastic text editor and the only one I use now because it does everything that I want of a text editor. Every programmer needs a good text editor, and this one is mine. Take a look in Appendix B for a list of tools, including text editors. Most offer a free trial, so give a few a test drive and find the one that suits your needs.

Don't think that there is no hope for your idea just because it's been done before. Just one improvement or betterment can make a huge difference (but if you can add a whole raft of improvements, so much the better!).

Problem Solving

Another reason that people want to learn to program is that they see programming as a tool that will help them solve problems, either at work or in their personal lives. They see a problem that they think programming could solve.

The variety of scale of such projects can be huge. The problem could be a small one (such as an application that does a simple numerical calculation). This might be something that is solved by a few lines of code (in fact, I've seen people solve an irritating problem that they have been facing for months or years with just one line of code!). Or the problem can be something far more complicated that needs a lot of coding (for example, an application that makes work or a hobby easier by making it computer-based rather than paper-based).

There are several factors that will decide whether the problem is something you should try to solve by learning to program yourself or by getting someone in who can already program.

How Big Is the Project?

The smaller the initial project, the better. The best way to learn how to program is by taking small steps and making small chunks. This way you get positive reinforcement along the way because you are actually writing programs, solving problems, and seeing yourself progress. Working on small projects also gives you a good programming foundation because you get to practice the basics a lot.

Nothing is more disheartening for learner programmers than to find themselves in the position where they have a massive project ahead of them that they don't seem to be making any progress on.

If the project that you want to work on is a big one and you don't want to waste time on smaller projects, then the best course of action for you to take is to break the project down into smaller parts and learn what you need to learn to prototype aspects of the program.

Another problem with jumping feet first into a big project is that as you learn more you'll discover you've done things wrong in the beginning and so will need to go back and rewrite huge segments of code. Planning and coding a big application takes practice to prevent you from making the coding equivalents of taking a wrong turn and going down dead ends. Also, the better you get at programming, the more efficient you become at writing code. An application that in the beginning might have taken you 1000 lines of code may only take you 300 when you know a little more. Seven hundred fewer lines of code mean a faster application and fewer lines of code to have to debug!

Is the Project Time Critical?

Time-critical projects are usually ones that are the worst to start off your programming career on. The pressure of time, followed by the fear of failure, makes it almost a no-win situation for most people. Add to that the fact that if you do take the burden upon yourself and run out of time, you'll feel pretty bad about it and might not carry on learning to program.

Only you know how you operate under pressure. Some people thrive under pressure, and if you are one of those people, then this might be just the kind of challenge you need to learn programming fast. However, most people aren't wired that way and find that the stress of deadlines looming affects their performance and inhibits their learning, which is why I don't recommend it.

Work or Hobby?

Is the project a work-related project or a hobby? A hobby project is one you can devote time to when you have it, but a work-related project is one where you might have more pressure on you to knuckle down and make progress.

As a rule, the less stress on you, the better. That enables you to learn without the pressure of having to deliver something or justify your progress.

However, don't discount work-based projects. Work might make available to you the time and resources you need to become a programmer.

Check out to whether your employer offers any programming-related training courses.

Because You Want to Contribute

Open source is becoming more and more common nowadays. Open source is a term used to indicate that the source code for a particular application or piece of software is made available freely to others to look at, experiment with, and improve upon. Open-source software is generally free software, and it owes its existence to the hard work and dedication of countless programmers all around the world.

Some people who have been making use of open-source software (especially those who have been active in the community testing software or suggesting new features) soon begin to feel that they should, and can, begin to contribute to the ongoing success of the project. And why not? They have access to the source code and a community of programmers who are willing to devote time and effort (and sometimes cash) to a project. Many people involved in these kinds of projects are extremely generous with their time and knowledge and will offer a helping hand to a beginner.

If you are involved in such a community, have a look around and see if they offer some support to budding programmers — you might be lucky!

Just for Fun

I've had conversations along the following lines many times:

Me: "So, you want to learn to program?"

Student: "Yes."

Me: "Why? Is it for work or a hobby project that you have in mind?"

Student: "Hmmm . . . well . . . I just want to learn because I think it will be fun."

This is not as crazy as it sounds. Some people do crosswords for fun, or play chess, or go running or hiking, or work on their car or truck, or go to the movies, or play games. Why not program for fun? It's challenging, it's mentally stimulating, you learn something, and it can lead to loads of other things. If you are one of the lucky ones who is learning to program "just for fun," you have a huge advantage because you will approach the subject in a relaxed state, give it all you've got for as long as you want, and then leave it for a while until you are ready for some more. In this state, you'll be surprised how much you learn and how effortless it will feel — people learning for fun are lucky!

Fame

Learning to program for fame? Forget it!

What to Learn?

The brief history of programming I gave you in the previous chapter should have made you aware of the fact that the term "programming" has massive scope — different languages, different applications, and different reasons. It can all seem overwhelming, and it can seem as if there's several lifetime's worth of studying to do.

Because of this it's important for you to work out early on what areas of programming you are interested in following.

The sooner you refine "programming" into something more specific, the better. Then you can narrow down your focus and concentrate of learning specifics instead of spending your time being generic.

Programming Avenues

There are two main programming areas that you can choose from:

Remember, just because you decide on one particular avenue of programming right now doesn't mean that you aren't free to change your mind later and pursue another. It also doesn't mean that you shouldn't get more programming languages under your belt later.

Coming to a decision now only helps to focus your attention on what's important to get you going. Once you are using one language comfortably, you can then experiment with others.

- ❑ Traditional programming
- ❑ Web programming

Within each of these are many subareas. Let's take a look at a few now.

Traditional Programming

Traditional programming is the term given to programming applications for computers. It might seem like an odd distinction to make since programs run on computers anyway, but it's helpful to distinguish them from applications that are important to the Internet.

It isn't technically accurate to say that all programs run on computers because many items that you have around the home contain code that can be thought of as a program — items such as DVD players, game consoles, calculators, even cars — none of these are computers, but they nonetheless contain small applications and code that determine how the item behaves and works.

Traditional programming is well established and until recently was the area that most programmers chose, partly because it was by far the largest segment but also because the Internet was still in its infancy.

Traditional programming is usually further subdivided into what programming languages people want to use. However, because there are so many languages to cover, and the differences between them subtle, I'll break down traditional programming into two types of programming:

- ❑ Commercial/application
- ❑ Learning/academic

Commercial/Application Programming

Commercial programming is the kind of programming that results in the creation of most of the applications that we see around us. There are several different "scales" of commercial programming but for our purposes here we won't worry about that.

There are a handful of applications that are ideally suited to commercial to programming commercial applications:

- ❏ C/C++
- ❏ Java
- ❏ Visual Basic

There are "big" languages in terms of being fully featured and powerful. However, going hand in hand with lots of features and flexibility is complexity, and these languages are probably the most difficult to learn. Of the three, Microsoft's Visual Basic is by far the easiest, C/C++ the most difficult.

The difficulty of a programming language comes down to how far it is removed from natural written language. Take a look at two simple examples to see the difference. Here is a code snippet in C++:

```
#include <iostream.h>
int main()
    {
    cout << "Hello, World!\n";
    }
```

Here it is in Java:

```
class helloworldjavaprog
{
    public static void main(String args[])
    {
        System.out.println("Hello, World!");
    }
}
```

And this one is Visual Basic:

```
Private Sub Form_Load()
    msgbox "Hello, World!"
End Sub
```

The difference should be immediately obvious! In C++ and Java, there are lots of symbols used within the code, whereas in Visual Basic the code mainly uses words, which people invariably find easier to read.

The next obvious question is "which language should I choose?" Well, if you want to develop applications for Windows, then you would be better off learning either C++ or Visual Basic. Learning C++ is going to give you more scope and possibly more opportunities, although it will take you longer to learn.

Another point to bear in mind is that Visual Basic makes creating the user interface (what your end users see of your application) a lot easier. Adding things like buttons, text boxes, and options is a lot easier with Visual Basic than it is with almost any other language.

However, all is not lost with C++ when it comes to user interface — it is possible to create effective user interfaces in C++, but the problem is that you need an integrated development environment (IDE) that uses a "visual" flavor of C++ or Java to do that. The main problem with these is that most of them come with quite a hefty price tag. It's okay if you are using the development package for business where it will pay for itself, but as a hobby it won't.

> There are shareware and freeware C++ and Java development environments that enable you to create effective user interface — check out Appendix B.

If you are developing software for operating systems other than Windows, then you might have to change the language that you plan on using.

C++ is still a good language to choose but Visual Basic isn't, because it's a Windows only application. The language of choice for those who want to write code that works on a variety of operating systems and platforms is Java. Java is easier to use than C++ and is very powerful, so you are not compromising functionality in order to gain extra benefits.

Learning/Academic Programming

If you are learning to program completely from scratch, then you want to make it easy on yourself. Of course, there are going to be constraints, such as the cost of the software and what you ultimately want to do, but if you are initially more interested in learning to program than you are in actually creating a specific application, it makes sense to make life as easy as possible.

There are languages that are specifically designed for teaching purposes. One such language is called Smalltalk. The problem with these languages is that while they are designed to provide maximum academic benefit, the students are learning a language that won't be of any use to them in the real world. Students are learning about concepts and the principals, but nothing that they can actually take away in the end. To do anything, they will then have to go away and learn a proper programming language.

Some languages are, however, good to use for learning purposes. Microsoft's Visual Basic is one. This language is easy to learn and suited to the beginner for a variety of reasons:

- ❑ It's easy to use — always a huge bonus!

- ❑ It's a real language that can be used for professional programming tasks!

- ❑ It's cheap — there are special academic deals available for those who qualify.

- ❑ It's well documented and comes with a lot of sample applications and code.

> Check with the Microsoft Visual Basic Web site for more details (msdn.microsoft.com/vbasic).

However, cheap doesn't mean free. So, when we look at Web programming I'll show you how to get a taste of Visual Basic for free.

Web Programming

The Internet has been on a huge rollercoaster growth trend for many years now. One of the main reasons that so many people own or have access to a computer is to get access to the Internet. To many people, the Internet is their main use for their computer.

The Internet represents a revolution in how information is transferred and at the same time it has changed programming. Programming is no longer about making standalone applications work, it's now also become a vital tool in controlling information and making it more compelling.

When it comes to Web programming, there are two separate areas of programming:

❑ Server-side programming

❑ Client-side programming

Server-Side Programming

Server-side programming is writing code very much like any other kind of code. However, instead of code carrying out an action or task on a computer for the end user, it instead carries out tasks on computers connected to the Internet that hold Web pages (these computers are generally referred to as *servers*). Server-side code can be used to carry out a wide range of tasks, the most common being sending a Web page to the browser of a person viewing a particular Web site. There is a lot that server-side programming can and does do:

❑ Control how pages are presented

❑ Control what data is displayed

❑ Store user preferences

❑ Communicate with databases

There are several languages that are used for server-side programming:

❑ **ASP (Active Server Pages).** Controls how pages are displayed along with a whole host of other things. Developed by Microsoft, this is a commercial system that ships with many Microsoft server operating systems.

❑ **PHP (Perl Hypertext Preprocessor).** Similar to ASP. Controls how pages are displayed along with a whole host of other things. This is an open source and freely available.

❑ **SQL (Structured Query Language).** A language that is used for reading from, writing to, and manipulating databases on the Web.

I've leaving out markup languages here used for displaying Web pages (such as HTML and XHTML).

As always, there is more to this picture than meets the eye. Take ASP, for example. There are several languages that are used to drive ASP, so things aren't as straightforward as they might seem.

We won't be covering server-side stuff in any detail in this book because it is beyond the scope of the material.

Client-Side Programming

Client-side programming differs from server-side programming in that this code is included within the actual Web page sent to the browser. This code is then read by the browser and interpreted and the code is run. We'll be looking at this in more detail later, however, for now let's just familiarize you with two important languages that began life and became very popular as client-side languages but have now achieved greater status that goes well beyond the Web (as you will see shortly!). These languages are:

❑ **JavaScript.** Developed by Netscape

❑ **VBScript.** A client-side language developed by Microsoft that is based on their popular language Visual Basic

JavaScript is a scripting language that has gained enormous popularity on the Internet by being widely supported by many browsers and operating systems while VBScript is a language for Windows and Microsoft's Web browser Internet Explorer.

You'll get a good opportunity to use both of these languages over the course of the book.

Both of these languages are quite powerful but they have an added advantage in that they are:

❑ Quick and easy to learn

❑ Excellent for educational purposes

❑ Real world and applicable

Most client-side programming languages aren't strictly programming languages but scripting languages, but the rules that they follow and how they work differ little and the difference is somewhat academic.

Before we finish this chapter, let's take a look at some myths surrounding programming and programming languages.

Programming Myths and Facts

Let's take a tour of the myths and beliefs that surround programming and see which have any substance and which are just urban myths.

Myth 1 — Programming Tools Cost a Lot of Money

FALSE!

This is the number one myth that surrounds programming. There are lots of people out there who love the idea of learning to program but they have a huge fear that the programming tools that they will need are going to cost a fortune. Not true, and this isn't a recent thing. For years, universities and colleges have made available free tools and compilers for learner programmers. Now there are more and better-quality free tools available than ever, so there has not been a better time to get into programming!

Bear in mind that learning to program and creating commercial software are two separate things and that many (but not all) of the licenses for free tools prohibit their use for commercial purposes. If in doubt, check the license carefully or contact the author/publisher.

Myth 2 — You Need a Degree in Computer Science to be a Programmer

FALSE!

Absolutely not. Any previous experience or background in programming or computers helps; there's no doubt about that, but the idea that anyone who gets into programming needs a degree of other qualification to get onto the programming ladder is nonsense.

Myth 3 — Learning to Program Takes Years

TRUE AND FALSE!

Programming is a huge field of study and you could quite easily spend a lifetime learning, refining, perfecting, and practicing your skills. Once you have perfected one language, there are plenty of others. And don't worry about running out of languages — developers will figure out new ones for you too (such as the .NET programming languages from Microsoft).

However, learning to program doesn't take too long. In fact, you'll be surprised just how quickly you can get started. Some aspects of programming take time to learn, but that's the same with anything. Getting into programming isn't hard, and building a firm foundation on which to build from doesn't take that long at all.

Myth 4 — Programming Is Just for Young People

FALSE!

Anyone can get into programming — young or old. As long as you are interested, have a sense of adventure, and are willing to put in the time, you can learn how to program.

Myth 5 — I'll Need a Top-of-the-Range Super-Duper Computer to Program On

FALSE!

There is little advantage to having a high-specification computer for programming. The development environment you use might load faster and compiling may be quicker, but for these small benefits there are also drawbacks.

The main drawback is that if you design a program on a high-end computer, you'll have to continually test the program on lower-specification machines to make sure that it still runs on them.

Myth 6 — Programming Is Addictive!

TRUE!

It sure is! There's a huge buzz to be had from making the computer do what you want, and the sense of power it gives even the beginner is truly amazing!

Myth 7 — Programming Languages Change All the Time

FALSE!

Like pretty much anything else in the computer world, programming languages go through cycles of improvement and change. However, if you choose to learn an established language (C++, Visual Basic, or even JavaScript and VBScript) the changes that it will experience are going to be small, and usually the main changes are in applications such as the IDE or compiler (the application that converts source code into an application).

Myth 8 — Once You've Learned One Programming Language, Learning Others Is Easier

TRUE!

Once you understand the basics of one language, learning others is not going to be hard. That's because the concepts are transferable from one language to another. Some languages can be quite similar (and sometimes small variations in the similarities can actually make things more difficult), while others can be quite different.

However, you can always rely on a variable being a variable, and operators will generally be similar from one programming language to another, as will be many other programming concepts, so while you might have to learn how to do something in a new language, you'll at least be familiar with whatever that "thing" is!

Summary

In this chapter, we've explored some of the most compelling reasons for learning to program and why it is a good thing. There are so many good reasons to learn programming, and while we've looked at some of the most common ones here, there are many other reasons — so whether you've come to this book with a reason that I've listed or a different reason, it's good to have you here either way!

In the next chapter, we take a look at how computers store and read code.

How Computers
"Read" Code

This chapter looks at how computers deal with the code they are given. If you get an understanding of how code is read by a computer, you will write better, more concise code right from the start!

Reading Code

To help you understand how a computer reads the code it is presented with, we'll start by looking at a page of generic code, shown in Figure 3-1.

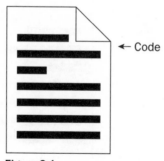

← Code

Figure 3-1

This is a page of code. Don't think of it as part of the code of an application, but think of it as the *all* of the code. There's no real code there, just black lines representing the code, but it will still give you enough of an idea as to how things work.

Top Down

Most people think that computers read the code from top to bottom, starting at the beginning and reading until it hits the end, as shown in Figure 3-2.

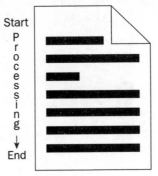

Figure 3-2

In this scenario, when the code is run the computer starts reading at the top and continues down, going through each line of code until it reaches the end.

"Top-to-bottom" or "top-down" processing used to be how things were done. It was considered both fast and easy. However, it was only fast and easy when code was small and not very complex (at least by today's standards). The trouble with doing this is that as the code is processed, it is all loaded into memory. (See Figure 3-3.)

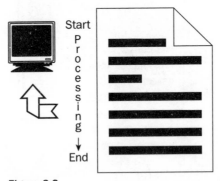

Figure 3-3

The more code you load into memory, the more system resources you need to cope. Refer to Figure 3-4.

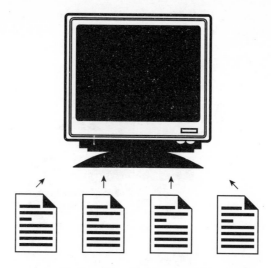

More code = More resources!

Figure 3-4

So, the more programs you run, the greater the demands on the system in terms of memory and processor, as shown in Figure 3-5.

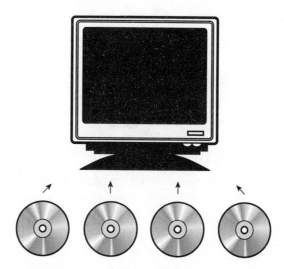

More programs = More resources!!!!!

Figure 3-5

Also, the bigger the program you are loading, the longer and longer it will take to load up if you are going to have to load up the whole thing each time. See Figure 3-6.

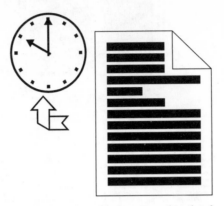

More code = More processing time!

Figure 3-6

There are even more drawbacks. One is that you have to write code in such a way that it is hard to properly test it until you have finished it. Testing individual parts becomes a nightmare. If you leave testing until the end, you have a lot of code to go through to find bugs. Refer to Figure 3-7.

Top down code is much harder to debug!

Figure 3-7

As you will see in later chapters, top-down processing still has its place when it comes to small projects but it quickly becomes infeasible for bigger projects or more complex coding. Even given the fact that top-to-bottom processing was a simpler solution than any other, it didn't stay in favor for very long.

Breaking Up Code

Rather than making code too complicated by writing code that we expect the computer to read and run all in one go, it is better to break up code and allow different parts of the code to handle different parts of the project.

Say, for example, that you were working on a simple program that works out how much tax is due on a purchase, as shown in Figure 3-8.

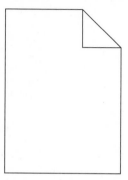

Tax calculator project - no code

Figure 3-8

You might end up with a situation where you have one portion of code that handles the input of the order total, as in Figure 3-9.

Code handling
input of order →
total

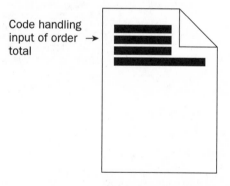

Tax calculator project

Figure 3-9

One part handles the working out of the tax due and adding that to the total, as shown in Figure 3-10.

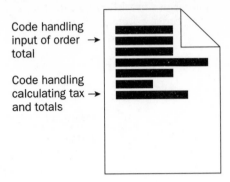

Tax calculator project

Figure 3-10

And finally (see Figure 3-11) we add the code to handle the displaying of the total and to carry out any final clearing up.

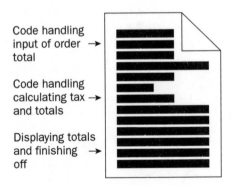

Tax calculator project

Figure 3-11

There are huge advantages to coding in this way.

❑ The code is broken up into smaller components, so it is easier to write and you can test it earlier and more often.

❑ Debugging any code errors is a lot easier because you know what part of the code handles what aspect of the program.

❑ You are in a position to reuse certain parts of your code in other projects more easily because they will be self-contained.

❑ Building up a big project from smaller, interconnected chunks enables you to build up a project over time and add more features as your skills improve!

Breaking up code into smaller chunks enables you to do a few other clever things. One is that you can write a portion of code that can be run and rerun as many times as required. A simple example of this might be a portion of code that is used to handle the addition of two numbers. In a top-down style of programming you would need to anticipate how many numbers you wanted to add together and repeat the code for each step. See Figure 3-12.

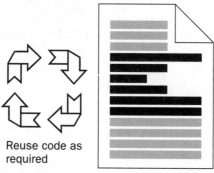

Reuse code as required

Figure 3-12

With this method, you can write a piece of code that handles the addition of numbers and just rerun it as required. This makes the overall code smaller and more responsive and easier to read and follow (the bigger the code, the more cumbersome it is, because it has to consume more memory and processor time, and as anyone who has used a PC for a while will know, both are usually in short supply!).

It also makes your code a lot more flexible. The reason why this is the case might not be immediately obvious but consider code that you've written that does number calculations. Let's say that you want a few things to happen after each calculation is done (you might want the total changed on the screen), then one way you could code for this is to add the code that carries out this updating at each point in the project where it is needed. See Figure 3-13.

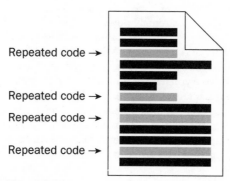

Repeated code →
Repeated code →
Repeated code →
Repeated code →

Figure 3-13

This is wasteful, not only of your time (having to type it out and then possibly debug the code several times because you made a mistake) but also of system resources. A far better way of writing code is to do the following, where you write the code in question once, as shown in Figure 3-14.

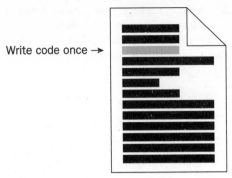

Figure 3-14

Once you run the code, you then run the code on demand from wherever it is required. This is called "calling" the code. See Figure 3-15.

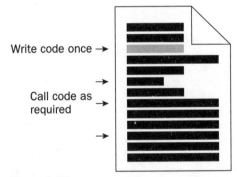

Figure 3-15

Running the code on demand is an extremely powerful step when you write code, and you'll see this in action a lot as soon as we start writing real code. Why? Because it means that for any particular task you need only write code for it once and refer to that when needed. There is no need to repeat yourself. But there are other benefits too. One is that if you find yourself having to change the code, you only need to change to it once, which will save you a lot of time in the long run. Imagine the earlier scenario, in which you have the code that updates totals on the screen and you want to change your program in some way that includes changing the code for the total update. Now, which is going to be easier, searching through the code and updating one area of the code or having to search through all of the code and find each and every instance where the updating is carried out and change each one? I think we can agree that changing the code once is not only going to be the easiest method but also the most sensible.

We've talked a lot about breaking up code and how it's important to writing good code. Now let me introduce you to some important terminology associated with code and code structure.

Code is broken into two basic structures:

❑ The statement

❑ The function or procedure

The Statement

The statement is the programming equivalent of the sentence. It is one line of computer instruction that can be understood by the system. In simple, nonprogramming terms a statement would be something like that shown in Figure 3-16.

```
Print current document

Change text to red and make it bold

Save current document
```

Figure 3-16

Figure 3-17 is an example of a statement in C++.

```
                    C++ code snippet

                    #include <iostream.h>
                    int main()
                       {
A statement →          cout << "Hello, World!\n";
                       }
```

Figure 3-17

Figure 3-18 shows an example of a statement in Visual Basic.

```
                    Visual Basic code snippet

                    Private Sub Form_Load()
A statement →          msgbox "Hello, World!"
                    End Sub
```

Figure 3-18

You can have one statement as shown in the preceding examples, or you can have many, as shown in Figure 3-19.

```
C++ code snippet

#include <iostream.h>
int main()
    {
    cout << "Hello, World!\n";
    cout << "Another statement here\n";
    cout << "And another!\n";
    cout << "Statements are what ...\n";
    cout << "... drive programs!\n";
    }
```

Figure 3-19

All statements are an instruction of some description, and do one of two things:

❑   Do something

❑   Wait

You have statements, but to give you greater control, you can organize statements into functions or procedures.

Functions/Procedures

If statements are the sentences of programming, then functions and procedures are the paragraphs.

> Another term that you might hear used for functions or procedures is "routine." This isn't commonly used and generally gives an old Pascal programmer away!

Figure 3-20 shows a function in C++.

```
C++ code snippet

                           #include <iostream.h>
                           int main()
                               {
A function  {              cout << "Hello, World!\n";
                               }
```

Figure 3-20

Figure 3-21 shows a function in Visual Basic:

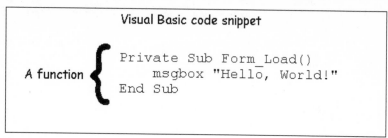

Figure 3-21

In certain languages (such as Pascal) function and procedure can have different meanings. For convenience, I'll now use the word "function" only.

Functions are the ultimate way to sort out your code into usable chunks. There might be times when you need only one statement but generally your code will make use of many statements and it is then that you will start to group them into functions.

The Sentences and Paragraphs of Programming

Before we continue, let's take a few short minutes to recap what's already been said. I think that it's important to do this here because we've covered some interesting and important terminology that is going to be the key to your programming later in the book. If we all speak the same language (no pun intended) as we move forward, things are going to be easier and there is going to be less chance that you will be confused.

Lines of Code

The lines of code that you write are called statements. These are normally the smallest building blocks of code, as shown in Figure 3-22.

```
                    Visual Basic code

           Private Sub Form_Load()
        →      if x > 4 then
        →          msgbox "Hello, World!"
Statements →   else
        →          msgbox "Not yet ..."
        →      end if
           End Sub
```

Figure 3-22

Line length is irrelevant, with both short and long lines of code being statements equally, as shown in Figure 3-23.

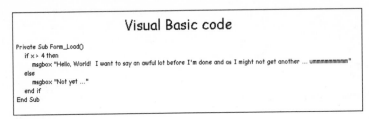

Figure 3-23

Note that sometimes when you are writing code statements that they might (depending on line length and type of text editor used) stray onto two or more lines, but bear in mind that this is still only one statement, as shown in Figure 3-24.

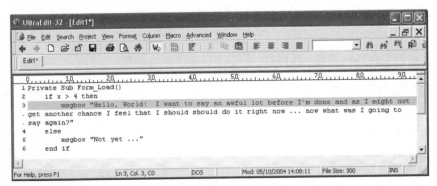

Figure 3-24

Paragraphs of Code

The sentences of code, or statements, are organized into paragraphs called *functions*. What the functions contain depends greatly on the language used and what you want the code to carry out, and many programming languages lay out restrictions as to what they can contain as well as giving you the syntax you need to write the code properly, as shown in Figure 3-25.

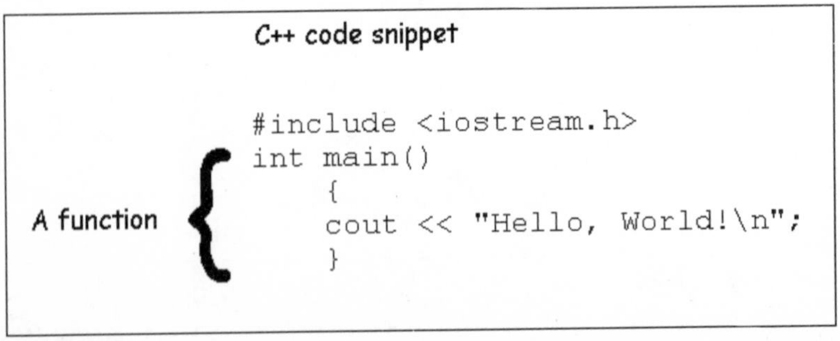

```
C++ code snippet

#include <iostream.h>
int main()
    {
    cout << "Hello, World!\n";
    }
```

A function

Figure 3-25

The syntax of the code is equivalent to the grammar of a language.

How many statements and how many functions there are in a project is dependent on the type of project you are undertaking and how complex it is — usually the bigger the project (that is, the more that it does and the more features the final application has) the more statements and functions it will contain. So, by simply looking at the code of a project you can tell, roughly, how big the final application will be.

Good programmers try to keep the final code they output as concise as possible. However, in the early stages of programming programmers might be more liberal with code and not bother making it as concise as they could, sacrificing the "size" of the code for readability.

Data Storage

Finally in this chapter, let's take a look at how code is stored before being run.

One of the simplest methods of inputting code into a system would be to sit there and type it in when needed. This would require no storage before use but it has loads of downsides:

❑   Time taken to input.

❑   Problems resulting from errors in transcribing the code.

❑   Problems distributing code (the code would have to be distributed in book form, making copying and piracy easy).

❑   Myriad other problems and issues too numerous to mention here!

Remember that all code starts life with someone sitting in front of a keyboard typing it in. There are many who think that this is the reason why modern software has so many bugs and problems — because of the human element. This may be the case but there is no other way to write code that seems to be making itself known to us (at least I'm still coding the old-fashioned way and not using some fantastic *Star Trek* system!).

To really make applications usable, you need a way to store the code so that it is available when you need it. Over the years, there have been many different solutions to such a problem:

❑   Paper punch cards

❑   Magnetic tape reels

❑   Magnetic cassettes

❑   Floppy disks (51/4 inch)

❑   Floppy disks (31/2 inch)

❑   Hard drives

❑   Networked systems

❑   CDs

❑   DVD

❑   Flash drives

❑   Internet distribution

Each of these systems enables you to store code in a way that can be accessed and run. One thing that you will notice is how, as time moves on, storage capacity increases dramatically. In the last 10 to 12 years alone we have seen hard drive capacities grow from tens of megabytes to hundreds of gigabytes — this means that a modern hard drive has a capacity tens of thousands of times greater than drives a decade ago.

Each of these systems enables the storage and retrieval of applications' programming code. Storage means that you only have to type or(more accurately) create the code once, storing it for future access. However, retrieval is equally important. This is what modern programming, in fact, all of modern computing, revolves around — the ability to store, access, and modify data.

As well as seeing an increase in storage capacity, we have seen a huge increase in the convenience surrounding the storage and retrieval of the data — loading programs stored on hard drives beats messing with punch cards, or even floppy disks, any day!

Data

But how is the data stored on these media? It is stored in the simplest form possible — binary. What is being read is a series of zeros and ones. If I were to store this paragraph in a text file, what would be stored on my hard drive would look as shown in Figure 3-26.

```
0100001001110101011101000010000001101000011011110110111001000
0001101001011100110010000000111010001101000011001010010000000110
0100011000010111010001100001001000000111001101110100011011101
1100100110010101100100000010000001101111011011100010000001110100
0110100001100101011100110110010010010000000110110101100101011001
0001101001011000010011111100010000000010000010010010110110000010
0000011010010111001100100000001110011011011101000011011110110110001
1001010110010000010000000110100101101110001000000111010001101000
0110010100100000011100110110100101101101011100000110110001100
0101110011011101000001000000110011001101111011110011001101101011001001110
0000011100001101111011110111001101101101010010110010011011000100110
1001010010000000100101100010000000110001001101001010110111001100001
0111001001110010010111000100000001000000101011110110100001100
0101110100000100000011010010101110011001000000110001001101001011001010110
10010101100011100110010110011010010110000001101100010110000
10000001101001011100110010000001100001001000000111001101101100101
01110010011010010110010101110010100100001101111011011001100010001000
0001111010010011010010110010010110111110111001100100000001100000010110
1110011001000000100000011011110110111101110110010010010011001000000110011
1000000010000001001010110100000010010010010010010000001110111
01100001011100110010000001101000011011110110010000001100110111101
0001101111011011100100110010100100000011101000110100000110100100101011
001100100000001110000110000010111001001100100001011001110110110010001
1000010111000001101000000100000011010001101111001001000000110001
001000000111010001100101011110000110100001000000010011001101010
01011011000110010100100101100001000000111011101101101010001100001011011
0100001000000111011101101111011110100001011010001110010001001001100010000001
10001001100101001000000111011101100111101110110101011011011000001
100100110010100100000011101101011011101111011101011011000110100001
1001000010000001100010011001010011101010
```

Figure 3-26

This creates a file that is 245 bytes in size — 1 byte for each character in the file, as shown in Figure 3-27.

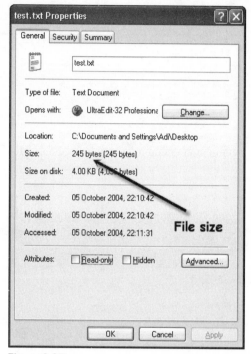

Figure 3-27

Programs are the same — but the code can be in one of two forms.

❑   Plain text

❑   Compiled

Plain text is text that is human readable — you are reading plain text here. Some code that you will come across will be stored and run in the plain text form — JavaScript and VBScript are good examples of this.

Compiled code is different. This is code that has been run through a program called a *compiler*. The compiler processes the plain-text code and changes it into something called "object code." Figure 3-28 shows an example of compiled code loaded into a text editor.

Object code is machine code, and this is what the system reads. The processor processes this code one instruction at a time. The computer's processor reads in and handles a specific number of zeros and ones at a time (for example, it might be designed to read 32 binary digits, or bits at a time). Because the system is designed to know how many bits (and also which bits) tell it what to do, it can search for the right sequence of bits and perform the next operation. Then it reads the next instruction, and so on.

There are advantages and disadvantages to either method.

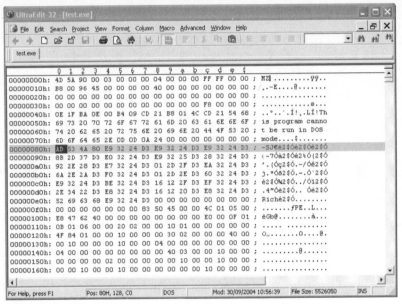

Figure 3-28

The main advantage to code stored in plain text is that it is easily read, changes can be made to it easily and quickly, and no special tools are required. However, this ease of reading the code and making changes is also its weakness because it allows others to copy the code, modify it, and claim ownership over it.

Compiled code is faster than plain-text code and offers the actual source code protection from copying and modification. You can't look at the compiled code and get back to the source code that way. This offers you a great deal of protection from prying eyes!

However, this also is a weakness as such, because you need special tools to compile and compiling is a one-way conversion. You need to keep a copy of the source code in case you need to make any subsequent changes to the code. In fact, you will need to keep many copies of the source code. Ideally, you would keep a copy every time you made a change to it — that way, if you made a change that caused a problem you could always go back to a working version. That's the ideal scenario but it is, more often than not, impractical to keep that many copies!

Summary

In this chapter, we've looked at the code of programming; what it is and how it's stored. While it's not vital that you understand everything about how the code is stored on the system and later retrieved, or what format that code is in, having an understanding of the different formats available can help you make an educated choice as to what is best suited to you.

This chapter has also given you more of the terminology you will encounter while reading programming books, talking to programmers, or viewing information on the Web.

4

From Concepts to Code —
The Language of Code

In this chapter, we are going to examine several elements of programming that allow you to take programming concepts and turn them into code. The ideal programming language would be one where you used the English language (or the language you are most familiar with) and gave the computer plain instructions that it could follow. For instance:

```
Print this document.

Make that item green.

Add the last two numbers together.
```

This would, in theory, be the easiest language to use because it is closest to a human language. It would be the highest-level language (the higher the level, the closer it is to a real language). But this kind of language is unrealistic because of the ambiguity of spoken/written language and the complexity of the brain necessary to handle and understanding it. For example, the following three statements are all the same — how would you make a computer recognize all three?

```
Print this document.
Print the current document.
Send this document to the printer.
```

There are more possibilities, all of which we would understand but a computer wouldn't.

Complex understanding is the ultimate goal, of course. Notice that in sci-fi (Star Trek, Star Wars, and many shows) humans interface with computers and robots using spoken language? Being able to do that now would be sweet!

Since we can't use our normal language to interact with computers, we have to use special languages, programming languages. In this chapter, we won't be looking at programming languages just yet; instead we will be looking at some of the elements that come together to create such languages. We begin by looking at the simplest scheme that a computer uses for communications — binary.

Binary

Binary is a number system. It differs from the normal decimal (base 10) system that we are used to because instead of having 10 component digits (0, 1 2, 3, 4, 5, 6, 7, 8, and 9), it has only two (0 and 1). Another name for the binary system is base 2. The name given to these digits is bits.

Many people find getting into binary really confusing because it uses 2 bits that are otherwise familiar to them in an unfamiliar way. If instead of using 0 and 1 it used _ and _ or _ and _ there would be less confusion.

Interpreting Binary

The easiest way to figure out how binary works is to compare it to the familiar decimal system.

Decimal	Binary
0	0
1	1
2	10
3	11
4	100
5	101
6	110
7	111
8	1000
9	1001
10	1010
11	1011

Notice how the increments occur. Since there are only 2 bits, the number appears to become bigger (have more digits) quicker, but don't let that fool you. Binary is read from right to left, with the bits increasing in value from right to left.

A simple way to look at binary numbers is to go back to the way children are taught numbers when they are little. Take the following number:

1010

Represented in decimal, you work out this number as follows:

Thousands	Hundreds	Tens	Units
1	0	1	0

Reading this gives us the value of the decimal number as *one thousand and ten*.

In binary, the column headings are slightly different and go up not in powers of 10, but powers of 2 (that is, they double).

Eights	Fours	Twos	Units
1	0	1	0

So, reading this gives the following:

1	x	8	=	8
0	x	4	=	0
1	x	2	=	2
0	x	1	=	0
			Decimal Total	10

Total up the right hand column to give you the answer you are looking for. Ten.

This means that the number is 1 eight and 1 two, giving, in decimal the number 10.

To read a bigger binary number, you just need a bigger grid. Take the following binary number:

10010111

Create a grid (remembering that the each column represents a doubling of the previous column):

One-Hundred-Twenty-Eights	Sixty-Fours	Thirty-Twos	Sixteens	Eights	Fours	Twos	Units
1	0	0	1	0	1	1	1

To work the number out in decimal, create a grid as we did previously and put the binary bits down the left-hand side.

1	x	128	=	128
0	x	64	=	0

Table continued on following page

0	x	32	=	0
1	x	16	=	16
0	x	8	=	0
1	x	4	=	4
1	x	2	=	2
1	x	1	=	1
			Decimal Total	**151**

So, in decimal, the binary number 10010111 is 151.

Large Numbers

Show kids numbers, and the first thing they do is try to write out the biggest number they can. Using 8 bits, the largest possible number is 11111111. This works out as:

1	x	128	=	128
1	x	64	=	64
1	x	32	=	32
1	x	16	=	16
1	x	8	=	8
1	x	4	=	4
1	x	2	=	2
1	x	1	=	1
			Decimal Total	**255**

Add more bits, and the number becomes bigger!

1111111111111111

1	x	32768	=	32768
1	x	16384	=	16384
1	x	8192	=	8192
1	x	4096	=	4096
1	x	2048	=	2048
1	x	1024	=	1024

1	x	512	=	512
1	x	256	=	256
1	x	128	=	128
1	x	64	=	64
1	x	32	=	32
1	x	16	=	16
1	x	8	=	8
1	x	4	=	4
1	x	2	=	2
1	x	1	=	1
			Decimal Total	65535

Bit Grouping

Conveniently, groupings of bits have names to make them easier to remember and discuss. Let's take a quick tour of the naming system.

Bit

A *bit* is a single binary digit. This is a bit:

0

As is this:

1

The maximum value of bit in decimal is obviously, 1.

Nybble

A grouping for four bits is called a *nybble* (sometimes called a nibble). Here is a nybble:

1010

The maximum value of a nybble in decimal is 15.

1111

1	x	8	=	8
1	x	4	=	4
1	x	2	=	2
1	x	1	=	1
			Decimal Total	15

Byte

A grouping of 8 bits is called a *byte*.

10101010

The maximum value of a byte in decimal is 255.

11111111

1	x	128	=	128
1	x	64	=	64
1	x	32	=	32
1	x	16	=	16
1	x	8	=	8
1	x	4	=	4
1	x	2	=	2
1	x	1	=	1
			TOTAL	255

Halfword

A grouping of 16 bits is called a *halfword*.

1010101010101010

The maximum value of a halfword in decimal is 65535.

1111111111111111

1	x	32768	=	32768
1	x	16384	=	16384
1	x	8192	=	8192
1	x	4096	=	4096

1	x	2048	=	2048
1	x	1024	=	1024
1	x	512	=	512
1	x	256	=	256
1	x	128	=	128
1	x	64	=	64
1	x	32	=	32
1	x	16	=	16
1	x	8	=	8
1	x	4	=	4
1	x	2	=	2
1	x	1	=	1
			Decimal Total	**65535**

Word

A grouping of 32 bits is called a *word*, as shown here:

10101010101010101010101010101010

The maximum value of a word in decimal is 4294967295:

11111111111111111111111111111111

1	x	2147483648	=	2147483648
1	x	1073741824	=	1073741824
1	x	536870912	=	536870912
1	x	268435456	=	268435456
1	x	134217728	=	134217728
1	x	67108864	=	67108864
1	x	33554432	=	33554432
1	x	16777216	=	16777216
1	x	8388608	=	8388608
1	x	4194304	=	4194304
1	x	2097152	=	2097152
1	x	1048576	=	1048576

Table continued on following page

1	x	524288	=	524288
1	x	262144	=	262144
1	x	131072	=	131072
1	x	65536	=	65536
1	x	32768	=	32768
1	x	16384	=	16384
1	x	8192	=	8192
1	x	4096	=	4096
1	x	2048	=	2048
1	x	1024	=	1024
1	x	512	=	512
1	x	256	=	256
1	x	128	=	128
1	x	64	=	64
1	x	32	=	32
1	x	16	=	16
1	x	8	=	8
1	x	4	=	4
1	x	2	=	2
1	x	1	=	1
			Decimal Total	**4294967295**

Doubleword

A grouping of 64 bits is called a *doubleword*, and is shown here:

1010101010101010101010101010101010101010101010101010101010101010

The maximum value of a doubleword in decimal is 18446744073709551615:

1111111111111111111111111111111111111111111111111111111111111111

Binary Math

You can work with binary numbers similarly to the way that you work with normal numbers. However, for the scope of this book, ploughing through masses of binary math theory won't be necessary. I'm going to show you a much easier way to work with binary, using a tool that has great power and flexibility — it has the added advantage of being free; it is shown in Figure 4-1.

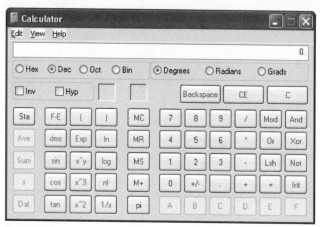

Figure 4-1

Yes, Windows calculator! If you use the Windows operating system, then this is the ideal application to use. If you are not a Windows user, then your system also should come with a calculator flexible enough for you to work with binary.

Using Windows Calculator

Here is a quick guide to using Windows Calculator with binary. The chances are that unless you use Windows Calculator often, instead of looking as it does in Figure 4-1, it will look as shown in Figure 4-2:

Figure 4-2

This is Windows Calculator in standard mode. To be able to make it capable of working with binary you need to switch it to scientific mode. To switch it to scientific mode click *View* and then *Scientific*, as shown in Figure 4-3.

Figure 4-3

The calculator changes to scientific mode and presents you with a whole raft of new buttons and features.

If you share your PC with someone else who might use Windows Calculator for some simple tasks, remember to switch it back to standard mode after you are done — just in case you give him or her a fright!

Now that you have it in scientific mode, you will notice the controls for changing the number format. Decimal is represented by Dec, while binary is represented by Bin. Refer to Figure 4-4.

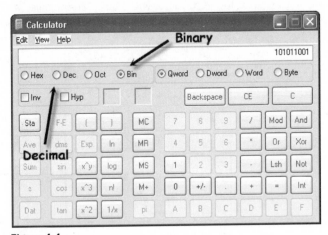

Figure 4-4

You also can use the menu to change the format. Click *View*, as shown in Figure 4-5.

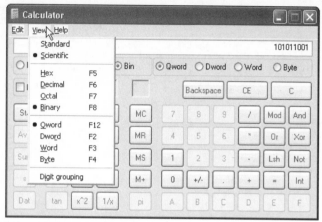

Figure. 4-5

Place Windows Calculator into normal decimal mode and type in a number. To see that number in binary, just switch the calculator from Dec . . . Refer to Figure 4-6.

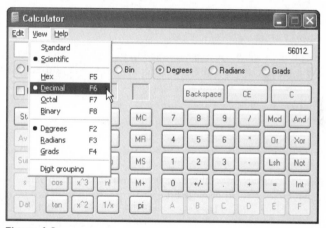

Figure 4-6

. . . to Bin, as shown in Figure 4-7 . . .

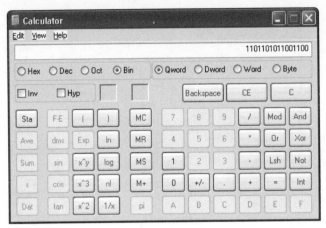

Figure 4-7

. . . and the decimal number is now displayed in binary form.

For any math you want to do, just use the calculator's normal functions and change the view to see it in binary, or vice versa. Addition, subtraction, multiplication, and division, it's all possible with the Windows Calculator. No need to get a pen and paper out to do it by hand.

Notice how there are other number formats included in the options on the calculator. Hex represents hexadecimal and Oct is octal. Octal is outside the scope of this book and not really relevant, but this chapter does spend some time in the hexadecimal system in a later section.

Why Binary?

A commonly asked question is "why is there a need to use binary?" Why not just use decimal?

The answer is simple — it allows information to be represented by two states — on and off. This means that in a computer system (or any other electronic system) information can be represented by switches, and changing these from on to off and back again enables it to work with binary. This is the basis for how processors and memory (both random access memory, or RAM, and hard drives) work.

Binary can also be represented as pulses of electricity down wires — the basis for networks and the Internet.

Binary might seem long-winded and cumbersome but it forms the signals sent down the nervous system of almost everything to do with the electronic transfer, processing, and storage of data. All around you, binary is flowing in circuits, along wires, and through the air.

Hexadecimal

Hexadecimal is a number system similar to decimal and binary, but on the face of it more complicated.

Why more complicated? Well, binary has 2 digits and decimal 10 digits. Hexadecimal on the other hand has 16.

0, 1, 2, 3, 4, 5, 6, 7, 8, 9, A, B, C, D, E, and F.

In some representations, the characters ~, !, @, #, $, and % are used instead of ABCDEF (respectively).

Interpreting Hexadecimal

Let's look at the hexadecimal (hex) number system and compare it to decimal; this will help you to familiarize yourself with the system.

Decimal	Hexadecimal
0	0
1	1
2	2
3	3
4	4
5	5
6	6
7	7
8	8
9	9
10	A
11	B
12	C
13	D
14	E
15	F
16	10
...	...
30	1E
31	1F
32	20
33	21

Notice how the increments occur. Because there are 16 digits, the number appears to grow more slowly than in the decimal system. As with binary, hexadecimal is read from right to left, with the bits increasing in value from right to left.

> *The word hexadecimal is peculiar because hexa is derived from the Greek hexi for 6 and decimal is derived from the Latin for 10. The older, and more accurate, term was the Latin sexidecimal, but that was abandoned because it was thought to be too risqué (not to mention that it also had an alternative meaning of base 60).*

Hexadecimal numbers have either an *0x* prefix to them or an *h* suffix. For example:

0x3F7D

For our purposes, we will forget about these because they merely make life more complicated and beginners get confused by them.

To convert a value from hexadecimal to binary, you merely translate each hexadecimal digit into its 4-bit binary equivalent. So, the previous number is translated as follows:

3   F   7   D

0011 1111 0111 1101

It's also easy to convert any binary string into hexadecimal. Take the following:

101111

Add zeros to the left-hand side so that the number of bits is divisible by 4 without remainder:

00101011

Now break the set up into 4-bit groups (a nybble):

0010 1111

Then convert each group into the appropriate hexadecimal number:

2 F

This gives:

2F

Done!

In fact, any nybble that you care to choose is directly representable by two hexadecimal digits.

> *This is the reason why a byte is usually displayed as two nybbles.*

Hexadecimal and Windows Calculator

In the same way that you can work with binary using Windows Calculator, you can do exactly the same thing with hexadecimal. You can switch the number format using the buttons of the calculator interface or through the menu system. Numbers can be converted to and from hex in the same way as with binary, as shown in Figure 4-8.

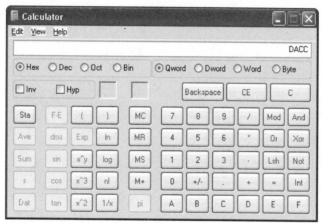

Figure 4-8

Representing Characters

So far we've looked at different ways of representing numbers but, as you are probably well aware, there is more to computing than just numbers. There's text, numbers, symbols, and so on: *characters*, as they are generically called. How do you go from binary (the system by which all computers operate on a fundamental level) to the characters that I am now typing and that you see around you all the time when you use a computer?

To handle character representation a system called ASCII was introduced (pronounced *as-kee*). *ASCII* stands for *American Standard Code for Information Interchange*. Since computers can only understand numbers, ASCII code is the numerical representation of a character such as "a" or "~" or an action of some description.

ASCII is a standard way to encode upper- and lowercase letters in the English alphabet, as well as numbers and special characters. It does this using binary, and it needs only 7 bits. Because it uses 7 bits, it is limited to representing 128 characters.

DECIMAL	OCTAL	HEX	BINARY		VALUE
000	000	000	00000000	NUL	(Null char.)
001	001	001	00000001	SOH	(Start of Header)
002	002	002	00000010	STX	(Start of Text)
003	003	003	00000011	ETX	(End of Text)

004	004	004	00000100	EOT	(End of Transmission)
005	005	005	00000101	ENQ	(Enquiry)
006	006	006	00000110	ACK	(Acknowledgment)
007	007	007	00000111	BEL	(Bell)
008	010	008	00001000	BS	(Backspace)
009	011	009	00001001	HT	(Horizontal Tab)
010	012	00A	00001010	LF	(Line Feed)
011	013	00B	00001011	VT	(Vertical Tab)
012	014	00C	00001100	FF	(Form Feed)
013	015	00D	00001101	CR	(Carriage Return)
014	016	00E	00001110	SO	(Shift Out)
015	017	00F	00001111	SI	(Shift In)
016	020	010	00010000	DLE	(Data Link Escape)
017	021	011	00010001	DC1	(XON)(Device Control 1)
018	022	012	00010010	DC2	(Device Control 2)
019	023	013	00010011	DC3	(XOFF)(Device Control3)
020	024	014	00010100	DC4	(Device Control 4)
021	025	015	00010101	NAK	(Negative Acknowledgement)
022	026	016	00010110	SYN	(Synchronous Idle)
023	027	017	00010111	ETB	(End of Trans. Block)
024	030	018	00011000	CAN	(Cancel)
025	031	019	00011001	EM	(End of Medium)
026	032	01A	00011010	SUB	(Substitute)
027	033	01B	00011011	ESC	(Escape)
028	034	01C	00011100	FS	(File Separator)
029	035	01D	00011101	GS	(Group Separator)
030	036	01E	00011110	RS	(Request to Send Record separator)
031	037	01F	00011111	US	(Unit Separator)
032	040	020	00100000	SP	(Space)
033	041	021	00100001	!	(exclamation)
034	042	022	00100010	"	(double quote)
035	043	023	00100011	#	(number sign)
036	044	024	00100100	$	(dollar sign)
037	045	025	00100101	%	(percent)
038	046	026	00100110	&	(ampersand)
039	047	027	00100111	'	(single quote)
040	050	028	00101000	(	(left/opening parenthesis)
041	051	029	00101001	)	(right/closing parenthesis)
042	052	02A	00101010	*	(asterisk)
043	053	02B	00101011	+	(plus)
044	054	02C	00101100	,	(comma)
045	055	02D	00101101	-	(minus or dash)
046	056	02E	00101110	.	(dot)
047	057	02F	00101111	/	(forward slash)
048	060	030	00110000	0	
049	061	031	00110001	1	
050	062	032	00110010	2	
051	063	033	00110011	3	
052	064	034	00110100	4	
053	065	035	00110101	5	
054	066	036	00110110	6	
055	067	037	00110111	7	
056	070	038	00111000	8	
057	071	039	00111001	9	

058	072	03A	00111010	:	(colon)
059	073	03B	00111011	;	(semi-colon)
060	074	03C	00111100	<	(less than)
061	075	03D	00111101	=	(equal sign)
062	076	03E	00111110	>	(greater than)
063	077	03F	00111111	?	(question mark)
064	100	040	01000000	@	(AT symbol)
065	101	041	01000001	A	
066	102	042	01000010	B	
067	103	043	01000011	C	
068	104	044	01000100	D	
069	105	045	01000101	E	
070	106	046	01000110	F	
071	107	047	01000111	G	
072	110	048	01001000	H	
073	111	049	01001001	I	
074	112	04A	01001010	J	
075	113	04B	01001011	K	
076	114	04C	01001100	L	
077	115	04D	01001101	M	
078	116	04E	01001110	N	
079	117	04F	01001111	O	
080	120	050	01010000	P	
081	121	051	01010001	Q	
082	122	052	01010010	R	
083	123	053	01010011	S	
084	124	054	01010100	T	
085	125	055	01010101	U	
086	126	056	01010110	V	
087	127	057	01010111	W	
088	130	058	01011000	X	
089	131	059	01011001	Y	
090	132	05A	01011010	Z	
091	133	05B	01011011	[	(left/opening bracket)
092	134	05C	01011100	\	(back slash)
093	135	05D	01011101	]	(right/closing bracket)
094	136	05E	01011110	^	(caret/circumflex)
095	137	05F	01011111	_	(underscore)
096	140	060	01100000	`	
097	141	061	01100001	a	
098	142	062	01100010	b	
099	143	063	01100011	c	
100	144	064	01100100	d	
101	145	065	01100101	e	
102	146	066	01100110	f	
103	147	067	01100111	g	
104	150	068	01101000	h	
105	151	069	01101001	i	
106	152	06A	01101010	j	
107	153	06B	01101011	k	
108	154	06C	01101100	l	
109	155	06D	01101101	m	
110	156	06E	01101110	n	
111	157	06F	01101111	o	

112	160	070	01110000	p	
113	161	071	01110001	q	
114	162	072	01110010	r	
115	163	073	01110011	s	
116	164	074	01110100	t	
117	165	075	01110101	u	
118	166	076	01110110	v	
119	167	077	01110111	w	
120	170	078	01111000	x	
121	171	079	01111001	y	
122	172	07A	01111010	z	
123	173	07B	01111011	{	(left/opening brace)
124	174	07C	01111100	|	(vertical bar)
125	175	07D	01111101	}	(right/closing brace)
126	176	07E	01111110	~	(tilde)
127	177	07F	01111111	DEL	(delete)

Notice how all of the preceding characters use 7-bit binary strings to represent the characters. As I said earlier, this allows for 127 characters to be represented. The set of characters represented form what is known as a character set.

Why 7-bit? All the essential characters were kept to the first 127 slots to reduce the amount of storage space needed for the data. In fact, plenty of early applications left out the eighth zero.

To provide more characters, such as accented characters and mathematical symbols, an 8th bit is often added, providing 256 characters in all. There are many different character sets, each representing different characters. This addition to the character set is known as an *extended character set*.

VALUE	DECIMAL	HEX
--	128	80
--	129	81
--	130	82
--	131	83
--	132	84
--	133	85
--	134	86
--	135	87
--	136	88
--	137	89
--	138	8A
--	139	8B
--	140	8C
--	141	8D
--	142	8E
--	143	8F
--	144	90
--	145	91
--	146	92
--	147	93
--	148	94
--	149	95
--	150	96

--	151	97
--	152	98
--	153	99
--	154	9A
--	155	9B
--	156	9C
--	157	9D
--	158	9E
--	159	9F
	160	a0
¡	161	a1
¢	162	a2
£	163	a3
¤	164	a4
¥	165	a5
¦	166	a6
§	167	a7
¨	168	a8
©	169	a9
ª	170	AA
«	171	AB
¬	172	AC
	173	AD
®	174	AE
¯	175	AF
°	176	B0
±	177	B1
²	178	B2
³	179	B3
´	180	B4
µ	181	B5
¶	182	B6
·	183	B7
¸	184	B8
¹	185	B9
º	186	BA
»	187	BB
¼	188	BC
½	189	BD
¾	190	BE
¿	191	BF
À	192	C0
Á	193	C1
Â	194	C2
Ã	195	C3
Ä	196	C4
Å	197	C5
Æ	198	C6
Ç	199	C7
È	200	C8
É	201	C9
Ê	202	CA
Ë	203	CB
Ì	204	CC

Í	205	CD
Î	206	CE
Ï	207	CF
Ð	208	D0
Ñ	209	D1
Ò	210	D2
Ó	211	D3
Ô	212	D4
Õ	213	D5
Ö	214	D6
×	215	D7
Ø	216	D8
Ù	217	D9
Ú	218	DA
Û	219	DB
Ü	220	DC
Ý	221	DD
Þ	222	DE
ß	223	DF
à	224	E0
á	225	E1
â	226	E2
ã	227	E3
ä	228	E4
å	229	E5
æ	230	E6
ç	231	E7
è	232	E8
é	233	E9
ê	234	EA
ë	235	EB
ì	236	EC
í	237	ED
î	238	EE
ï	239	EF
ð	240	F0
ñ	241	F1
ò	242	F2
ó	243	F3
ô	244	F4
õ	245	F5
ö	246	F6
÷	247	F7
ø	248	F8
ù	249	F9
ú	250	FA
û	251	FB
ü	252	FC
ý	253	FD
þ	254	FE
ÿ	255	FF

The – symbol indicates that no character is specified.

Using ASCII you can take text strings and convert them into strings of zeros and ones and back again. There is no loss in data and no ambiguity.

Take the following string:

```
Programming is great!
```

By consulting the ASCII table, these characters can be converted onto binary bytes. Here I have done just that for you:

```
0101000001110010011011110110011101110010011000010110110101101101011010010110111001100111001000000110100101110011001000000110011101110010011001010110000101110100001000
01
```

Character	Binary
P	01010000
R	01110010
O	01101111
G	01100111
R	01110010
A	01100001
M	01101101
M	01101101
I	01101001
N	01101110
G	01100111
	00100000
I	01101001
S	01110011
	00100000
G	01100111
R	01110010
E	01100101
A	01100001
T	01110100
!	00100001

To convert a binary string back to ASCII isn't hard. If you have to do it by hand, the trick is that you break the binary string up into bytes before trying to work on it. Working on a long train of ones and zeros is hard work, and the scope for mistakes is high!

```
01010000 01110010 01101111 01100111 01110010 01100001 01101101 01101101 01101001
01101110 01100111 00100000 01101001 01110011 00100000 01100111 01110010 01100101
01100001 01110100 00100001
```

Then work through the table:

```
   P        r        o        g        r        a        m        m
01010000 01110010 01101111 01100111 01110010 01100001 01101101 01101101

   i        n        g                 i        s                 g
01101001 01101110 01100111 00100000 01101001 01110011 00100000 01100111

   g        e        a        t        !
01110010 01100101 01100001 01110100 00100001
```

No data is lost in the process.

The nice thing about modern programming is that you rarely need to worry about or bother with using binary representations of characters; most of this is handled for you automatically. However, there are times when knowing the relationship between binary and characters can come in handy (for one thing, it gives you insight into how data is stored in memory and on the hard drive). See Figure 4-9

Figure 4-9

It is important to remember that the displaying of the actual characters has nothing to do with the binary code. The binary (or hexadecimal or octal) numbers are translated, and the appropriate characters are displayed by the application or operating system.

So far you've seen different number formats in operation and looked at how numbers can be used to represent characters for display, manipulation, transfer, or storage. Next, we will move on to look at mathematical and logical operators.

Operators

A lot of programming is about manipulating data, both textual and numerical in nature. Operators enable you to work with data and compare information.

Let's start by taking a look at some basic operators to get you familiar with what they do and how they work. It's important to realize that not all operators have the same symbol in all programming languages (and this can be one of the biggest stumbling blocks that trip up students when they try learning a second programming language). For now, if you understand what these do, then that will help you significantly later on.

Operators fall into five categories, each of which will be described in the following sections:

❑ Arithmetic

❑ Assignment

❑ Comparison

❑ Logical

❑ String

Arithmetic Operators

These operators are likely to be the operators most familiar to you because these are math operators that you are used to using for normal math.

There are seven common arithmetic operators:

Operator	Description	Example	Result
+	Addition	If x = 6 x + 4	10
–	Subtraction	If x = 6 x - 2	4
*	Multiplication	If x = 6 x * 2	12
/	Division	If x = 6 x / 3	2
++	Increment (add one)	If x = 6 x++	7
--	Decrement (subtract one)	If x = 6 x--	5
%	Modulus (division remainder)	7%2 10%4 12%6	1 2 0

Assignment Operators

Assignment operators are used to assign a value. These will be used extensively later when we come to using variables (the x in the previous examples is an example of a variable that has been assigned the value of 6).

There are six assignment operators:

Operator	Example	Is Equivalent to . . .
=	x = 6 x = y	x = 6 x = y
+=	x += y	x = x + y
-=	x -= y	x = x - y
*=	x *= y	x = x * y
/=	x /= y	x = x / y
%=	x %= y	x = x % y

In the preceding examples, x and y are both variables. Variables need to have unique names (unless you are reusing them) and for us here, x and y do just fine!

Comparison Operators

Comparison operators are used to compare two things. You will find that when you get to working with code in Chapter 7, "The Structure of Coding," these will be really useful.

There are six comparison operators. Each of these returns either true or false, depending on whether the outcome of the comparison is true or false.

Operator	Description	Example
==	Equal to	5 == 8 (returns false) 8 == 8 (returns true) "cat" == "dog" (returns false) "cat" == "cat" (returns true)
!=	Not equal to	5 != 8 (returns true) 8 != 8 (returns false)
>	Greater than	5 > 8 (returns false) 8 > 3 (returns true)
<	Less than	5 < 8 (returns true) 8 < 3 (returns false)

Operator	Description	Example
>=	Greater than or equal to	5 >= 8 (returns false) 8 >= 3 (returns true) 8 >= 8 (returns true)
<=	Less than or equal to	5 <= 8 (returns true) 8 <= 3 (returns false) 3 <= 3 (returns true)

Logical Operators

Logical operators enable you to introduce logic to the code you write and enable you to make combinations of the preceding operators.

There are three logical operators.

Operator	Description	Example
&&	And	x = 7 y = 2 (x < 12 && y > 1) returns true In English, the preceding states "x is less than 12, and y is greater than 1." x = 7 y = 2 (x < 12 && y < 1) returns false
||	Or	x=6 y=1 (x==6 || y==5) returns true In English, the preceding states "x is equal to 5, and y is equal to 5." x=6 y=1 (x==5 || y==5) returns false x=6 y=1 (x==6 || y==1) returns true

Table continued on following page

Operator	Description	Example
!	Not	x=6 y=3 !(x==y) returns true In English, the preceding states "x is not equal to y." x=3+3 y=4+2 !(x==y) returns false

String Operators

String operators are operators that work on strings. Strings are usually snippets of text. Here are two sample strings:

```
string1 = "Hello "
string2 = "World!"
```

Using string operators, you can join (or concatenate) strings together.

```
string3 = string1 + string2
```

The variable string3 will now hold the value Hello World!

One thing that newcomers to strings seem to find hard to cope with is spaces. That is, keeping track of spaces between strings and making sure that the end string makes sense.

For example, in the preceding example I could have had the following:

```
string1 = "Hello"
string2 = "World!"
```

Then I could have concatenate the strings.

```
string3 = string1 + string2
```

However, now string3 will holds the value HelloWorld!

One fix for this would have been to add the space when carrying out the concatenation:

```
string3 = string1 + " " + string2
```

Now string3 will be correct and have the value Hello World!

We'll look at this in much more detail in later chapters, but for now if you have the basics in place, it'll be a lot easier and hopefully make much more sense.

Summary

In this chapter, we've taken a look at how to go from concepts to code. We've examined some of the number formats that you might come across along with how binary, hexadecimal or octal can be used to represent characters using ASCII. We've also examined briefly why binary is important in computing and how it is at the core of almost everything to do with data in the electronic world.

We've also taken a look at operators and how they enable you to take simple data and begin to work with it, which, ultimately, is what computing is all about.

The next chapter takes a look at the tools of programming.

The Tools for Programming

In this chapter, we'll look at some of the applications, both free and commercial, that you will be using throughout the remainder of this book.

> *Most of what you need in the way of software in this book will be free and available for downloading from the Internet.*

What you choose to use depends on you, but this chapter looks at programming from the point of view of several different languages, so you get broad coverage and experience.

Make Your Workspace Your Own

The area in which you work is as much a programming tool as is any piece of kit or software you need. In fact, it may be one of the most important factors in your early programming career, because a poorly thought out, uncomfortable workspace means that you enjoy programming less and consequently spend less time doing it!

The Keyboard

No matter what kind of programming you plan to do or what programming language you choose to use, one thing you are going to have to do is type code. When it comes to programming, you will spend time behind the keyboard, like the one shown in Figure 5-1.

There are many different types of keyboard. Today, they seem to come in all sorts of shapes and sizes and connection types (wired, wireless). In general, it's the style and layout of the keys that are of interest, and these come in three categories:

- ❑ Traditional
- ❑ Ergonomic
- ❑ Bizarre/futuristic

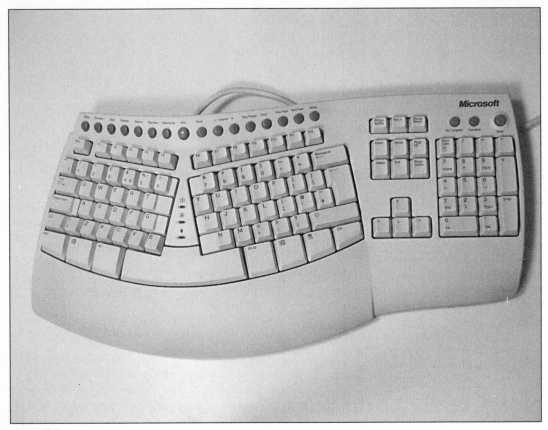

Figure 5-1

Be wary of anything too bizarre. Oddly laid out keyboards can be hard to become accustomed to and make you less efficient when away from your computer system.

Get a keyboard you are comfortable with. Ergonomic keyboards make typing for longer easier but many require you to "relearn," to some extent, how to type. In the short term this may seem a real pain, but in the longer term it can be enormously beneficial.

Whatever you choose to type with, here are a few pointers:

❏ Make sure that the keyboard is comfortable to use. Some require more pressure on the keys than others, and if yours is not comfortable for general typing, then long coding sessions are going to be less enjoyable.

❏ Don't jump into the most radical ergonomic keyboard you see. Take wild claims with a pinch of salt, and always try a new style of keyboard before committing to it.

❏ If your current keyboard is worn out or has a sticky key, replace it!

Workspace

Get used to keyboard work early, and customize your workspace. Make it as comfortable as possible and get a good quality chair to sit in. If your back is uncomfortable or if you are at the wrong height for the keyboard, your concentration will suffer and the time you can spend programming will be shorter and more uncomfortable. This will undoubtedly affect your concentration, learning, and performance.

Make sure that you have good lighting and, if possible, good air flow. Because you are going to be sitting still, try to make the area warm, but not hot. Add plants and whatever else makes you feel happy and comfortable.

Desk

Make sure that you have plenty of space on your desk when you are programming. Clutter is bad for the mind and makes things harder on you than necessary. As a beginning programmer, you are going to be referring to many books (hopefully this one!) and other materials. Make space for books and papers that you will be using.

You will also find making and taking notes useful, so make sure that you have a pen and ample supply of paper and sticky notes. A hardbound notebook is ideal for keeping track of your projects and your progress.

Monitor

Make sure you are at a comfortable angle to your keyboard and monitor. If glare off the screen is a problem, then you might want to either reposition your system or install a glare filter. Because you will be doing a lot of text work and probably reading what you've typed a lot, make sure that the font of the application you are using it easily readable.

Fonts

Change the font size and type to what you can read best. Simple fonts such as Courier New or Arial are much better (see Figure 5-2) than fancy fonts such as cursive types (see Figure 5-3).

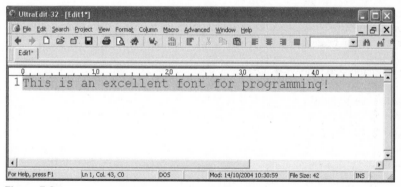

Figure 5-2

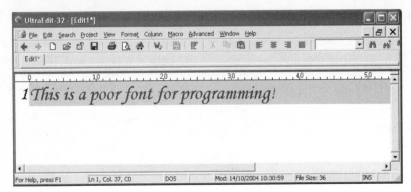

Figure 5-3

Make sure that the font size is also appropriate. If you use a font such as Courier New, then a font size of 12 or 14 point is appropriate, as shown in Figure 5-4.

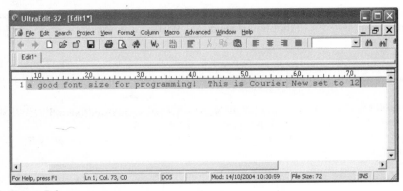

Figure 5-4

A size 16-point font or above is too big to effectively get enough code on the screen, as shown in Figure 5-5.

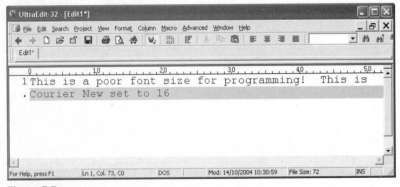

Figure 5-5

A font that is too small becomes just plain unreadable, and it will be especially hard to make out operators (-, +, *, /, and so on) and parentheses and braces, as shown in Figure 5-6.

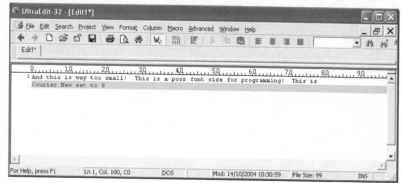

Figure 5-6

Unless your program offers some sort of syntax highlighting (that is, the programming application highlights different aspects of the code with different colors), it is better to leave the font as black. Syntax highlighting can be a real bonus for coding, but it does mean that you need to learn what the different colors mean and how that relates to the programming language you've chosen. The text editor that I will be using, UltraEdit, can be set to use syntax highlighting (as shown in Figure 5-7).

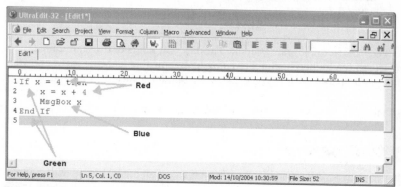

Figure 5-7

For the beginner, having to deal with loads of colors as well as figuring out the code can be traumatic and highlighting might best be disabled. In UltraEdit, as with most other applications that use syntax highlighting, this feature is easily switched off until you are ready for it (see Figure 5-8).

Choose Your Language

There are many languages that you can choose from. The nice thing is that many can carry out similar tasks, and if you choose carefully, based on what you think you want to do, you can find one that will suit your needs (for a while anyway, until you need to do something different).

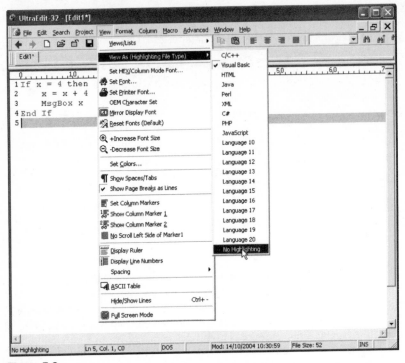

Figure 5-8

Chapter 2, "Why Learn to Program?," looked at different kinds of programming languages and at what they could be used for. In this chapter, I'm going to assume that learning to program is the main objective that you have, and I'll look at how you can best do that for a variety of languages.

One factor that controls what language you will use to program is how you are learning to program.

Learning to Program

Learning to program is very much like learning a foreign language. Just as with a foreign language, some of the elements of what you are learning will be familiar, while others will be uncannily similar but work in a very different way than you would expect. People say that learning a third language is easier than learning the second, and this is true. Most people think that this is so because having a second language under your belt means that you can draw from that common ground when learning the next, however, I believe that this isn't entirely accurate. I think that the reason why learning becomes easier is that you learn not to expect languages to follow similar rules. When there are commonalities, it makes life easier but if there aren't many, you aren't half as frustrated and annoyed by it.

Learning to program differs from real programming in a number of ways. How much it differs depends a lot on the learning route you take.

School/College

School or college is the traditional route to learning programming. Before you touch any code, you are taken though, in detail, the history of programming and how present-day programming is heavily influenced by the progress made over the years. What you notice is that many of the things that we think of as being "modern" concepts have, in fact, been around for a long time.

Going through the history of programming can be very interesting, and getting exposure to older languages and ideas not only makes you appreciate how much easier and more intuitive programming is today, but also helps you understand much of the logic and structure of modern coding.

After covering the history of programming, you will then probably move on to look, in quite some detail, at the concepts behind the code. The logic of code and the processing and manipulation of data will be covered in detail.

You will also get to do some coding! The programming that you do will be to support the material that you cover, giving real meaning to the concepts.

How much of the programming that you can actually apply to real-world problems depends a lot on what languages are used in the course of the class. Languages such as Java and C++ enable you to create real applications that can be put to work on real problems, while other languages (Smalltalk for example) cannot.

If you are fortunate enough to be taught using a language that has real-world significance, you can quickly start applying what you learn. In fact, I would absolutely recommend that you do so because you will expand your knowledge of programming much faster by actually programming. The more you program, the more you solidify the foundation knowledge. By setting yourself tasks, you are stretching yourself, thereby expanding your skills and gaining new experience. This experience is invaluable when it comes to projects that you might have to do and also gives you an advantage when it comes to any exams!

Tips

- ❏ Take plenty of notes.

- ❏ Practice regularly and work on your own "out-of-hours" projects.

- ❏ Many students are entitled to cheap "student licenses" for software and programming tools — if you can, take advantage of these offers as they can save you thousands of dollars!

- ❏ If you are given the opportunity to use more than one language, take it!

Work-Based Training

More and more businesses see training their employees as a valuable part of keeping their workforce flexible and giving them an edge over their competitors. Because of this, work-based training is becoming more and more common.

Work-based training differs a lot from the traditional school or college programming route. First, the history of programming is viewed as irrelevant because it takes too long to cover and isn't seen as an important use of the training time.

Another difference is that in the workplace the training usually delves straight into whatever language is needed — it is unlikely that anyone would be taught more than one language simultaneously. You might be given a choice, but all the choices will be real languages that have commercial significance.

The time that the training takes will also be shorter — a lot shorter — but that's possible because the training will be much more specific and task-oriented. The basics that you need will be covered at the start, but after that the elements of programming will be covered as required. This allows the training to flow better and means that you get a better mix of theory and practical experience.

You will more than likely be provided with all the materials that you need, such as:

❑ Texts

❑ Software

❑ Sample code

❑ Support

If you are given access to online resources or paid-for communities, make good use of these while they're available — they can be a great resource that can really boost your programming career and help give you a tremendous head start.

Tips

❑ If you get a choice of languages to learn, do some research first and choose the one of greatest interest/benefit to you.

❑ If you are given access to a "learn at your own pace" system, use it in that way and don't feel that you have to rush.

❑ Keep all materials you are given (books, notes, software) and annotate them — this is a great skill booster!

❑ Keep all source code you produce — this will be great way to judge your progress later on!

Hobby Programmer

Hobby programmers are lucky programmers because they are motivated by their own desire to learn. This means they aren't usually under any time pressure or pressure to produce. This relaxed state is one of the best states for learning and absorbing information and making progress. Hobby programmers are also, oddly enough, more motivated to learn and try out new things than those learning in a more controlled environment.

There are disadvantages too. You have to provide all your learning materials, which might cost you a bit. You'll also have to structure your learning time around everything else that you do, and that can sometimes mean that you don't always get around to programming as often as you'd like.

As a hobby programmer, you can take as long as you like or take as little time as you want over things. You also can make choices about what you want to learn, and there is no pressure on you to learn everything or in a particular order. The basics need covering initially so that you are in a position to actually program, but after that you have a freedom to learn only the areas that are important to you.

Tip

- ❏ Try to get some programming practice in daily initially — the more often you practice the better your programming will be and the faster you will progress.

- ❏ Program is short bursts initially — no more than an hour.

- ❏ If you find that a problem becomes frustrating, walk away from it for a while and come back later. You might just find that a short break from what you are doing improves your concentration and skill.

- ❏ Keep notes of what you are doing and where you are up to — there's nothing worse than forgetting where you are!

- ❏ If you find that things have become tough, a great tip is to backtrack a little and go over familiar ground again before you move to new areas.

The Languages

If you are new to programming, then the first thing you need to do is choose a language that you are going to learn. There are several languages that are ideally suited for learning. The languages that we are going to be using in this book are:

- ❏ C++
- ❏ Java
- ❏ VBScript
- ❏ JavaScript

These have been chosen by me for a variety of reasons:

- ❏ They can be used for real-world applications.
- ❏ They are easy to learn.
- ❏ They can be used to demonstrate programming concepts.
- ❏ They can all be learned using free tools!

How I Will Teach You to Program

Before we go any further, let's take a look at what you are going to learn in the pages of this book.

- ❏ **The fundamentals.** This book teaches you the basics of programming. These basics are the fundamental knowledge that you need no matter what language you choose and no matter what you want to do. Most of this will be applicable to whichever language you choose to use.

- ❏ **The basics of the various languages.** This book covers the basics of these languages. This will give you a head start in using the languages and the applications.

- ❏ **Example applications.** In the process of learning to program, we'll be creating some interesting code that you can use and modify for your later projects.

There are some things that we won't be covering. This book isn't a *Complete Guide to C++* or *Everything You Need to Know about Java* — if it were, this book would be the first volume of many! Also, as a beginner to programming, you don't need that kind of information just yet!

Why Not Buy a Book Covering a Specific Language?

Almost all the books on the market that cover specific languages just aren't suited to beginners.

Why? The problem with books covering specific programming languages is that they assume that you are already a programmer and that you don't need any coverage of the basics. Those books that do cover the basics only do so in the form of a primer and don't give much page coverage to the knowledge you need to create a firm foundation.

The other problem with the texts and manuals covering specific programming languages is that they, more often than not, cover commercial languages, meaning that you need to spend money on expensive commercial packages that are too complex for the learner.

Be very careful about buying books that have "learning edition" copies of software applications bundled with the CD — most of these software packages are disabled in some way and don't offer you the tools you need to do proper programming.

The Tools

Let's now look at the tools you need to start to learn to program!

We'll divide the tools up into two convenient categories:

- ❑   General tools and utilities
- ❑   Programming-specific tools

General Tools and Utilities

There are a few tools that make programming easier, and they are listed in the following subsections.

Text Editor

A text editor is a handy tool because you can use it for a variety of different programming languages. There are many to choose from (both free and commercial), and I recommend the following:

- ❑   Windows Notepad (free)
- ❑   UltreEdit (commercial)

Windows Notepad

This is the standard text editor that comes loaded with the Windows operating system (every version of Windows has had a version of Notepad included (shown in Figure 5-9).

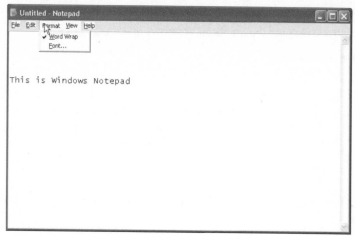

Figure 5-9

To find Notepad click Start and then All Programs (Windows XP — on other operating system click on Programs) then click on Accessories and then on the Notepad icon (shown in Figure 5-10).

Notepad

Figure 5-10

Notepad is a very basic text editor with no special programming facilities, and it has no special features specifically designed for programming. Nonetheless Notepad has been a firm favorite among programmers for years. The basic Save facility is shown in Figure 5-11.

Figure 5-11

- **Cost**: Free
- **Availability**: Free with the Microsoft Windows operating systems
- **Features**: Very basic

UltraEdit

UltraEdit is in my opinion the best text editor available on the market. This is shown in Figure 5-12.

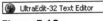

Figure 5-12

It isn't free, but it comes jam-packed with loads of features that are ideally suited to programmers — features such as:

- Syntax highlighting
- Line numbering
- Advanced save features (see Figure 5-13)

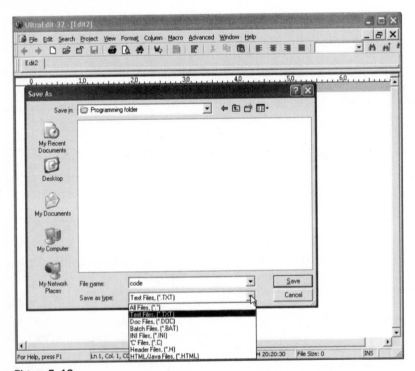

Figure 5-.13

❑ **Cost**: $35 (trial download available)

❑ **Availability**: www.ultraedit.com

❑ **Features**: Fully featured

Utilities

Utilities are tools that help make your job easier and quicker. They're not directly relevant to programming, but are tools that make your actual programming time quicker and easier and stop you from having to fight with your system.

Winzip

A programmer can produce a lot of files, and they can start to build up quickly and become hard to navigate and store.

A compression tool can help you store all the files relating to a particular project (or aspect of a project) all in one place, and one of the best compression tools available is Winzip, shown in Figure 5-14.

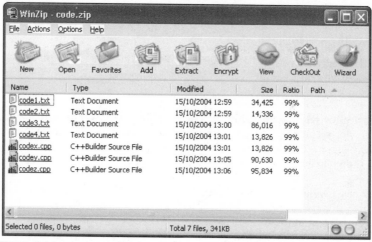

Figure 5-14

Compressing your project files into a single compressed file has huge advantages. It reduces clutter — all the files that you need can be found in one place, making the whole job a lot tidier. This way you can keep all the files you created, saving the changes you've made to the code along the way. Compressed files also (rather obviously) save a lot of disk space. The compressed .zip file detailed here holds nearly 315 KB of data but when compressed shrinks to an incredible 2 KB. Text compresses incredibly but there is also a great disk space saving to be made from compressing test files that you create along the way. Here a 215 KB executable has been compressed down to 170 KB (see Figure 5-15). Not as good a compression ration as that achieved then compressing the source code, but still a space saver.

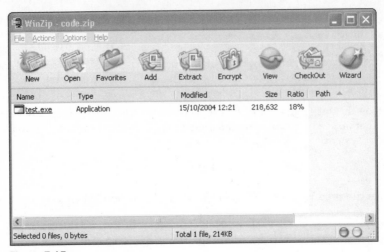

Figure 5-15

❑ **Cost**: $29 (trial download available)

❑ **Availability**: www.winzip.com

❑ **Features**: Fully featured

UltraCompare

When you are dealing with a lot of different files containing code where there may be very little differences between one and another, it can be handy to quickly scan files for changes. One tool that I've found extremely capable of doing this is UltraCompare (by the makers of the text editor UltraEdit). This application is shown in action in Figure 5-16.

UltraCompare has a variety of useful compare features:

❑ **File compare**. Scan for differences in files

❑ **Folder compare**. Scan for differences in files contained in a folder

❑ **Binary compare**. Scan binary files for changes

Being able to spot changes in files, as shown in Figure 5-17, can be useful when you are looking for changes made and can be extremely valuable when looking for errors that have crept into the code.

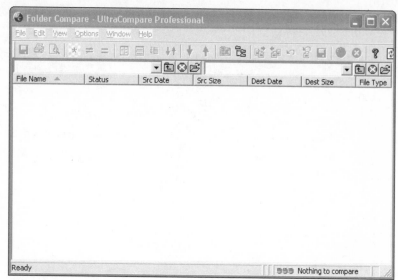

Figure 5-16

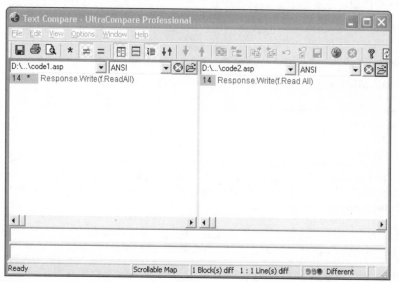

Figure 5-17

UltraCompare can be used to spot multiple differences between files and even to look for just the similar lines in files and disregard changes (see Figure 5-18).

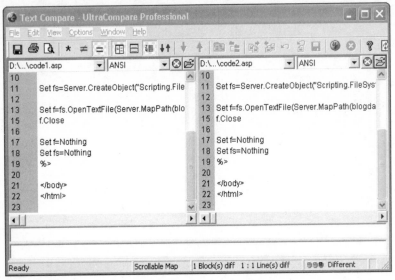

Figure 5-18

- ❏ **Cost**: $30 (trial download available)
- ❏ **Availability**: www.ultraedit.com
- ❏ **Features**: File, folder and binary compare

SnagIt

Sometimes it's really handy to take a screenshot or screen capture of what you are doing and save that. This might be because you are compiling help files for people using your application or may be that you are just keeping a record of the progress of your application. Whatever the reason, the ability to take professional screenshots can be very valuable.

One of the best programs for taking screenshots is SnagIt by TechSmith and can be seen in Figure 5-19. This enables you to take professional-quality screenshots that you can use in documentation or on the Web.

This program allows you to take a variety of different kinds of screenshots:

- ❏ Full-screen capture
- ❏ Windows
- ❏ Menus
- ❏ Screen objects
- ❏ Specific regions
- ❏ Capture text
- ❏ Capture video

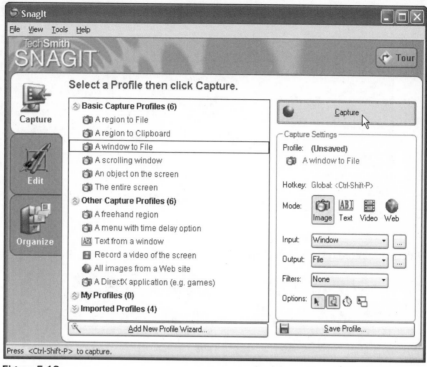

Figure 5-19

You can then output these in a variety of file formats.

- **Cost**: $39.95 (trial download available)
- **Availability**: www.snagit.com
- **Features**: Fully functional screen and video capture ability

Programming Tools

Now it's time to look at the tools of the programming trade. Programming tools are the actual tools you will use to write, create, or run the code and will be used a great deal over the remainder of the book.

Some of the tools you need are just tools that you will use to run the code that you create in a text editor, while others are specific to the language that you are using.

From this point forward, this book assumes that you are fairly confident and competent at working your way around the Windows operating system. We will be using several components of the operating system, in particular:

- Windows Explorer, shown in Figure 5-20

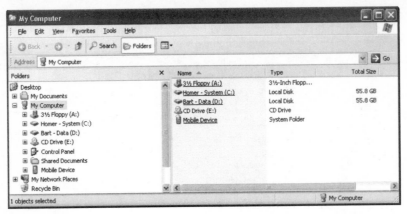

Figure 5-20

❑ Internet Explorer, shown in Figure 5-21

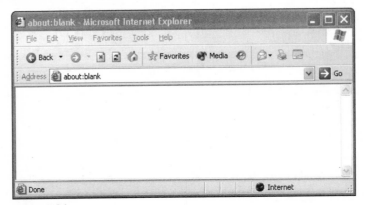

Figure 5.21

❑ The command window, shown in Figure 5-22

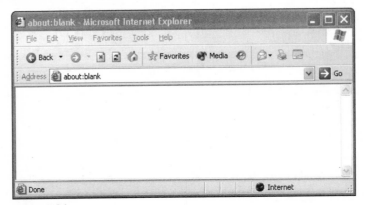

Figure 5-22

Let's take a look at the tools that we will be using.

Java

Java is a programming language developed by Sun Microsystems in 1995 that was primarily designed for use on the Internet. Java was created deliberately to be similar to C++ language but much simpler to learn and use than C++. Java can be used to create fully functional applications that can be run on a single computer or be distributed among servers and computers on a network system.

The main power of Java is that it is known as a *platform-independent language*, meaning that it has been designed specifically to run of different types of system (Macintosh and PC for instance) and different operating systems. The code itself is called *bytecode*, and this code does not depend on any specific aspect of the hardware or software — the running of the code is controlled by a special runtime environment.

To start programming in Java you need two things:

❑   **The Java Software Development Kit (SDK).** This is used to develop Java applications and it contains tools and information you need. This download is called J2SE (Java 2, Special Edition) and is shown in Figure 5-23.

Figure 5-23

❑   **The Java Virtual Machine (VM) runtime environment.** The Java Virtual Machine is needed on each machine that will run the Java code. This download is called Java VM (this is included with the SDK, but every machine that runs your code will need it installed).

Figure 5-24

Windows XP does not come with the Java VM installed but all other Windows operating systems do.

Both of these are available for download from the official Java Web site, which you can visit at
http://java.sun.com/j2se.

Installation of these downloads is easy. Double-click them, as shown in Figure 5-25.

Figure 5-25

You then agree to the license and choose where to install it to on your PC. The installation then proceeds, as shown in Figure 5-26.

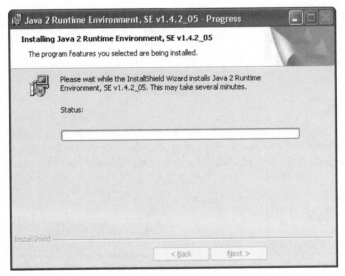

Figure 5-26

The installation may take many minutes and completes by installing the VM runtime environment. This is shown in Figure 5-27.

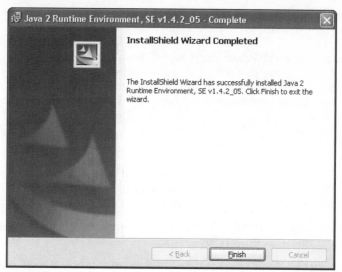

Figure 5-27

Once the software is installed, use Windows Explorer to navigate to the installation directory (the default is c:\j2sdk1.4.2_06) to check that it has been properly installed (see Figure 5-28).

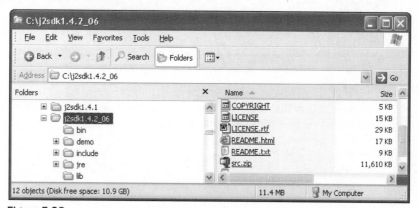

Figure 5-28

Once this is installed it is ready to use later.

C++

Many people believe that to be able to program with and use C++ you need expensive applications — compilers and development environments. This is simply not true. One of the major side effects of a language becoming a popular and well-used academic language is that there are plenty of free tools that spring up around it — created by teachers and professors for academic use.

Before we go any further, a word about the phrase *academic use:* When a program or application is said to be for academic use that means that it can be used freely for learning purposes — so a programming tool or compiler described like that can generally be used freely within the context of learning. These tools can be used by students and teachers alike to further their knowledge of the subject.

But there are usually limits as to what you can do. Here are a few of the common limits placed on academic software:

❑ **The software cannot be used for any commercial purposes.** What that usually means is that you are allowed to create applications using the tools but you are prohibited from selling anything you create. Generally giving away what you create is legal.

❑ **There is no support for the tools.** There may be some sort of informal support system in place but expect to get what you pay for — in this case, nothing!

❑ **At your own risk.** A common phrase with all software nowadays, but again expect it to apply doubly so for free academic software.

Expect the documentation to be basic. This isn't always the case but is often true.

To be absolutely sure of your rights, check the licensing agreement accompanying the application, and if you are in any doubt as to what you can or can't do, then contact the company or author of the application.

Stay legal!

Now with that out of the way, let's take a look at some of the C++ tools that are available.

Borland C++ compiler

One of the best free compilers available is from Borland. They make available for free their command line compiler from the Borland C++ Builder application.

The current download is available from:
`www.borland.com/products/downloads/download_cbuilder.html`

The current version is version 5.5, and the download size is 8.7 MB.

Download the latest version of the software (shown in Figure 5-29) from the Web site.

Figure 5-29

Once the package has downloaded, double-click it to run it and begin the installation process, as shown in Figure 5-30.

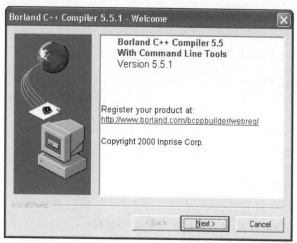

Figure 5-30

The default installation location of the application is C:\Borland\BCC55 (shown in Figure 5-31). Stick to this location unless you really have no choice.

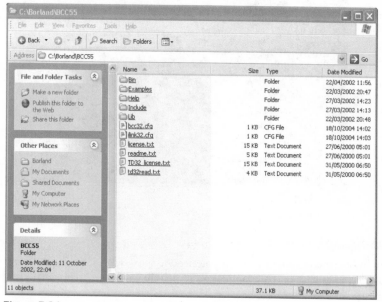

Figure 5-31

To get the software to work you have to create two new configuration files. Don't worry, you don't have to do anything complicated.

The two files are:

```
bcc32.cfg
ilink32.cfg
```

The contents of the files are as follows. First, `bcc32.cfg`:

```
-I"c:\Borland\Bcc55\include"
-L"c:\Borland\Bcc55\lib"
```

And secondly, `ilink32.cfg`:

```
-L"c:\Borland\Bcc55\lib"
```

Create these files in an application such as UltraEdit or Windows Notepad and save them in `C:\Borland\BCC55`.

This application is command line only — there is no help for writing code here at all, and all code will have to be created in a text editor. This code is then processed and compiled by the application and an executable file is created. The compiler in action can be seen in Figure 5-32.

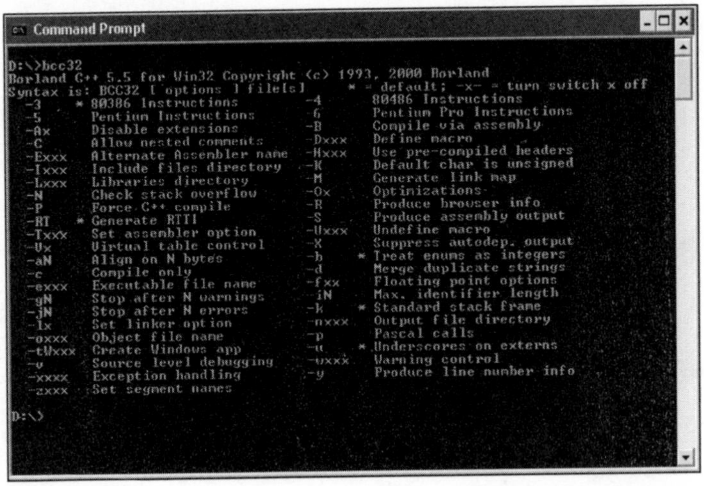

Figure 5-32

Scripting Languages

This last section offers a quick tour of what you need to work with scripting languages such as VBScript or JavaScript. The simplicity of these languages is such that you don't need an awful lot to be able to work with them. The basics are:

❑ **Text editor.** To create the code with

❑ **Compliant Web browser.** To run the code

That's it!

Compliant browsers depend on the scripting language used:

❑ **VBScript.** Internet Explorer (this has to be running on the Windows operating system)

❑ **JavaScript.** Nearly all modern browsers, including Internet Explorer, Netscape Navigator, Opera, and Mozilla

Summary

In this chapter, you've toured the tools that you need to get stuck in coding. You've looked at the tools that you need for a variety of languages that are covered in this book.

I'd suggest you download what you need now because this will save you a lot of time, effort, and hassles later and means that you are all set to begin coding immediately.

As for a text browser, I recommend UltraEdit because of the amazing features it makes available to the programmer, but there is no requirement to use this and you can always choose the text editor installed on your operating system or download one of the many free versions available. What is important is that you have one installed and are comfortable using it.

Simple Coding

This chapter you will get really involved with some serious code! There's a lot that we are going to be covering in this chapter, but don't worry — even if you haven't done any coding before we will take it nice and easy, doing everything step by step.

In this chapter, you will get exposure to the following programming and coding concepts:

- ❑ Commenting code
- ❑ Variables
- ❑ Strings
- ❑ Processing input
- ❑ Outputs
- ❑ Simple math

That's a lot of material to cover, so let's get going!

Commenting Code

Commenting code is the process of leaving cues as to what the code means within the actual code itself. These comments can be for yourself or for other programmers who will look at your code. Comments are not read by any compiler or interpreter while processing code — they are there entirely for the benefit of humans reading the code.

It's odd that we start this chapter talking about writing stuff in the code that has no bearing on what the computer actually does. The comments that you create are only for the benefit of (and the eyes of) people as opposed to being for the computer.

One of the most important things you have to do while programming, and doubly so while you are learning, is to comment your code.

Not only are comment tags handy for adding comments to your code, but they are also a great way to remove lines of code that are causing trouble or are no longer needed without actually having to physically remove them.

How you comment code depends on the language you are using. In this chapter, we will be looking at VBScript, JavaScript, and a little C++ and so we should look at how to comment code in these languages.

VBScript Comments

VBScript is one of the easiest languages to learn because its structure is so similar to that of English.

Comments in VBScript are easy — VBScript makes use of apostrophes to comment code. So, if you are writing code comments would look like this:

```
' This line is a comment.
' As is this one and the one below.
' I am a comment too!
```

There is no structure regarding what follows the apostrophe so all the following are valid comments:

```
'              Lots of whitespace at the beginning
' comment starts lowercase
' Symbols * ( ) / &£^ {}
```

What you do need to make sure is that the apostrophe you use is a simple apostrophe and not the curly ones you find in some word processors. Figure 6-1 shows an enlarged image of the simple style apostrophe, while Figure 6-2 shows an incorrect curly one.

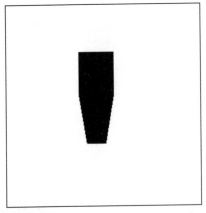

Figure 6-1

Another style of comment that you can use is the REM statement. For VBScript this is:

```
REM This is a comment.
REM It stands for "remark."
```

We call REM a VBScript statement because both it and the apostrophe actually do something — they tell the interpreter to ignore what follows! This makes it a statement.

Figure 6-2

REM stands for remark, and it gives rise to statements that you might have heard programmers say such as:

"That line is remmed out."

"I remmed out the line of code that was causing problems."

You can mix and match apostrophes and remarks in your code, and this won't cause any problems at all.

```
REM This is a remark.
' This is a comment.
REM Another remark
' Another comment
```

One type of comment your code should have is the tombstone comment block that appears at the beginning of the code to give a rundown of what the code does. Two styles of comment mean two types of tombstone comment block.

One that uses the apostrophe:

```
' Tombstone comments
' Widget 1.0.2
' Author: A. N. Other
' 22-10-04
'
' Code starts below
```

And one that uses the REM statement:

```
REM Tombstone comments
REM Widget 1.0.2
REM Author: A. N. Other
REM 22-10-04
REM
REM Code starts below
```

As you will see later, you will be able to add comments to the end of lines containing code, such as this for example:

```
x = x + 1 ' This takes x and adds 1 to the value.
```

For now though, don't worry too much about that — as we write code, you will get experience in commenting.

Things to Watch For

Make sure that you use only apostrophes and not double quotes, commas, or anything like that.

```
" This is not a comment.
, This isn't a comment either.
```

Also make sure that you leave a space between the apostrophe or REM statement and the comment. If you don't, the comment will not be ignored.

```
'Not a valid comment
REManother invalid comment
```

Both of the following are also valid comments because the first apostrophe or REM turns the second into simply a comment that's ignored.

```
REM REM A valid comment
' ' Another valid comment
```

These are also valid:

```
' REM valid too
REM ' Also valid!
```

A common problem that people have if they are familiar with HTML (Hypertext Markup Language) is that they try to use HTML comment tags (which are <!-- and -->) instead of the correct ones. This will not work within script and will cause an error!

Quick Exercise

Work through these quick questions just to make sure that you have VBScript comments figured out.

What do you use to define comments in VBScript?

Which of the following are NOT valid VBScript comments?

```
'Comment 1

' Comment 2

REM comment 3

REM_Comment4

" Comment 5
```

```
REM      Comment 6

' REM Comment 7

REM ' comment 8

<!-- Comment 9 -->
```

Is this comment valid?

```
x = x + 1 ' A comment following code
```

JavaScript Comments

JavaScript comment tags are simple tags — the first we will look at is the simple two forward slashes, as follows:

```
//
```

Just prefix this onto any comments you make.

```
// Comments go here.
```

You can do all the same things with a JavaScript comment tag as you can with a VBScript tag.

Here is a set of comments:

```
// Comments
// More comments
// Even more
```

You can create a tombstone comment block too:

```
// Tombstone comments
// Widget 1.0.2
// Author: A. N. Other
// 22-10-04
//
// Code starts below.
```

If you are going to do something like that though, you are better off using the multiline comment tags:

```
/*
Comments go here.
*/
```

There are great for tombstone comment blocks:

```
/*
Tombstone comments
Widget 1.0.2
Author: A. N. Other
```

```
22-10-04

Code starts below.
*/
```

Remember that the order is as follows:

Open with slash star:

```
/*
```

Close with star slash:

```
/*
*/
```

Add the comments between the two:

```
/*
Comments go here.
*/
```

Things to Watch For

The main causes of errors are that people either use the wrong slashes:

```
\\ Invalid comments!!!!
```

They don't leave whitespace between the slashes and the comment:

```
//Invalid comments
```

Or they use weird combinations:

```
/\Invalid!
\/Also invalid
```

With multiline comments, you need to make sure that you get the order of slash star and star slash right:

```
*/
Invalid comments!
/*
```

Quick Exercise

Work through these quick questions just to make sure that you have JavaScript comments figured out.

How do you define comments in JavaScript?

Which of the following are NOT valid JavaScript comments?

```
\\ Comment 1
```

```
// Comment 2
```

```
/*
Comments 3
*/

//Comment 4

/*Comment 5

/* Comment 6
```

C++ *Comments*

C++ comment tags follow the same rules that JavaScript comment tags do and include single-line comments and multiline comments:

```
// Single line comment
```

And:

```
/*
Multiline comments
Look like this
*/
```

The same rules as for JavaScript apply, and you can use tombstone comment blocks in exactly the same way (in fact, tombstone comment blocks are very important in C++ and are used extensively).

```
/*
C++ Project
Widget 3.1.9
Author: A. N. Other
22-10-04

Code starts below.
*/
```

Things to Watch For

The problem areas with C++ comment tags are exactly the same as those for JavaScript, the main difference being that if you make mistakes it is the compiler that will pick up on it rather than the interpreter. The compiler will detail the location of the error, but might be a bit ambiguous as to the actual error.

Common C++ comment errors are:

Using the wrong slashes:

```
\\ This will cause problems!!!!
```

Not leaving whitespace between the slashes and the comment:

```
//This is incorrect!
```

With multiline comments, you need to make sure that you get the order of slash star and star slash right:

```
*/
This comment block will
throw errors.
/*
```

Quick Exercise

Work through these quick questions just to make sure that you have C++ comments figured out.

True/False: C++ comment tags are like VBScript comments.

How do you define comments in C++?

Which of the following are NOT valid C++ comments?

```
// Comment 1

\/ Comment 2

/*
Comments 3
*/

*/
Comments 4
/*

' Comment 5

REM Comment 6
```

Variables

Variables are the cornerstone of most programming because they allow you to work with and manipulate data.

There are lots of definitions floating about as to what a variable is, some very complex and some very simple. You might hear things such as it being a "location in memory that can be referenced and accessed." While not inaccurate, this is a really complicated way of defining the term.

I much prefer to think of a variable as a named placeholder for data that you can reference. I've created a pictorial representation in Figure 6-3.

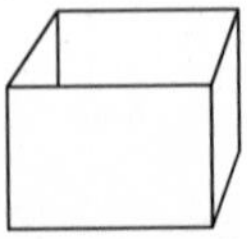

Variable

Figure 6-3

You load the data into a variable, and it can then be accessed and manipulated by the code, as shown in Figure 6-4.

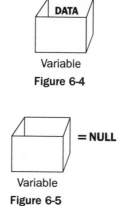

Variable

Figure 6-4

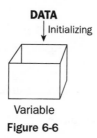

= NULL

Variable

Figure 6-5

An empty, null, variable (as depicted in Figure 6-5) is like a bucket or basket waiting to be filled — waiting to be given purpose. When you load a value into a variable, this is called *initializing* the variable (see Figure 6-6).

DATA
↓ Initializing

Variable

Figure 6-6

The variable can hold data of all kinds — a few of the commonest types of data that variables can hold are:

❑   Test strings (see Figure 6-7)

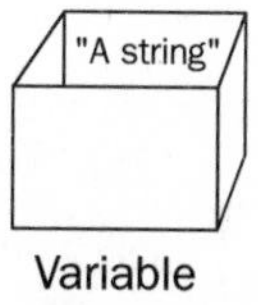

Variable

Figure 6-7

❑   Numbers

  ❑   Floating point (see Figure 6-8)

Variable

Figure 6-8

❑   Integers (see Figure 6-9)

Variable

Figure 6-9

❑   Boolean values — true and false (see Figure 6-10)

Variable

Figure 6-10

The great thing about variables is that they are very versatile. You can easily change what the variable holds.

There are two ways that a variable can be updated:

❑   The variable can be changed completely (see Figure 6-11). The data type can stay the same or it can be changed. This is an example of a variable usually being reused for a different purpose within the code.

Generally, this isn't recommended because, as you will see later, it encourages problems and makes mistakes more likely.

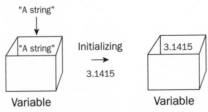

Figure 6-11

❑   The variable can be updated. This means that the program has worked on the data held and made some change to it. This is the most common way that variables are used in code (Figure 6-12).

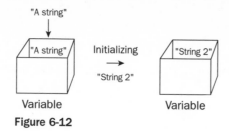

Figure 6-12

Variables in Action

Let's make some progress programming and make use of a few variables. For this part of the book, we'll look at JavaScript because it's quick, it's simple, no compiling is required, it effectively demonstrates the point, and it works in a way similar to other browsers.

Variable Run Through

OK, let's run through some code that looks at how variables work. We'll be making quite some progress here and introducing some key concepts that you probably haven't seen before. However, these next few pages will give you some good hands-on programming experience.

Creating a Template

Since we are going to be using JavaScript, the first thing that you are going to need is a template to allow you to run the code in the browser. For what we are going to do here the following template will do just fine.

```
<html>
<head>
<title>JavaScript Test Template</title>
<script language="JavaScript">
<!--
/*
Code goes below this comment block
*/

// -->
</script>
</head>
<body>

</body>
</html>
```

See the HTML comment tags used inside the <script> and </script> tags in this example? This is done so that the code won't cause an error in some Web browsers.

Most of the contents of the file are HTML, and if you have experience in creating your own Web pages, then much of it will be familiar to you already. Just in case though, here's a quick run-through of the code.

There three lines start out the file, open the head of the page (where your code will go), and add a title to the page.

```
<html>
<head>
<title>JavaScript Test Template</title>
```

The next eight lines are called a script block — it is the block that will hold the JavaScript that you are going to be creating.

```
<script language="JavaScript">
<!--
/*
Code goes below this comment block
*/

// -->
</script>
```

The remaining five lines close the header of the HTML file, open, and closes the body of the page (which would be the place where the contents of the page would go), and finally close the page.

```
</head>
<body>

</body>
</html>
```

Take this code, copy it out into a text file, and save it as `jstemplate.htm`. This is a file that you can open in a Web browser to test your code.

The browser that I recommend that you use to run JavaScript examples is Internet Explorer (although the code should work in most other modern browsers).

Once you have this file completed, open it up in a text editor (Windows Notepad or UltraEdit, for example). Figure 6-13 shows the code in UltraEdit.

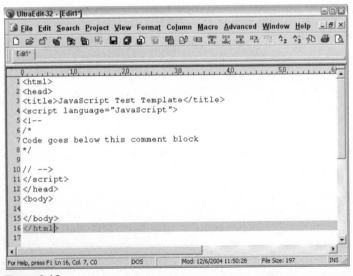

Figure 6-13

Writing Code

OK, let's write some code that looks at variables in action.

Since we are dealing with variables, let's create two variables. For simplicity, we'll call them x and y. To do this we use the var keyword to declare (another word for create) the variables.

```
<html>
<head>
<title>JavaScript Test Template</title>
<script language="JavaScript">
<!--
/*
Code goes below this comment block
*/
var x
var y
// -->
</script>
</head>
<body>
</body>
</html>
```

We could have declared the variables on one line, as follows:

```
<html>
<head>
<title>JavaScript Test Template</title>
<script language="JavaScript">
<!--
/*
Code goes below this comment block
*/
var x, y
// -->
</script>
</head>
<body>
</body>
</html>
```

At the moment, both variables have been declared, but are undefined and therefore null.

To define them, we write the following:

```
<html>
<head>
<title>JavaScript Test Template</title>
<script language="JavaScript">
<!--
/*
Code goes below this comment block
*/
var x = 3
var y = 4
// -->
```

```
</script>
</head>
<body>
</body>
</html>
```

Now x holds the value 3 and y holds the value 4. These are numbers that they hold (integers of whole numbers at that) and not the alphanumeric characters 3 and 4. If you wanted the variable to hold the alphanumeric characters 3 and 4, then you would need to write the following:

```
<html>
<head>
<title>JavaScript Test Template</title>
<script language="JavaScript">
<!--
/*
Code goes below this comment block
*/
var x = "3"
var y = "4"
// -->
</script>
</head>
<body>
</body>
</html>
```

You can now go on to prove that the variables now hold values by getting the script to display the values in a pop-up box as follows:

```
<html>
<head>
<title>JavaScript Test Template</title>
<script language="JavaScript">
<!--
/*
Code goes below this comment block
*/
var x = 3
var y = 4
alert(x)
alert(y)
// -->
</script>
</head>
<body>
</body>
</html>
```

Save the file and load it in the browser. When the page loads up two pop-ups will be displayed, as shown in Figures 6-14 and 6-15.

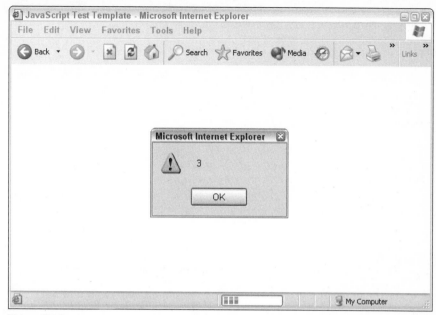

Figure 6-14

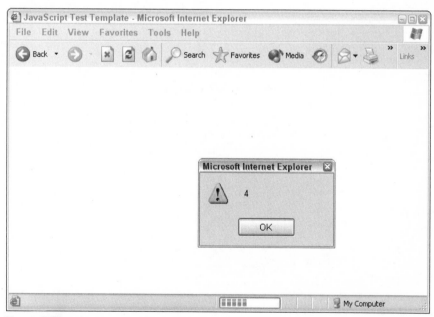

Figure 6-15

The pop-up boxes show the value of the variables. Now you can set to work on the values held by the variables and use the pop-up boxes to show you how the values change.

Take a look at the following code alteration.

*From now on I'm only going to show the JavaScript part of the code and omit the HTML component —
just remember that you need the HTML as well.*

```
<script language="JavaScript">
<!--
/*
Code goes below this comment block
*/
var x = 3
var y = 4
alert(x)
alert(y)
var x = 10
var y = 7
alert(x)
alert(y)
// -->
</script>
```

What happened here? Well, take a look at the pop-ups that are generated (see Figures 6-16, 6-17, 6-18,
and 6-19).

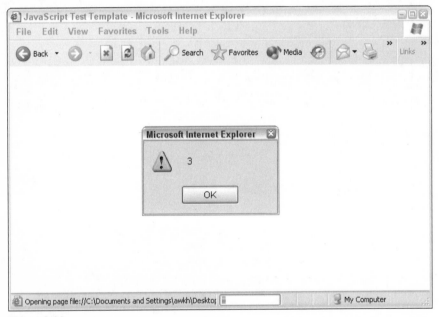

Figure 6-16

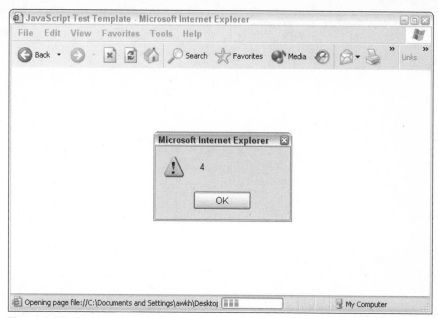

Figure 6-17

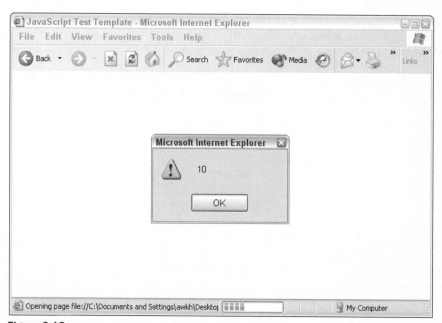

Figure 6-18

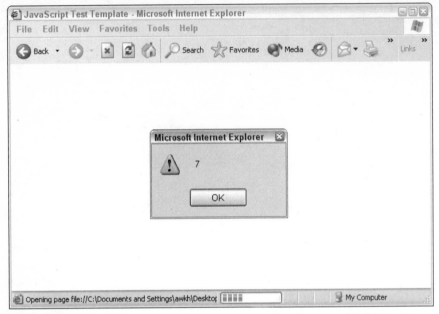

Figure 6-19

The values for the variables are declared and then displayed in Figures 6-16 and 6-17. These are the same values as before. But look at the code. After that, we declare them again, this time with different values and display them again in pop-ups which clearly show the values have been replaced by the new values.

In that example we replace integers with other integers, but there's no rule that says that we have to do that. The following code replaces the integer values with text strings.

```
<script language="JavaScript">
<!--
/*
Code goes below this comment block
*/
var x = 3
var y = 4
alert(x)
alert(y)
var x = "Hello"
var y = "World!"
alert(x)
alert(y)
// -->
</script>
```

Let's go back to numeric values for a moment. I want to show you that you can do a lot more than just have static numbers displayed when you use variables. Take a look at the following code:

```
<script language="JavaScript">
<!--
/*
Code goes below this comment block
```

```
*/
var x = 3
var y = 4
var answer
var answer = x + y
alert(answer)
// -->
</script>
```

Here we've introduced a new variable called `answer`:

```
var answer
```

We then define `answer` as the sum of `x` and `y`:

```
answer = x + y
```

And display the answer in a pop-up:

```
alert(answer)
```

The pop-up result is shown in Figure 6-20.

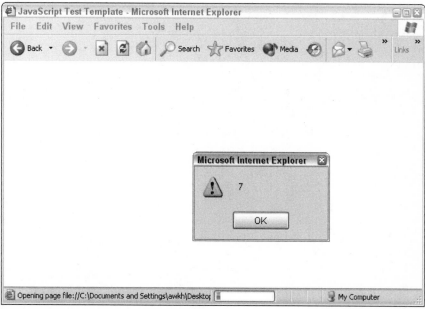

Figure 6-20

As you can see, what has been displayed is the result of the sum 3 + 4. From this you can see that we have the beginnings of true programming because we have the ability to manipulate stored data.

You can reuse variables too. Take a look at the following code, which reuses the same variables over and over.

```
<script language="JavaScript">
<!--
/*
Code goes below this comment block
*/
var x = 3
var y = 4
var answer
var answer = x + y + x + y + x
alert(answer)
// -->
</script>
```

Figure 6-21 shows the value of answer.

This is the equivalent of doing the following:

```
<script language="JavaScript">
<!--
/*
Code goes below this comment block
*/
var x = 3
var y = 4
var answer
var answer = 3 + 4 + 3 + 4 + 3
alert(answer)
// -->
</script>
```

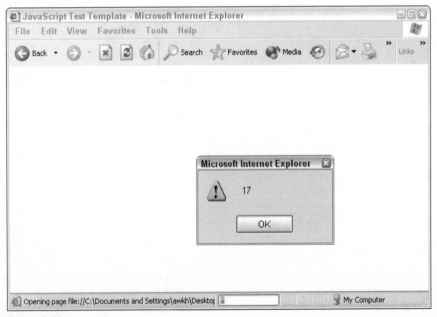

Figure 6-21

A quick and simple way to redefine a variable with an answer to a sum is:

```
<script language="JavaScript">
<!--
/*
Code goes below this comment block
*/
var x = 3
var y = 4
var x = x + y
alert(x)
// -->
</script>
```

The pop-up gives the value of x now as 7 and not 3 (see Figure 6-22). This new value will remain until the value of the variable is changed again or reset by rerunning the code.

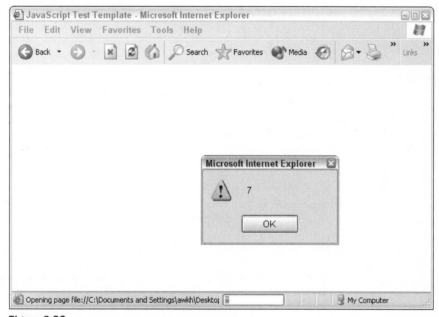

Figure 6-22

Have you noticed how we add `var` before each variable? In some languages when you first use a variable you need to define it explicitly before using it, after which you can use it without doing so. In JavaScript you do that just like that:

```
var myVariable
```

Afterward you can just use the variable without adding the var.

```
myVariable = "something ..."
```

JavaScript is a language that is less strict and allows you to get away without doing that. It's one of the areas you will find that varies from language to language. These niggling things that change from language to language can make learning them tricky.

Naming Variables

So far you've seen three variables:

```
x
y
answer
```

In the context of the code, what do you think of these variables? Are they effective? Do they tell you anything important? Are they descriptive?

Well, answer is to some degree, but x and y are pretty vague.

You could comment the code to make the variables stand out and be descriptive:

```
<script language="JavaScript">
<!--
/*
Code goes below this comment block
*/
var x = 3 // variable x - arbitrary number
var y = 4 // variable y - arbitrary number
var answer = x + y // variable answer - sum of x + y
alert(answer)
// -->
</script>
```

This works, but it is cumbersome because for it to be effective you'd have to comment each line that uses the variables, or do so every so often if it is used more than once. This adds a lot of bulk to the code.

A far better method is to be more methodical and thorough about naming the variables in the first place.

Before looking at naming variables and making them easy to understand, you first need to know what you can or can't use in a name.

Here's a quick rundown of the dos and don'ts of variable naming that apply pretty much across the board for most languages.

Don'ts

❑ Variable names cannot contain numbers at the beginning, as shown in Figure 6-23.

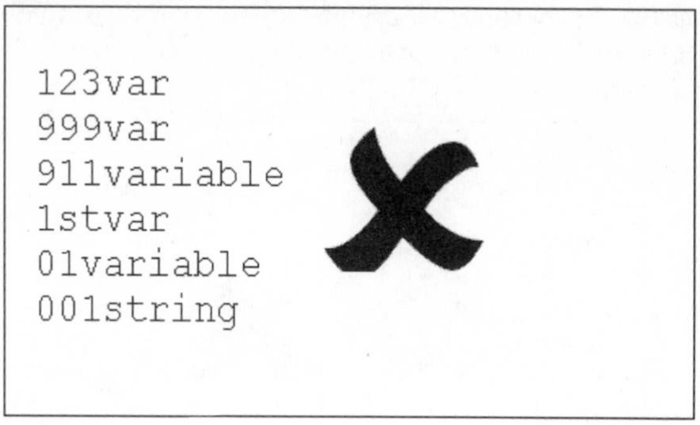

```
123var
999var
911variable
1stvar
01variable
001string
```

Figure 6-23

❏   Variable names cannot contain arithmetic operators — refer to Figure 6-24.

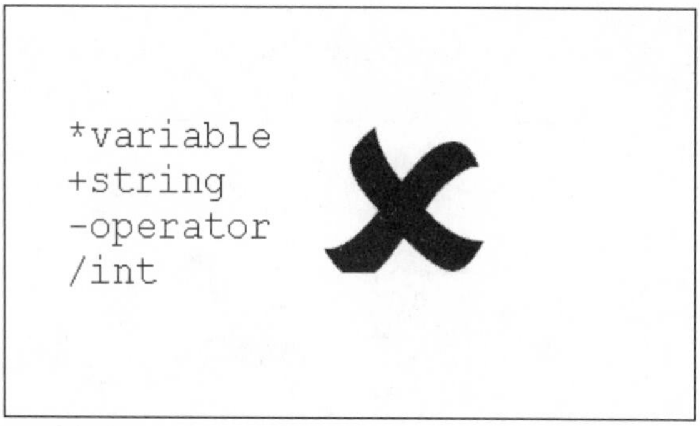

```
*variable
+string
-operator
/int
```

Figure 6-24

❏   Variable names cannot contain punctuation — refer to Figure 6-25.

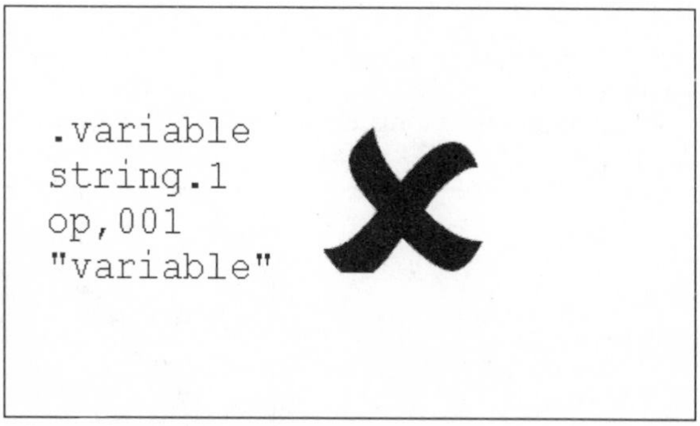

```
.variable
string.1
op,001
"variable"
```

Figure 6-25

❑ Variable names cannot consist of a keyword or reserved word that applies to the language, as shown in Figure 6-26.

```
var
alert
prompt
```

Figure 6-26

❑ Variable names cannot contain a space, as shown in Figure 6-27.

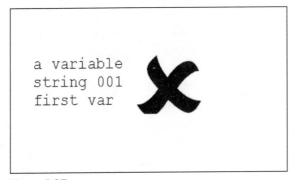

```
a variable
string 001
first var
```

Figure 6-27

Dos

❑ Variables can contain numbers as long as they aren't at the beginning, as shown in Figure 6-28.

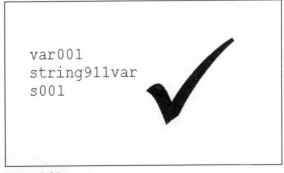

```
var001
string911var
s001
```

Figure 6-28

❏   Underscores are allowed in variable names, as shown in Figure 6-29.

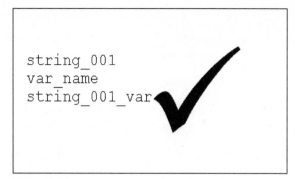

Figure 6-29

❏   Variables can contain mixed case, as indicated in Figure 6-30.

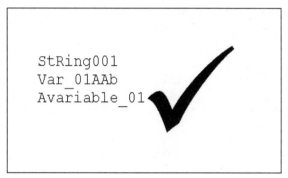

Figure 6-30

Naming of Variables

There are several ways that you can make the naming of variables clearer to and more effective for any programmer who has to come along afterward and read the code.

Let's look at a few schemes that you can use.

Clearer Naming

The first thing you can do to make variable names clearer is to use clearer naming. Take our earlier example:

```
x
y
answer
```

Which do you think is clearest? Well answer is of course.

In an application, you might have a statement like this:

```
z = x * y
```

where z is the product of x and y multiplied together. The math is quite clear, but what the variables actually represent is lost. Far better would be something like this:

```
totalvalue = subtotalprice * taxrate
```

That's a lot clearer and makes the code and the logic of the math easier to follow. It also makes logic errors in the code easier to spot. Take a look at this:

```
totalvalue = subtotalprice - taxrate
```

Subtracting the tax rate from the subtotal doesn't make sense does it? When the variables are named clearly, just by reviewing the code some errors become far more obvious.

Capitalization

Another thing that makes reading code easier is if you take care and capitalize the first letter of each word in the variable name. Take a look at these two lines of code:

```
totalvalue = subtotalprice - taxrate

TotalValue = SubTotalPrice - TaxRate
```

I think that you'll agree that the second one is a lot easier to read because the capitalization draws the eye to the word better.

A modification that makes reading the code easier and might be less work is to not capitalize the first letter of the variable. Take a look at this:

```
TotalValue = SubTotalPrice - TaxRate

totalValue = subTotalPrice - taxRate
```

Try to do this as often as often as possible because it really makes the code easier to read and interpret.

Use Underscores

Another way to clarify the variables is to make use of underscores in the variable names to augment the use of capitalization.

A good routine is to use underscores between words that have initial capitals, because this also aids in the reading of the code. Take a look at the following:

```
totalvalue = subtotalprice - taxrate

TotalValue = SubTotalPrice - TaxRate

totalValue = subTotalPrice - taxRate

totalValue = subTotal_Price - taxRate
```

The longer the variable names, the more that this scheme helps:

Take a look at these with and without the underscores:

```
totalValueBeforeTax
totalValue_Before_Tax
cpuCoreTempCelsius
cpuCore_Temp_Celsius
minFileSizeMb
minFile_Size_Mb
```

I think you will agree that the variable names containing both capitalization and underscores are easier to read than those without.

Naming Notation

Believe it or not there is notation for naming variables. This is called Hungarian Notation and was developed by a Microsoft programmer called Charles Simonyi, who just happened to be Hungarian, hence the name.

The purpose of Hungarian Notation was to bring order to the chaos of creating and representing variable names. It works by prefixing the name of the variable with letters that identify the type of information the variable holds.

For example, if you have a variable that held a text string, you could call it something like:

```
stringUser_Name
```

That would work but the problem would come when programmers started to shorten it (as programmers are apt to do!). Very soon you'd end up with:

```
strgUser_Name
sUser_Name
strUser_Name
```

And probably a lot more. Far better to offer a standard prefix.

There are a lot of prefixes, many of which needn't bother you right now and some that are unlikely to be of any use to you at all, but here are a few to get you started:

Prefix	Type	Example
Str	String	strUser_Name
C	Character	cStudent_Grade
Dt	Date (and time)	dtStart
Cur	Currency	curTotal
B	Boolean (true and false)	bIs_Valid
Int	Integer	intAge

There are lots more types, but for now this is probably enough to get you going. As you need more types and prefixes, we'll introduce them as we go.

Quick Exercise

Here are some quick questions to test your knowledge of variables and using them.

1. Explain in simple terms what a variable is.

2. Identify the variables in this code:

```
<script language="JavaScript">
<!--
/*
Code goes below this comment block
*/
var curTotal_Price = 3
var curTotal_Price = 4
curTotal = curTotal_Price + curTotal_Price
alert(curTotal)
// -->
</script>
```

3. Describe ways to make variables easier to spot and read.

4. Look at the following code and come up with better, more descriptive variable.

```
<script language="JavaScript">
<!--
/*
Code goes below this comment block
*/
var name = "A. N. Other"
var zipcode = 09090
var age = 27
var member = true
// -->
</script>
```

Strings

Let's now shift our attention away from variables and start to look at what they hold. So far we've mainly looked at variables that hold numbers (or to be more accurate, integers). Let's now have a look at another type of data that variables can hold — strings.

What Are Strings?

Technically, a string is a sequence of two or more characters. A string can contain alphanumeric characters (letters and numbers) as well as whitespace and symbols (such as punctuation).

One character would be just a character, although some languages look at one character as a string and almost all don't mind dealing with single characters as strings.

Here are some variables that hold strings:

```
var strTest_String1 = "Hello, World!"
var strTest_String2 = "123xyz"
var strTest_String3 = "[*^£/\¬"
```

It's important for you to realize that the string itself is what's contained within the quotation marks and does not include the quotation marks. So, the actual strings are:

```
Hello, World!
123xyz
[*^£/\¬
```

You can get JavaScript code to display text strings in much the same way as it displays numbers. Take a look at this code:

```
<script language="JavaScript">
<!--
/*
Code goes below this comment block
*/
var strName = "A. N. Other"
alert(strName)
// -->
</script>
```

The output of this is shown in Figure 6-31.

That's nothing new; if the code can display numbers, then displaying text is no real big deal. But now it's time to take a look at how you can manipulate variables and the text strings that they contain.

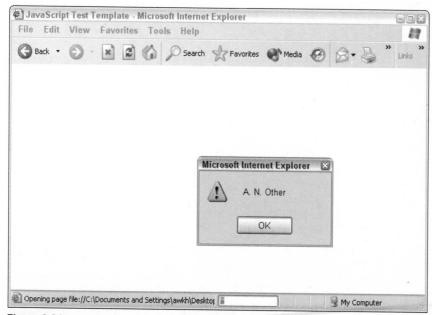

Figure 6-31

String Manipulation

Take a look at the following code:

```
<script language="JavaScript">
<!--
/*
Code goes below this comment block
*/
var strFirst_Name = "Andy"
var strMiddle_Initials = "N"
var strLast_Name = "Other"
alert(strFirst_Name)
alert(strMiddle_Initials)
alert(strLast_Name)
// -->
</script>
```

Running this code will cause three pop-up boxes to be displayed, as shown in Figure 6-32.

Figure 6-32

Now, that's interesting, but not very functional. It would be far better if you could manipulate the data and join the three parts of the name together to show it in one pop-up. Can this be done? Of course it can!

The process of joining text strings together is known as concatenation and is a basic string manipulation function.

Concatenating strings in JavaScript involves using the + operator. So, to concatenate the previous strings into a new variable and then display that you could write the following:

```
<script language="JavaScript">
<!--
/*
Code goes below this comment block
*/
var strFirst_Name = "Andy"
var strMiddle_Initials = "N"
var strLast_Name = "Other"
alert(strFirst_Name + strMiddle_Initials + strLast_Name)
// -->
</script>
```

The output pop-up from this is shown in Figure 6-33.

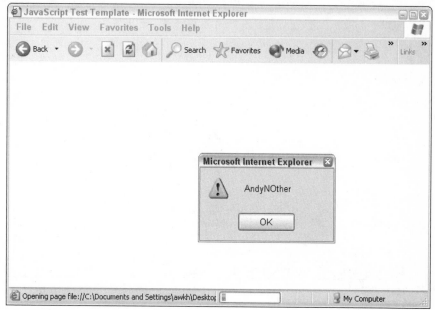

Figure 6-33

Do you notice something wrong with that output though? Notice how there are no spaces between the individual strings as concatenated. To add the spaces, you can input strings into the concatenation statement like this:

```
<script language="JavaScript">
<!--
/*
Code goes below this comment block
*/
var strFirst_Name = "Andy"
var strMiddle_Initials = "N"
var strLast_Name = "Other"
alert(strFirst_Name + " " + strMiddle_Initials + ". " + strLast_Name)
// -->
</script>
```

Figure 6-34 shows that the output in now formatted properly.

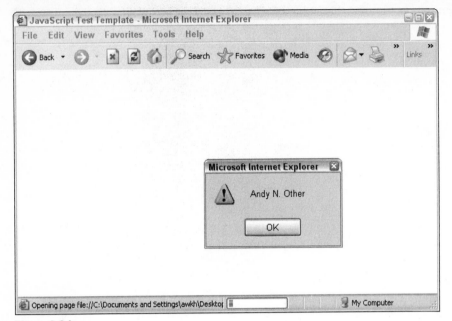

Figure 6-34

There are improvements that you could do to the code. First, if you wanted to work purely with variables, you could make the single whitespace character and the full stop two variables.

```
<script language="JavaScript">
<!--
/*
Code goes below this comment block
*/
var strFirst_Name = "Andy"
var strMiddle_Initials = "N"
var strLast_Name = "Other"
var strSpace = " "
var strFull_Stop = "."
alert(strFirst_Name + strSpace + strMiddle_Initials + strFull_Stop + strSpace +
strLast_Name)  // this should be typed as one line of code
// -->
</script>
```

This code now does exactly the same thing as the earlier code, but it is a little bit tidier.

You might want to concatenate the parts of the name up into a single string that you can use in more than one place. In that case, do the following which, if you need to reuse the full name a few times, will save you a lot of typing!

```
<script language="JavaScript">
<!--
/*
Code goes below this comment block
*/
var strFirst_Name = "Andy"
```

```
var strMiddle_Initials = "N"
var strLast_Name = "Other"
var strSpace = " "
var strFull_Stop = "."
var strFull_Name = strFirst_Name + strSpace + strMiddle_Initials + strFull_Stop +
strSpace + strLast_Name   // this should be typed as one line of code
alert(strFull_Name)
// -->
</script>
```

See that huge, ugly line of code? While it works, having to read across the page that far or word-wrapping the line can make it difficult to read and problems harder to spot. You can use concatenation to join the line up in two stages as follows:

```
<script language="JavaScript">
<!--
/*
Code goes below this comment block
*/
var strFirst_Name = "Andy"
var strMiddle_Initials = "N"
var strLast_Name = "Other"
var strSpace = " "
var strFull_Stop = "."
var strFull_Name = strFirst_Name + strSpace + strMiddle_Initials
strFull_Name = strFull_Name + strFull_Stop + strSpace + strLast_Name
alert(strFull_Name)
// -->
</script>
```

The concatenation is done in two stages:

```
var strFull_Name = strFirst_Name + strSpace + strMiddle_Initials
```

By the end of this stage, the variable strFull_Name holds the following value:

```
Andy N
```

You can test this if you want by adding the following line to the code:

```
<script language="JavaScript">
<!--
/*
Code goes below this comment block
*/
var strFirst_Name = "Andy"
var strMiddle_Initials = "N"
var strLast_Name = "Other"
var strSpace = " "
var strFull_Stop = "."
var strFull_Name = strFirst_Name + strSpace + strMiddle_Initials
alert(strFull_Name)
strFull_Name = strFull_Name + strFull_Stop + strSpace + strLast_Name
alert(strFull_Name)
// -->
</script>
```

Running this, you can confirm the value of the variable, as shown in Figure 6-35.

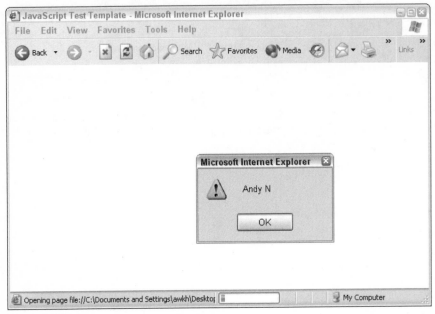

Figure 6-35

The second line takes the variable and tacks on to the end of that the remainder:

```
strFull_Name = strFull_Name + strFull_Stop + strSpace + strLast_Name
```

Processing Inputs

Variables are important when you are dealing with inputs into your program. We'll be going into detail about inputs later on in this book but for now we'll just look at how variables are used to deal with inputs and a little about how that can be made use of.

JavaScript code can take in inputs from the user using a JavaScript prompt. Here is the code for a simple prompt:

```
<script language="JavaScript">
<!--
/*
Code goes below this comment block
*/
var strYour_Name = prompt('Please enter your name:', 'Enter your name')
var strGreeting = "Welcome " + strYour_Name + "!"
alert(strGreeting)
// -->
</script>
```

Figure 6-36 shows how all the variables come together to build up the full name.

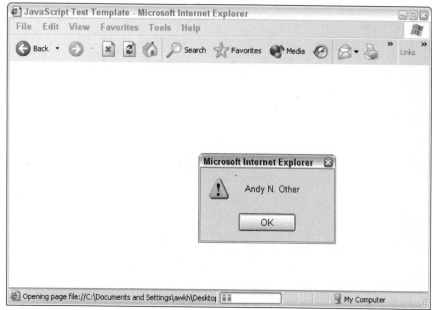

Figure 6-36

Run this code and a prompt is displayed and that asks you to enter your name (any text will do for that matter). The text that you enter is held in the variable strYour_Name (see Figure 6-37).

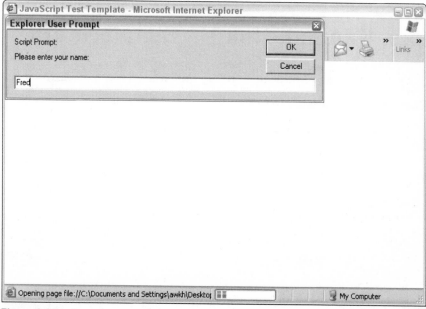

Figure 6-37

This is then concatenated with a greeting and stored in a variable called `strGreeeting` and then displayed in a pop-up box (see Figure 6-38).

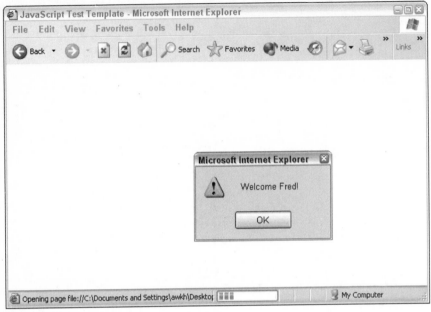

Figure 6-38

Once you have the input from the user stored in the variable you can then treat it as any other string that you have in a variable.

Variable Manipulation — Simple Math

Let's finish this chapter by taking a look at some variable manipulation and carrying out some simple math. Along the way, we'll pick up some more information about how variables behave.

Take a look at the following code:

```
<script language="JavaScript">
<!--
/*
Code goes below this comment block
*/
var intNum1 = 7
var intNum2 = 12
var intNum3 = 2
var intNum4 = 15
var intNum5 = prompt('Please enter a number:', 'Enter a number')
// -->
</script>
```

We can now alter the code and start to do some math.

The simplest math is to just add up the first four integers:

```
<script language="JavaScript">
<!--
/*
Code goes below this comment block
*/
var intNum1 = 7
var intNum2 = 12
var intNum3 = 2
var intNum4 = 15
var intNum5 = prompt('Please enter a number:', 'Enter a number')
alert(intNum1 + intNum2 + intNum3 + intNum4)
// -->
</script>
```

That's simple, but notice how we aren't doing anything with the input from the prompt, intNum5. Let's add that to the final alert and see what happens.

```
<script language="JavaScript">
<!--
/*
Code goes below this comment block
*/
var intNum1 = 7
var intNum2 = 12
var intNum3 = 2
var intNum4 = 15
var intNum5 = prompt('Please enter a number:', 'Enter a number')
alert(intNum1 + intNum2 + intNum3 + intNum4 + intNum5)
// -->
</script>
```

That's simple, but notice how we aren't doing anything with the input from the prompt, intNum5. Let's add that to the final alert and see what happens.

```
<script language="JavaScript">
<!--
/*
Code goes below this comment block
*/
var intNum1 = 7
var intNum2 = 12
var intNum3 = 2
var intNum4 = 15
var intNum5 = prompt('Please enter a number:', 'Enter a number')
alert(intNum1 + intNum2 + intNum3 + intNum4 + intNum5)
// -->
</script>
```

This just adds up all the numbers and displays the answer in a pop-up, as in Figure 6-39.

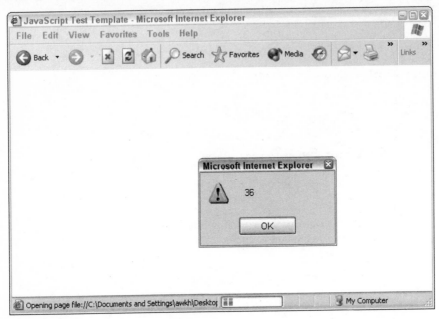

Figure 6-39

Run the code now; enter a number into the prompt, and take a look at the answer, and you should see something odd happen.

What you should notice is that whatever you enter into the prompt, instead of being added to the total of the numbers, is concatenated to the number total. So, if the total of intNum1, intNum2, intNum3, and intNum4 is 36, whatever you entered into the prompt is concatenated to this, so if you entered 100, the total will be 36100. This is obviously incorrect and is an error in the code. This exposes a potential problem in having the system (in this case the interpreter, but it could be a compiler) interpret what data type is stored in a variable.

Let's examine what's happening.

In this case, the code is taking what we wanted to be interpreted as integers and interpreting them instead as a string. The problem is that the addition operator and the concatenation operators are the same.

There are ways around this. With JavaScript one of the easiest ways around this is to take the value stored in the variable and multiply it by 1. This has no effect on the math but does change how it views the value of the variable, subsequently treating it as a number and not a string.

```
<script language="JavaScript">
<!--
/*
Code goes below this comment block
*/
var intNum1 = 7
var intNum2 = 12
var intNum3 = 2
var intNum4 = 15
var intNum5 = prompt('Please enter a number:', 'Enter a number')
intNum5 = intNum5 * 1
alert(intNum1 + intNum2 + intNum3 + intNum4 + intNum5)
// -->
</script>
```

Figure 6-40 shows that the code now interprets the value as a number correctly.

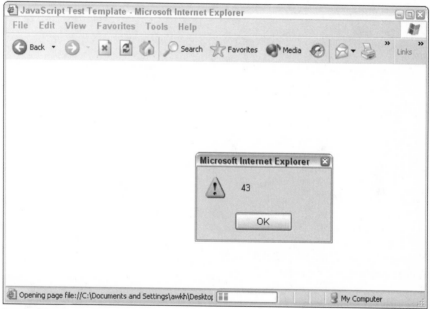

Figure 6-40

Remember to check for these kinds of problems in any outputs your code gives. This should serve as a stark reminder as to how easy it is to get an output that you don't expect.

Summary

That's enough for now. You've covered a lot of ground and in the coming chapter you'll be making a lot of use of variables in a variety of languages. For now, you've received enough information about variables to enable you to move onto new areas and progress with your coding.

In this chapter, you've taken a look at the workhorse of most programming language — the variable. The variable handles the data and is used in statements that process data. Learn to give variables clear, decent names, and add comments to the code to remove any ambiguity and make the code easier to follow.

There's been a lot of information in this chapter and a lot of code examples, I'd recommend that you look through the code examples and experiment with your own variations. Remember that the more you experiment with the code, the more you learn, the more you'll remember, and the faster you'll progress.

Experiment, experiment, experiment!

The Structure of Coding

So far we've looked at pretty simple code, and one thing about simple code is that it can only do simple things. If you want your code to do more, you need to know more about coding schemes that build upon what you've looked at so far and take it to a higher level.

In this chapter, we are going to look at how to get your code to carry out real work. To be able to do this you need to add structures to your code that will enable your code to do more.

We are going to cover four types of structure that add power to your code:

- ❏ Functions
- ❏ Conditionals
- ❏ Loops
- ❏ Arrays

Knowing how to leverage these structures will enable you to write code that will be able to carry out many more tasks than the simple code that you've looked at up until now.

The Purpose of Structure

From the point of view of learning how to write code, there is nothing better than simple code. It's easy to follow, quick to write, lets you experience the high of getting something to work, and gives you practice at writing real code and getting into the mindset of coding. However, eventually (often quite quickly!) you will find you want to do things that are more complicated or beyond what you can accomplish with simple code.

But there's another reason why adding structure to your code is important — it allows you to do more work with less code. See, another problem with simple code is that it isn't very compact and the more you want to do, the more code you end up having to write. The more code you write, the more scope there is for errors in the code and the harder those errors are to find.

Just as you organize letters into words, sentences, and paragraphs, you need to organize your code into manageable structures.

Benefits

As you progress through this chapter, you will notice that the structures that we apply to code have many benefits. Here are a few you will undoubtedly notice:

❑ Less code equals more power

❑ Make the code easier to read and follow

❑ Enable you to break your code into logical parts

❑ Make it easier to spot where errors are

❑ Make reusing code easier

Examining Structure

We are going to use the C++ language to look at structure, so you need the following ready on your system:

❑ A text editor (Windows Notepad, UltraEdit, or something similar)

❑ A C++ compiler (refer to Chapter 5, "The Tools for Programming," for details about setup information)

Quick Introduction to C++

Before we move along, let's have a quick introduction to C++ to get you up to speed.

If you've been working through the code so far, then the basic C++ structure you're going to see here isn't going to be much of a challenge to you.

Examine Source Code

The basic C++ code structure that we are going to work from is shown here:

```
// C++ code template
#include <iostream.h>
void main()
    {
        // Code goes here!!!!
    }
```

You may see a lot of new things here. Don't worry; here's what it all means. Let's work through it line by line.

```
// C++ code template
#include <iostream.h>
void main()
    {
        // Code goes here!!!!
    }
```

The first line is a simple comment. Just as in JavaScript, anything after the // will be overlooked by the compiler that will turn the code into a program.

```
// C++ code template
#include <iostream.h>
void main()
    {
        // code goes here!!!!
    }
```

This second line is an instruction to the compiler and isn't really anything to do directly with the code we are going to write. This line tells the compiler to include a file, iostream.h, in the code that we are writing. This is called a *header file* and is added to the code to provide support for IO, or inputs and outputs. Without this, you can't work with keyboard inputs and screen outputs.

Another one you are likely to use is called string.h; it adds support for string handling to the code. If you want you can add this to the code even if you aren't going to be using it here; write the following:

```
// C++ code template
#include <iostream.h>
#include <string.h>
void main()
    {
        // Code goes here!!!!
    }
```

If you happen to use any header files that you don't need, the compiler will ignore them (I'll even prove this to you later in this chapter).

If you are curious you'll probably have found that all these header files (iostream.h, string.h, and many more) are stored on your PC with the compiler. You can see these in Figure 7-1.

Don't worry about what these files are and what they contain. Just think of them as ready-made code that you can add to your application when you need them to handle particular tasks for you. You don't need to know how they work — that's a job for the compiler!

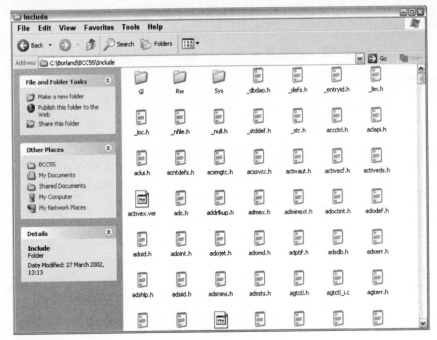

Figure 7-1

```
// C++ code template
#include <iostream.h>
void main()
    {
        // code goes here!!!!
    }
```

This line is used to define something that we are going to cover in a moment — a function. There are two parts to the statement:

❑ **main().** This declares the name of the function, in this case, called main. The parentheses at the end have a purpose that we will look at shortly.

❑ **void.** This is a keyword used to specify that the function we will be writing will not take values passed to it from other functions (called *parameters*) and neither will it pass parameters to other functions. It's not needed, but it does help you know what the function does and whether it is linked to any other function.

Don't dwell too much on this information at this stage — examples and practice later on will make it all clear.

```
// C++ code template
#include <iostream.h>
void main()
    {
        // Code goes here!!!!
    }
```

This line is the beginning of the actual code for the function. It has to start with the opening curly brace. It doesn't have to be on a separate line, but this helps you to know that it is there and to avoid errors if it is!

```cpp
// C++ code template
#include <iostream.h>
void main()
    {
        // Code goes here!!!!
    }
```

Next is where the code would go. There's no code here, just a comment, but it is where the code would go. You can add as many lines of code here as are needed and also use comments to tell yourself (in the future) what the code does.

```cpp
// C++ code template
#include <iostream.h>
void main()
    {
        // Code goes here!!!!
    }
```

This is the end of the function. This is a closing curly brace, and it is required. Just as with the opening curly brace it doesn't need to be on a separate line, but it helps if it is.

Compiling C++

We can now compile this code. To do this we need the Borland compiler. Type the preceding code into a text editor (see Figure 7-2) and save it.

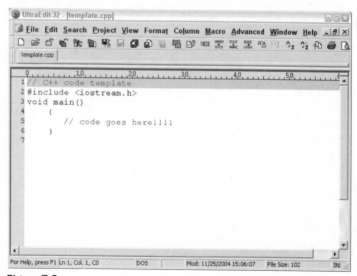

Figure 7-2

When you save this code remember to give it a file extension .cpp. This tells the compiler that it is a file that contains C++ source code. The source file is shown in Figure 7-3; this one is called test.cpp.

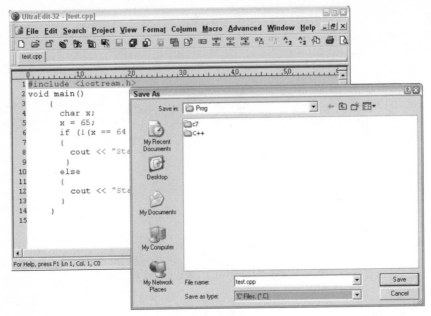

Figure 7-3

I've saved this file in a folder called Prog on the D drive (d:\) of my machine, and I called it template.cpp. This is shown clearly in Figure 7-4.

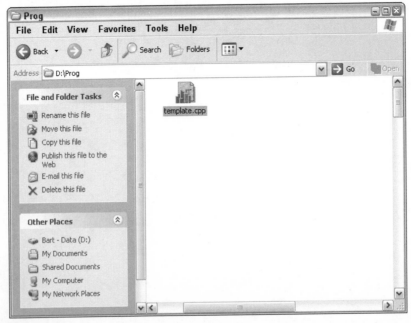

Figure 7-4

Now to compile it. Compiling is easy — you just need to call up the compiler and tell it where the source file is.

First open a Command Prompt or a Command window. The shortcut for the command prompt is normally located in the Accessories folder on the Start Menu (click Start, then All Programs) or click Start, Programs for all non–Windows XP machines, then go to Accessories and click on Command Prompt (see Figure 7-5).

Figure 7-5

You can also click Start, then Run and type the following:

cmd

Then click OK. Either method will bring up the window, as shown in Figure 7-6.

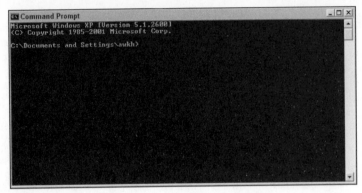

Figure 7-6

Now call the compiler and point it to the source code file. To do this you need to know two things:

❑   Where the compiler is installed

❑   Where the source code files are

If you installed the compiler in the default location, then that will be stored at:

```
c:\borland\bcc55\bin\bcc32.exe
```

If you didn't, then you need to go looking for it! Either way, this is the path to the compiler and typing this in (or copying it into) the Command Prompt window will run the compiler (see Figure 7-7).

Figure 7-7

However, this does nothing other than bring up a big list of instructions about how to use the compiler. If you just want it to compile, then point it to the files. To do this, you type in the path to the compiler, followed by the path to the source code file, as shown in Figure 7-8.

Figure 7-8

Since my path to the source file is d:\prog\template.cpp, all I have to do is type in this:

```
c:\borland\bcc55\bin\bcc32.exe d:\prog\template.cpp
```

And press the Enter key.

It now compiles the file (see Figure 7-9).

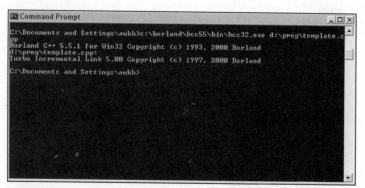

Figure 7-9

After compiling is done (should only take a few seconds), you can then check the folder where the source code was stored. See anything there? No, probably not! That's because the files are likely in the root of the drive where the source code was — in this case, d:\.

You'll now find a few new files in there (Figure 7-10). They will all be called `template`, but there will be three:

- ❑ `template.exe`
- ❑ `template.obj`
- ❑ `template.tds`

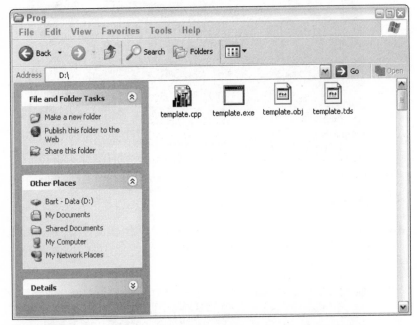

Figure 7-10

All you are interested in is the executable file, `template.exe`. You can run this by either double-clicking it or through the command prompt. If you run it by double-clicking it, then chances are that it'll just pop up and disappear. To run it through the Command Prompt window type:

    d:\template.exe

Then press Enter. The file will run but it won't do anything (see Figure 7-11).

Figure 7-11

To get it to place the output files into the appropriate folder, you need to move into that folder before running the compiler. You can do this by typing the following:

```
cd prog
```

Then pressing Enter (as in Figure 7-12).

Figure 7-12

This issues the change directory command (directory is another name for folder). You must be in the appropriate drive to do this; otherwise, you'll have to change drive letters too. So, if I started off with the Command Prompt window in c:\ (as seen in Figure 7-13), then I'd change to d:\prog by typing in the following commands:

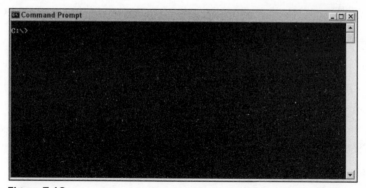

Figure 7-13

```
d:
```

Then press Enter, followed by:

```
cd prog
```

followed by Enter again.

Figure 7-14 confirms I'm in the appropriate folder/directory.

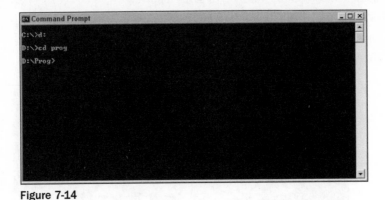

Figure 7-14

Now all you have to type is:

```
c:\borland\bcc55\bin\bcc32.exe template.cpp
```

And the output files are placed in d:\prog automatically.

You can shorten it more. Windows has the ability to store path information within the operating system so that when you try to run an executable it checks all the paths specified for that executable and runs it if it finds it. If the application cannot be found then an error message will be displayed.

To set this in Windows XP, do the following (you need to be logged in as an Administrator to do this):

1. Right-click My Computer, and then click Properties.

2. Click the Advanced tab.

3. Click Environment variables.

4. Click the PATH variable, and then click Edit to alter the value.

5. Go to the end of the existing path specified and add a semicolon (if not already present), then add the path to the compiler.

```
c:\borland\bcc55\bin
```

To run the compiler now all you need to type is:

```
bcc32
```

Then press Enter. Much easier! This new command is shown in action in Figure 7-15.

```
Command Prompt                                                        _ □ ×

D:\Prog>bcc32
Borland C++ 5.5 for Win32 Copyright (c) 1993, 2000 Borland
Syntax is: BCC32 [ options ] file[s]     * = default; -x- = turn switch x off
      -3   * 80386 Instructions        -4      80486 Instructions
      -5     Pentium Instructions       -6      Pentium Pro Instructions
      -Ax    Disable extensions         -B      Compile via assembly
      -C     Allow nested comments      -Dxxx   Define macro
      -Exxx  Alternate Assembler name   -Hxxx   Use pre-compiled headers
      -Ixxx  Include files directory    -K      Default char is unsigned
      -Lxxx  Libraries directory        -M      Generate link map
      -N     Check stack overflow       -Ox     Optimizations
      -P     Force C++ compile          -R      Produce browser info
      -RT  * Generate RTTI              -S      Produce assembly output
      -Txxx  Set assembler option       -Uxxx   Undefine macro
      -Vx    Virtual table control      -X      Suppress autodep. output
      -aN    Align on N bytes           -b    * Treat enums as integers
      -c     Compile only               -d      Merge duplicate strings
      -exxx  Executable file name       -fxx    Floating point options
      -gN    Stop after N warnings      -iN     Max. identifier length
      -jN    Stop after N errors        -k    * Standard stack frame
      -lx    Set linker option          -nxxx   Output file directory
      -oxxx  Object file name           -p      Pascal calls
      -tWxxx Create Windows app         -u    * Underscores on externs
      -v     Source level debugging     -wxxx   Warning control
      -xxxx  Exception handling         -y      Produce line number info
      -zxxx  Set segment names

D:\Prog>
```

Figure 7-15

Congratulations! You've written and compiled a C++ application. Well done! OK, it does nothing yet, but at the same time you accomplished a lot too. You've:

❑ Written code

❑ Saved it in the appropriate format

❑ Saved it in the appropriate place

❑ Used the command prompt

❑ Run the compiler

❑ Pointed the compiler to the source code

❑ Tested the executable that was created

❑ Learned about navigating files and folder in the command prompt

❑ Modified the PATH information for Windows

I think that's quite a lot!

Functions

If that was the first C++ application you've written, then the next thing you are going to want to do is write some more code and compile it! I don't blame you. Writing code is both fun and addictive, especially when you are making progress and getting results.

Armed with all this new-found knowledge, we can now start to look at what we set out to look at earlier — functions.

You've already seen a function.

```
void main()
    {
        // Code goes here!!!!
    }
```

This function is an empty one, but a function nonetheless. It has a name (`main`) and the scope to contain code, although this one does not.

Functions called main have a special meaning in C++ — they are functions that will be automatically run. So any code you place into this function will be run when the executable is run (after it has been compiled of course).

We can now add some code and start making executables that actually do something!

Let's start with the ever popular Hello, World! code:

```
// C++ code template
#include <iostream.h>
void main()
    {
        cout << "Hello, World!" << endl;
    }
```

There's only one line in this code that differs from what you've seen so far:

```
// C++ code template
#include <iostream.h>
void main()
    {
        cout << "Hello, World!" << endl;
    }
```

There are five parts to this line that we need to look at:

```
cout
```

```
<<
```

```
"Hello, World!"
```

```
endl
```

```
;
```

Let's start with `cout`. This is an *instruction* (that happens to be contained within the `iostream.h` file) that outputs text to the screen — nothing complex there.

Next let's look at `<<`. This is called an *insertion operator*, and its job is to pass something (data) from one part of the program to another. In this case, it is used to pass the string that follows to the `cout` instruction so that it can be displayed on the screen.

The next part is the string to be displayed. This is the simple `"Hello, World!"` string. Everything inside the quotes is outputted to the screen.

Next comes another insertion operator, meaning that something else is being passed to the `cout` instruction. And that something is `endl`. This is used to insert a new line.

Finally, we have the statement closing semicolon (`;`). Unlike JavaScript, this is required in C++.

If you compile this and run the code, you get what you expect. The program runs and the function called `main` is run. The statement is executed and the text is displayed (as shown in Figure 7-16).

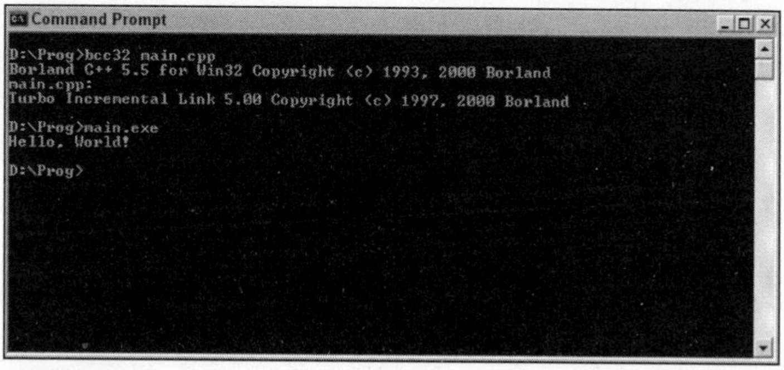

Figure 7-16

Everything works as you expect it to.

> *Just a quick aside . . . remember I said earlier that you could add header files that won't be needed to the source code and not affect the final code. Well, when I compile the preceding code the final code is 112,640 bytes, but if I add a line to the code to include the `string.h` header (which this code doesn't use) the file is still exactly the same size!*

Now we've established what a simple function is:

```
// C++ code template
#include <iostream.h>
void main()
    {
        cout << "Hello, World!" << endl;
    }
```

But a function can do more than one thing. Here is another function that has two simple statements:

```cpp
// C++ code template
#include <iostream.h>
void main()
    {
        cout << "Hello, World!" << endl;
        cout << "How are you?" << endl;
    }
```

More Functions

Having one function is a start, but to really do some programming you need more than one function.

Take a look at this code:

```cpp
#include <iostream.h>

void hello()
    {
        cout << "Hello, World!" << endl;
    }

void hello2()
    {
        cout << "Hello, World, MK II!" << endl;
    }

void main()
    {
        cout << "main function" << endl;
    }
```

This code has three functions:

```
hello
```

```
hello2
```

```
main
```

However, if you compile this code and run it you'll find something interesting, as shown in Figure 7-17.

Figure 7-17

Only the function main is run, which is run as default. To make the others run, you put all of them in the code, like this:

```
#include <iostream.h>

void hello()
    {
        cout << "Hello, World!" << endl;
    }

void hello2()
    {
        cout << "Hello, World, MK II!" << endl;
    }

void main()
    {
        cout << "main function" << endl;
        hello();
        hello2();
    }
```

If you compile this and run the code, you'll get the output shown in Figure 7-18.

Figure 7-18

What these two lines do is run the other two functions after `main` is run. Logically, you might think that this code will work:

```
#include <iostream.h>

void hello()
    {
        cout << "Hello, World!" << endl;
        hello2();
    }

void hello2()
    {
        cout << "Hello, World, MK II!" << endl;
    }

void main()
    {
        cout << "main function" << endl;
        hello();
    }
```

However, there's a problem with this — you are calling a function that hasn't yet been defined (or processed by the compiler). This generates an error because the compiler likes to see the functions before calling them, so while the preceding code generates errors, the next one won't because the function `hello2` is called after it appears in the code:

```
#include <iostream.h>

void hello2()
    {
        cout << "Hello, World, MK II!" << endl;
    }

void hello()
    {
        cout << "Hello, World!" << endl;
        hello2();
    }

void main()
    {
        cout << "main function" << endl;
        hello();
    }
```

You also can call functions more than once:

```
#include <iostream.h>

void hello2()
    {
        cout << "Hello, World, MK II!" << endl;
    }
```

```
void hello()
    {
        cout << "Hello, World!" << endl;
        hello2();
    }

void main()
    {
        cout << "main function" << endl;
        hello();
        hello2();
    }
```

The results of this code are shown in Figure 7-19.

Figure 7-19

You do need to be careful when you call the same function more than once though, because the compiler might complain about ambiguity in the code. The following code generates the error shown in Figure 7-20.

```
#include <iostream.h>

void hello2()
    {
        cout << "Hello, World, MK II!" << endl;
        hello();
    }

void hello()
    {
        cout << "Hello, World!" << endl;
        hello2();
    }

void main()
    {
        cout << "main function" << endl;
        hello();
    }
```

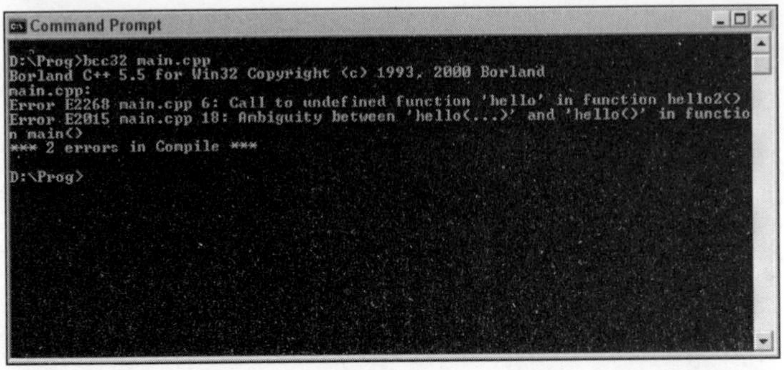

Figure 7-20

You'll be using a lot of functions over the course of this chapter, so we'll leave the discussion on functions at that for now. Just remember though; functions are the basic subdivision of code. Just as statements are the equivalent of sentences, functions are the equivalent of paragraphs. To move between functions you use calls. Remember to have the function appear before you call it and you should be OK.

Quick Exercise

Take a look at the following code examples and work out (without compiling and running if possible) what's wrong with each one.

Code Sample 1:

```
#include <iostream.h>

void hello()
    {
        cout << "main function" << endl;
    }
```

Code Sample 2:

```
#include <iostream.h>

void main()
    {
        cout << "main function" << endl;
        hello();
        hello2();
    }

void hello()
    {
        cout << "Hello, World!" << endl;
        hello2();
    }

void hello2()
    {
        cout << "Hello, World, MK II!" << endl;
    }
```

Code Sample 3:

```
void main()
    {
        cout << "main function" << endl;
    }
```

Conditionals

If there is one thing that will truly make you appreciate the power of programming, it's conditionals. Conditionals enable you to run code based on feedback about certain parameters so that you can choose what statements to run and which not to run. Conditionals revolve around answers to questions. And these answers are almost exclusively true/false or yes/no answers to simple questions.

It's not just programming that relies of conditionals — in day-to-day life we ourselves use conditionals. Here's a simple one:

```
For breakfast, would you rather have toast or cereal?
```

That's a conditional, and the answer you come to decides what you'll do next. You can say yes to toast, yes to cereal, yes to both, or no to both. In fact, those are the only answers possible. If you choose not to answer the question, then in theory you've just said no to both, and if you add another option then you've changed the parameters of the question.

As you might have worked out now, conditionals revolve around making a decision, and the nice thing about dealing with computers and programming is that if you ask it to come to a decision based on some data, if it can, it will!

Programming Decisions

Every computer programming language has a way to test the value of things and then make decisions based on the findings. In C++ the way to do this is to use the If statement.

Here is a simple C++ If statement:

```
if (condition)
    {
        // do statements here if the condition is true
    }
else
    {
        // do these statements if the condition is false
    };
```

The If statement tests the condition given (more on these conditions shortly) and either finds it to be true or false. If the condition is true, then one statement, or set of statements, is executed, while if it is false, another statement or set of statements is run.

Conditions

Take a look at the following code:

```cpp
#include <iostream.h>
void main()
    {
    int x;
    cout << "Pick an integer: ";
    cin >> x;
    if (x == 7)
    {
      cout << "You win the C++ lottery!" << endl;
      cout << "Thank you for playing the C++ lottery" << endl;
    }
    else
    {
      cout << "Thank you for playing the C++ lottery" << endl;
    }
    }
```

If you create this code, save it, compile it, and run the application, you get a program that looks like Figure 7-21.

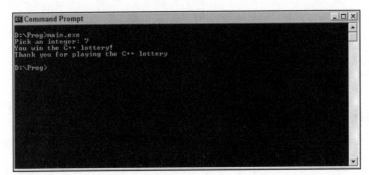

Figure 7-21

This code makes use of a conditional. Let's walk through the code and take a look at how it works:

```cpp
#include <iostream.h>
void main()
    {
    int x;
    cout << "Pick an integer: ";
    cin >> x;
    if (x == 7)
    {
      cout << "You win the C++ lottery!" << endl;
      cout << "Thank you for playing the C++ lottery" << endl;
    }
    else
```

```
    {
      cout << "Thank you for playing the C++ lottery" << endl;
    }
  }
```

The first few lines are just basic C++ code. You should know what all this means by now.

```
#include <iostream.h>
void main()
    {
      int x;
      cout << "Pick an integer: ";
      cin >> x;
      if (x == 7)
      {
        cout << "You win the C++ lottery!" << endl;
        cout << "Thank you for playing the C++ lottery" << endl;
      }
      else
      {
        cout << "Thank you for playing the C++ lottery" << endl;
      }
    }
```

Next is the opening curly brace of a function, the `main` function.

```
#include <iostream.h>
void main()
    {
      int x;
      cout << "Pick an integer: ";
      cin >> x;
      if (x == 7)
      {
        cout << "You win the C++ lottery!" << endl;
        cout << "Thank you for playing the C++ lottery" << endl;
      }
      else
      {
        cout << "Thank you for playing the C++ lottery" << endl;
      }
    }
```

This line now declares a variable that we are going to be using. I've unimaginatively called this variable x.

```
#include <iostream.h>
void main()
    {
      int x;
      cout << "Pick an integer: ";
      cin >> x;
      if (x == 7)
      {
        cout << "You win the C++ lottery!" << endl;
```

```
              cout << "Thank you for playing the C++ lottery" << endl;
          }
          else
          {
              cout << "Thank you for playing the C++ lottery" << endl;
          }
      }
```

This line sends a line of text to the screen. Notice that I didn't add endl to the end of that line.

```
      #include <iostream.h>
      void main()
          {
          int x;
          cout << "Pick an integer: ";
          cin >> x;
          if (x == 7)
          {
              cout << "You win the C++ lottery!" << endl;
              cout << "Thank you for playing the C++ lottery" << endl;
          }
          else
          {
              cout << "Thank you for playing the C++ lottery" << endl;
          }
      }
```

Now we come to something new. In the previous statement you saw cout. In this statement you see cin. While cout is an instruction that sends strings to the screen, cin is used to receive input from the keyboard. This input is then inserted into the variable x using the insertion operator, >>.

If you run this code, you'll notice that the number you enter is placed on the same line as the outputted text asking you to type in an integer. This is a side effect of not using endl.

```
      #include <iostream.h>
      void main()
          {
          int x;
          cout << "Pick an integer: ";
          cin >> x;
          if (x == 7)
          {
              cout << "You win the C++ lottery!" << endl;
              cout << "Thank you for playing the C++ lottery" << endl;
          }
          else
          {
              cout << "Thank you for playing the C++ lottery" << endl;
          }
      }
```

Now for the meat of the conditional — the test. This line of code tests to see if the value of x is 7. This is a simple test, but it enables you to test for a condition and run statements based on that.

```
#include <iostream.h>
void main()
    {
      int x;
      cout << "Pick an integer: ";
      cin >> x;
      if (x == 7)
      {
        cout << "You win the C++ lottery!" << endl;
        cout << "Thank you for playing the C++ lottery" << endl;
      }
      else
      {
        cout << "Thank you for playing the C++ lottery" << endl;
      }
    }
```

These statements are run if the condition comes out as being true, that is, the value entered is actually 7.

```
#include <iostream.h>
void main()
    {
      int x;
      cout << "Pick an integer: ";
      cin >> x;
      if (x == 7)
      {
        cout << "You win the C++ lottery!" << endl;
        cout << "Thank you for playing the C++ lottery" << endl;
      }
      else
      {
        cout << "Thank you for playing the C++ lottery" << endl;
      }
    }
```

Here is the else. Statements below this are run if the condition is not true.

```
#include <iostream.h>
void main()
    {
      int x;
      cout << "Pick an integer: ";
      cin >> x;
      if (x == 7)
      {
        cout << "You win the C++ lottery!" << endl;
        cout << "Thank you for playing the C++ lottery" << endl;
      }
      else
      {
        cout << "Thank you for playing the C++ lottery" << endl;
      }
    }
```

There it is. C++ code that makes use of conditionals to determine which statements are run and which aren't.

There are, though, different ways to do the same thing in C++. The code that I have created in the next example does the same thing as the previous code, but doesn't make use of `else`.

```cpp
#include <iostream.h>
void main()
    {
      int x;
      cout << "Pick an integer: ";
      cin >> x;
      if (x == 7)
        cout << "You win the C++ lottery!" << endl;
        cout << "Thank you for playing the C++ lottery" << endl;
    }
```

The main difference in this code from the previous code are these lines:

```cpp
#include <iostream.h>
void main()
    {
      int x;
      cout << "Pick an integer: ";
      cin >> x;
      if (x == 7)
        cout << "You win the C++ lottery!" << endl;
          cout << "Thank you for playing the C++ lottery" << endl;
    }
```

What happens with this code is this: If the condition is true, then the two statements are processed, but if the condition is false, only the last one is processed.

But, as you can see, this kind of code can be ambiguous, and on top of that, what happens in a case such as this?

```cpp
#include <iostream.h>
void main()
    {
      int x;
      cout << "Pick an integer: ";
      cin >> x;
      if (x == 7)
        cout << "You win the C++ lottery!" << endl;
        cout << "What about this statement..." << endl;
        cout << "Thank you for playing the C++ lottery" << endl;
    }
```

How are these statements run?

The answer is that if the condition is true, then the all the statements are executed, but if it is false all but the first are run. This can be a handy shortcut which means that you can write less code, but it also is more ambiguous than writing it all out in full and can be more confusing.

More on Conditionals

Take a look at this code that creates a simple C++ calculator:

```cpp
#include <iostream.h>
void main()
    {
        float num1;
        float num2;
        char op;
        float ans;
        cout << "Please enter a number: ";
        cin >> num1;
        cout << "Please enter another number: ";
        cin >> num2;
        cout << "Press A to add the two numbers."
             << endl
             << "Press S to subtract the two numbers."
             << endl
             << "Press M to multiply the two numbers."
             << endl
             << "Press D to divide the two numbers."
             << endl;
        cin >> op;
        if (op == 65)
          ans = num1 + num2;
        if (op == 83)
          ans = num1 - num2;
        if (op == 77)
          ans = num1 * num2;
        if (op == 68)
          ans = num1 / num2;
        cout << "The answer is " << ans << endl;
    }
```

This code enables you to take two numbers that you can enter and perform an operation on them based on an input. It uses a lot of what we've looked at so far in this chapter. Let's look at some of the highlights of the code.

```cpp
#include <iostream.h>
void main()
    {
        float num1;
        float num2;
        char op;
        float ans;
        cout << "Please enter a number: ";
        cin >> num1;
        cout << "Please enter another number: ";
        cin >> num2;
        cout << "Press A to add the two numbers."
             << endl
             << "Press S to subtract the two numbers."
             << endl
```

```
        << "Press M to multiply the two numbers."
        << endl
        << "Press D to divide the two numbers."
        << endl;
    cin >> op;
    if (op == 65)
      ans = num1 + num2;
    if (op == 83)
      ans = num1 - num2;
    if (op == 77)
      ans = num1 * num2;
    if (op == 68)
      ans = num1 / num2;
    cout << "The answer is " << ans << endl;
  }
```

These four lines define the variables we are going to be using in the code. There are two new types here:

❑   **float.** A floating-point number (a number that can make use of a decimal point for precision, such as 3.141592654).

❑   **char.** A character. As you will see shortly, these are stored in an odd way by the code.

```
#include <iostream.h>
void main()
  {
    float num1;
    float num2;
    char op;
    float ans;
    cout << "Please enter a number: ";
    cin >> num1;
    cout << "Please enter another number: ";
    cin >> num2;
    cout << "Press A to add the two numbers."
        << endl
        << "Press S to subtract the two numbers."
        << endl
        << "Press M to multiply the two numbers."
        << endl
        << "Press D to divide the two numbers."
        << endl;
    cin >> op;
    if (op == 65)
      ans = num1 + num2;
    if (op == 83)
      ans = num1 - num2;
    if (op == 77)
      ans = num1 * num2;
    if (op == 68)
      ans = num1 / num2;
    cout << "The answer is " << ans << endl;
  }
```

Here are a few combinations of `cout` and `cin` that enable you to enter the two numbers.

```cpp
#include <iostream.h>
void main()
    {
        float num1;
        float num2;
        char op;
        float ans;
        cout << "Please enter a number: ";
        cin >> num1;
        cout << "Please enter another number: ";
        cin >> num2;
        cout << "Press A to add the two numbers."
             << endl
             << "Press S to subtract the two numbers."
             << endl
             << "Press M to multiply the two numbers."
             << endl
             << "Press D to divide the two numbers."
             << endl;
        cin >> op;
        if (op == 65)
          ans = num1 + num2;
        if (op == 83)
          ans = num1 - num2;
        if (op == 77)
          ans = num1 * num2;
        if (op == 68)
          ans = num1 / num2;
        cout << "The answer is " << ans << endl;
    }
```

These lines give us the nicely formatted output that you see in Figure 7-22.

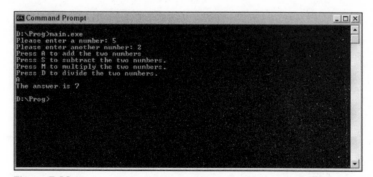

Figure 7-22

```cpp
#include <iostream.h>
void main()
    {
```

```
    float num1;
    float num2;
    char op;
    float ans;
    cout << "Please enter a number: ";
    cin >> num1;
    cout << "Please enter another number: ";
    cin >> num2;
    cout << "Press A to add the two numbers."
         << endl
         << "Press S to subtract the two numbers."
         << endl
         << "Press M to multiply the two numbers."
         << endl
         << "Press D to divide the two numbers."
         << endl;
    cin >> op;
    if (op == 65)
      ans = num1 + num2;
    if (op == 83)
      ans = num1 - num2;
    if (op == 77)
      ans = num1 * num2;
    if (op == 68)
      ans = num1 / num2;
    cout << "The answer is " << ans << endl;
  }
```

This is the third keyboard input into the program; this time this will define the operation carried out on the two numbers you entered earlier.

```
#include <iostream.h>
void main()
    {
    float num1;
    float num2;
    char op;
    float ans;
    cout << "Please enter a number: ";
    cin >> num1;
    cout << "Please enter another number: ";
    cin >> num2;
    cout << "Press A to add the two numbers."
         << endl
         << "Press S to subtract the two numbers."
         << endl
         << "Press M to multiply the two numbers."
         << endl
         << "Press D to divide the two numbers."
         << endl;
    cin >> op;
    if (op == 65)
      ans = num1 + num2;
    if (op == 83)
      ans = num1 - num2;
```

```
    if (op == 77)
      ans = num1 * num2;
    if (op == 68)
      ans = num1 / num2;
  cout << "The answer is " << ans << endl;
}
```

This is the main driving force of the code. The code looks at the operator that was entered and carries out an operation on the numbers based on that. One thing for you to notice is how the input from the keyboard is a letter (A, S, M, or D), but in the code we check for the numbers 65, 83, 77, or 68. This is so because when characters are stored as char, it is the decimal representation on the ASCII code that is stored. You don't need to worry too much about this, but the letters are represented as follows:

A	B	C	D	E	F
65	66	67	68	69	70

G	H	I	J	K	L
71	72	73	74	75	76

M	N	O	P	Q	R
77	78	79	80	81	82

S	T	U	V	W	X
83	84	85	86	87	88

Y	Z	Space			
89	90	32			

A	b	c	d	e	f
97	98	99	100	101	102

G	h	i	j	k	l
103	104	105	106	107	108

Table continued on following page

M	n	o	p	q	r
109	110	111	112	113	114

S	t	u	v	w	x
115	116	117	118	119	120

Y	z				
121	122				

```cpp
#include <iostream.h>
void main()
    {
      float num1;
      float num2;
      char op;
      float ans;
      cout << "Please enter a number: ";
      cin >> num1;
      cout << "Please enter another number: ";
      cin >> num2;
      cout << "Press A to add the two numbers."
           << endl
           << "Press S to subtract the two numbers."
           << endl
           << "Press M to multiply the two numbers."
           << endl
           << "Press D to divide the two numbers."
           << endl;
      cin >> op;
      if (op == 65)
        ans = num1 + num2;
      if (op == 83)
        ans = num1 - num2;
      if (op == 77)
        ans = num1 * num2;
      if (op == 68)
        ans = num1 / num2;
      cout << "The answer is " << ans << endl;
    }
```

The final statement is the one that displays the answer on the screen. Figure 7-23 shows the application in action.

This program works quite well but there is one problem — check out the result if, instead of pressing one of the prescribed keys (A, S, M, or D), you press something else (see Figure 7- 24).

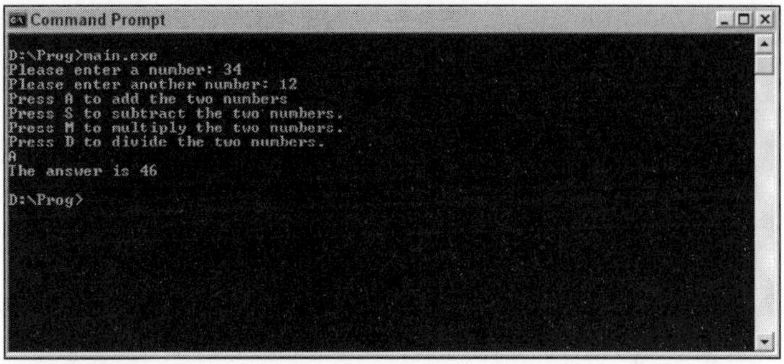

Figure 7-23

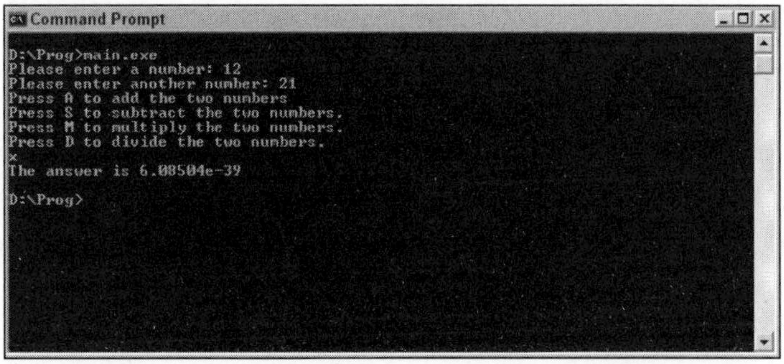

Figure 7-24

The answer is most certainly incorrect, and the code cannot handle the input that you gave it. We need to do something about this.

```cpp
#include <iostream.h>
void main()
    {
    float num1;
    float num2;
    char op;
    float ans;
    cout << "Please enter a number: ";
    cin >> num1;
    cout << "Please enter another number: ";
    cin >> num2;
    cout << "Press A to add the two numbers."
        << endl
        << "Press S to subtract the two numbers."
        << endl
        << "Press M to multiply the two numbers."
        << endl
        << "Press D to divide the two numbers."
        << endl;
    cin >> op;
```

```
            if (op == 65)
            {
               ans = num1 + num2;
               cout << "The answer is " << ans << endl;
            }
            if (op == 83)
            {
               ans = num1 - num2;
               cout << "The answer is " << ans << endl;
            }
            if (op == 77)
            {
               ans = num1 * num2;
               cout << "The answer is " << ans << endl;
            }
            if (op == 68)
            {
               ans = num1 / num2;
               cout << "The answer is " << ans << endl;
            }
            if (op != 65 && op != 83 && op != 77 && op != 68)
            {
               cout << "No valid operation was chosen!" << endl;
            }
      }
```

Not only have we had to add the highlighted code, but we've also added curly braces to make the code less ambiguous.

But what does the statement that was added do? Well, it is controlled by this string of conditions:

```
            if (op != 65 && op != 83 && op != 77 && op != 68)
```

There are two operators here that you haven't seen yet.

```
      !=
```

```
      &&
```

The != operator stands for *not equal to* while && represents *and*. Therefore, in English, what this is saying is:

```
      If op is not equal to 65 and op is not equal to 83 and op is not equal to 77 and op
      is not equal to 68, then . . .
```

Here is another way to represent not equal to:

```
      if (!(op == 83))
```

The condition here is:

```
      If op is not equal to 83 then . . .
```

This is the equivalent of writing:

```
if (op != 83)
```

So, it is testing for all the valid inputs and if none of them are found, then the statement is run. Concise and quite clever.

For this condition to be true, all of the conditions contained within it have to be true and if one is false, then the overall result is false.

Along with &&, another operator that you will find useful with conditionals is the || operator. This represents *or* and can be used just like &&.

Here is an example:

```
if (op != 65 || op != 83 || op != 77 || op != 68)
```

In English, this is stating:

```
If op is not equal to 65 or op is not equal to 83 or op is not equal to 77 or op is
not equal to 68 then ...
```

This is very different from using && with the main difference being that for the overall condition to be false, all the conditions that went to making it up need to be false; otherwise, it will return a true.

Quick Exercise

Take a look at the following code examples and work out (without compiling and running them if possible) which statement is run.

Code Sample 1

```
#include <iostream.h>
void main()
  {
    int x;
    x = 7;
    if (x == 7)
    {
      cout << "Statement 1" << endl;
     }
    else
    {
      cout << "Statement 2" << endl;
    }
  }
```

Code Sample 2

```
#include <iostream.h>
void main()
    {
```

```
        int x;
        x = 7;
        if (!(x == 7))
        {
          cout << "Statement 1" << endl;
         }
        else
        {
          cout << "Statement 2" << endl;
        }
      }
```

Code Sample 3

```
    #include <iostream.h>
    void main()
       {
         char x;
         x = 65;
         if (x == 64 || x != 65 || x == 66)
         {
           cout << "Statement 1" << endl;
          }
         else
         {
           cout << "Statement 2" << endl;
         }
       }
```

Code Sample 4

```
    #include <iostream.h>
    void main()
       {
         char x;
         x = 65;
         if (x == 64 && x == 65 && x == 66)
         {
           cout << "Statement 1" << endl;
          }
         else
         {
           cout << "Statement 2" << endl;
         }
       }
```

Code Sample 5

```
    #include <iostream.h>
    void main()
       {
         char x;
         x = 65;
         if (!(x == 64 && x == 65 && x == 66))
         {
```

```
      cout << "Statement 1" << endl;
    }
  else
  {
      cout << "Statement 2" << endl;
    }
}
```

Loops

Another really important task you need to be able to do with code is to look through the same piece of code a number of times. Useful applications of this might not be immediately apparent but for now let's just look at how to loop.

For Loops

One type of loop that you will come across is the For loop.

```
for ( <initialisation> ; <terminating condition> ; <increment> )
{
  // statement (or block of statements)
}
```

Here's some code that loops:

```
#include <iostream.h>
void main()
  {
    int counter;

    for (counter = 1; counter < 20; counter++)
      {
        cout << "Going loopy " << counter << endl;
      }
  }
```

If you compile and run this code, you'll get the output shown in Figure 7-25.

Figure 7-25

The loop, called a `for` loop, is controlled by this line of code:

```
for (counter = 1; counter < 20; counter++)
```

This consists of three parts:

❑ **counter = 1.** This is initialization point of the loop, or where we want it to start. This is the value given to the control variable. In this case the value of `counter` is set to `1`.

❑ **counter < 20.** This is the termination condition. When this condition results in a false answer, the loop stops. In this case, while `counter` is less than 20, the loop will repeat.

❑ **counter++.** This is the increment. Here `counter++` means that the value of counter is incremented by 1 during each loop. `counter--` would mean that the value should be decremented (decreased) by 1 for each loop.

The code that follows works backward, from 20 to 0. Notice in Figure 7-26 how it doesn't go down to 0. That's because the condition is set to look while `counter` is greater than 0.

Figure 7-26

```
#include <iostream.h>
void main()
  {
    int counter;

    for (counter = 20; counter > 0; counter--)
      {
        cout << "Going loopy " << counter << endl;
      }
  }
```

One simple modification will enable it to count all the way down to 0.

```
#include <iostream.h>
void main()
  {
    int counter;

    for (counter = 20; counter >= 0; counter--)
```

```
    {
      cout << "Going loopy " << counter << endl;
    }
}
```

Infinite Loops

The main thing to watch out for with loops is what are called *infinite loops*. This is where you make a mistake in the code which results in the terminating condition not being achieved, which means that, in effect, the loop continues forever (or until you stop it or it crashes your computer).

Here is an example of such a loop:

```
#include <iostream.h>
void main()
  {
    int counter;

    for (counter = 20; counter <= 20; counter--)
      {
        cout << "Going loopy " << counter << endl;
      }
  }
```

This code loops forever because the termination condition can never be false because decrementing the value of counter takes it further away from being greater than 20, not closer.

While Loops

The While loop is another type of loop that you might find useful.

```
while ( <condition> )
{
  // statement (or block of statements)
}
```

This is different from the For loop because this continues until a condition is met by an input or some other means, rather than an increment or decrement to a value built into the code.

Here is an example:

```
#include <iostream.h>
void main()
    {
      int num;
      cout << "Enter a number greater than 7: ";
      cin >> num;
      while (num <= 7)
         { cout << "Try again: ";
           cin >> num;
         }
    }
```

This code is shown in action in Figure 7-27.

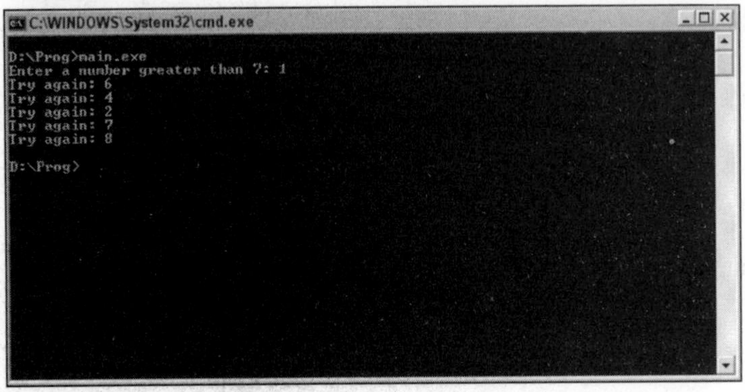

Figure 7-27

Basically, this code keeps looping this statement until it gets the input it requires:

```
#include <iostream.h>
void main()
    {
      int num;
      cout << "Enter a number greater than 7: ";
      cin >> num;
      while (num <= 7)
          { cout << "Try again: ";
            cin >> num;
          }
    }
```

Do While loop

Another C++ loop is the Do While loop.

```
do
  {
    // statement (or block of statements)
  }
while ( <condition> )
```

This is pretty much like the While loop. Here is an example that will make it clear:

```
#include <iostream.h>
void main()
    {
      int num;
      do
        {
          cout << "Enter a number greater than 7: ";
```

```
        cin >> num;
        }
    while (num <= 7);
}
```

In you input a value that satisfies this (any integer greater than 7), it ends gracefully (as shown in Figure 7-28).

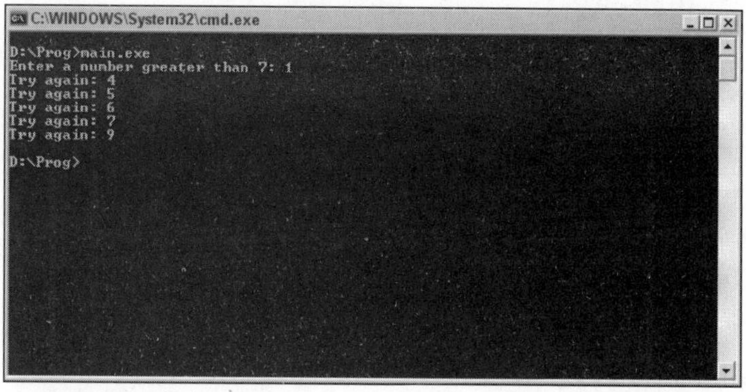

Figure 7-28

Quick Exercise

Take a look at the following code examples and work out (without compiling and running them if possible) the answers to the questions.

Code Sample 1

How many times will this code loop?

```
#include <iostream.h>
void main()
  {
    int counter;

    for (counter = 5; counter < 18; counter++)
      {
        cout << "Going loopy " << counter << endl;
      }
  }
```

Code Sample 2

How many times will this code loop?

```
#include <iostream.h>
void main()
  {
    int counter;
```

```
    for (counter = 10; counter > 0; counter--)
      {
        cout << "Going loopy " << counter << endl;
      }
  }
```

Code Sample 3

Is this an infinite loop?

```
#include <iostream.h>
void main()
  {
    int counter;

    for (counter = 10; counter <= 5; counter--)
      {
        cout << "Going loopy " << counter << endl;
      }
  }
```

Code Sample 4

Is this an infinite loop?

```
#include <iostream.h>
void main()
  {
    int counter;

    for (counter = 10; counter <= 15; counter--)
      {
        cout << "Going loopy " << counter << endl;
      }
  }
```

Code Sample 5

What numbers will satisfy this While loop?

```
#include <iostream.h>
void main()
    {
        int num;
      cin >> num;
      while (num <= 14)
         { cout << "Try again: ";
           cin >> num;
         }
    }
```

Code Sample 6

What numbers will satisfy this While loop?

```
#include <iostream.h>
void main()
    {
        int num;
     cin >> num;
     while (num < 12)
        { cout << "Try again: ";
          cin >> num;
        }
    }
```

Arrays

So far, the variables used in the code have been used to hold single values. However, there are times when it is useful to group lots of values together under a single name.

This is where arrays come in.

You can think of an array as a sequence of mailboxes, each individually numbered (see Figure 7-29).

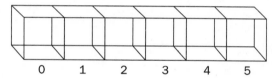

Figure 7-29

These mailboxes are identified by numbers, and the numbers begin at 0 as opposed to 1 (giving rise to the golf course that IBM had that was numbered 0 to 17!).

If you were creating an array to hold your seven assignment scores in a subject, you would number them 0 to 6 (as in Figure 7-30).

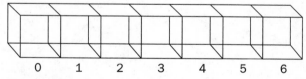

Figure 7-30

Arrays need to be declared in the same way as variables. You could call this array grades, and the individual elements of the array could be referenced as grades[0], grades[1], all the way to grades[6].

Here is code that will take seven grades and then displays them along with the average.

```
#include <iostream.h>
void main()
    {
    float grades[7];
    int i;
    float tot;
    cout << "Please enter grade 1: ";
    cin >> grades[0];
    cout << "Please enter grade 2: ";
    cin >> grades[1];
    cout << "Please enter grade 3: ";
    cin >> grades[2];
    cout << "Please enter grade 4: ";
    cin >> grades[3];
    cout << "Please enter grade 5: ";
    cin >> grades[4];
    cout << "Please enter grade 6: ";
    cin >> grades[5];
    cout << "Please enter grade 7: ";
    cin >> grades[6];
    cout << "Your grades are: " << endl;
    for (i = 0; i < 7; i++)
    {
       cout << grades[i] << endl;
       tot += grades[i];
    }
    cout << "Average: " << (tot/7) << endl;
    }
```

The working application is shown in Figure 7-31.

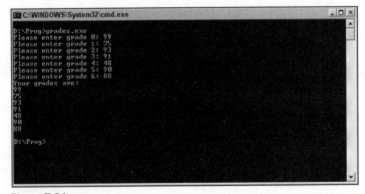

Figure 7-31

Two-Dimensional Array

The array we've looked at so far is called a one-dimensional array. This type of array just contains a single line of placeholders for data. A two-dimensional array is represented by a rectangular grid of placeholders (see Figure 7-32).

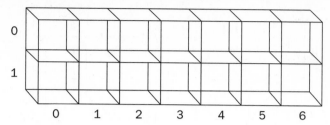

Figure 7-32

To declare an array such as the one shown in Figure 7-32, you'd use this line of code:

```
int array_values[5][7];
```

This type of array would be useful where you wanted to say . . . store the results of seven assignment scores for five different subjects.

Values are set using code such as this:

```
array_values[2][6] = 56;
```

And values accessed like this:

```
x = 2;
y = 6;
cout << array_values[x][y];
```

It is with arrays that loops really come into play. Take a look at this code, which can be used to loop through and populate an array:

```
for (x = 0; x <= 6; x++)
  for (y = 0; y <= 4; y++)
  {
    cout << "Enter a value for the element " << x << " : " << y << " : ";
      cin >> array_values[y][x];
  }
```

Multidimensional Array

Multidimensional arrays are arrays of three or more dimensions. Figure 7-33 is a representation of a three-dimensional array.

You declare them with code such as this:

```
int letters[5][5][7];
```

Otherwise, working with this kind of array is the same as one- and two-dimensional arrays we've already looked at.

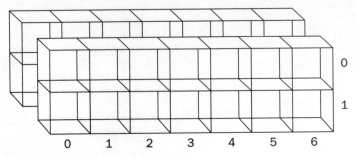

Figure 7-33

Quick Exercise

Take a look at the following code examples and work out (without compiling and running if possible) the answers to the questions.

Code Sample 1

What's wrong with this code?

```
#include <iostream.h>
void main()
    {
        float grades[6];
    int i;
    float tot;
    cout << "Please enter grade 1: ";
    cin >> grades[1];
    cout << "Please enter grade 2: ";
    cin >> grades[2];
    cout << "Please enter grade 3: ";
    cin >> grades[3];
    cout << "Please enter grade 4: ";
    cin >> grades[4];
    cout << "Please enter grade 5: ";
    cin >> grades[5];
    cout << "Please enter grade 6: ";
    cin >> grades[6];
    cout << "Please enter grade 7: ";
    cin >> grades[7];
    cout << "Your grades are: " << endl;
    for (i = 0; i < 7; i++)
    {
      cout << grades[i] << endl;
      tot += grades[i];
    }
    cout << "Average: " << (tot/7) << endl;
```

Code Sample 2

Describe this array:

```
int letters[5][4][7];
```

Code Sample 3

What does this code do?

```
array_values[3][2][6] = 22;
```

Summary

In this chapter, you've had a lot of hands-on experience both with C++ and a variety of different code structures. You've accomplished a lot in this chapter, and you should give yourself a pat on the back for completing it.

In this chapter you've looked at:

❑   Functions

❑   Conditionals

❑   Loops

❑   Arrays

If you've worked through all the examples, then what I suggest you do now is take a fresh look at the examples in this chapter and look at ways to modify them. See if you can take the code given to you and make it do more. For example, take the code from later examples and break it up into separate functions (the calculator example is ideal for this).

I also hope that this chapter has whetted your appetite to get more involved with code and programming!

Problem Solving

Programming is mostly about solving problems. Many people seem to think that programming is about learning to write code, writing and then testing the code before compiling it into useful applications, and making those applications available to others. While all this is true, and these are all the real steps that you will have to take to be a programmer, it misses the real point of programming — which is that programming is about problem solving. The programming language is simply the tool you use to do the job.

It's a bit like fiction writing. If you want to be the next Stephen King, Tom Clancy, John Grisham, or J. K. Rowling, you aren't going to get anywhere if all you concentrate on is spelling, grammar, and using a word processor! It's about using the tools you have access to and applying them to solve a problem.

For example, if you are writing code that adds sales tax to an order total, the code you need to write solves the problem of how to calculate the total sales tax and how to add that tax to the total. If you are creating a more complicated application, such as a game, then this solves a lot of little problems, a few of which are detailed here:

- ❑ Making things move on screen
- ❑ Making the game interact with the player
- ❑ Responding to player input
- ❑ Keeping track of the objectives of the game
- ❑ Keeping score
- ❑ Creating harder/easier levels to the game
- ❑ How to save the game and allow it to be reloaded later

So, as you can see, a programmer needs to be a good problem solver, and in this chapter we take a look at the problem solving and how best to solve programming problems by applying logic to them.

The Basics of Problem Solving

Because problem solving is a core skill that the programmer needs to master, we're now going to spend some time looking at schemes that make problem solving quicker, easier, and more accurate.

To look at problem solving, you need an example to work through. Consider the following. You've been approached to write a calculator application. The client wants you to create an application that is capable of converting temperatures between two common units of measure:

❑   Fahrenheit to centigrade (or Celsius)

❑   Centigrade (or Celsius) to Fahrenheit

The client doesn't seem to care how it does this, he just wants an application where he can enter one temperature and convert it to another.

How do you approach writing such an application? I'm going to assume that you don't know much about the conversion process but that you can write simple code in C++.

Let's now look at what problems you need to solve to be able to write this application and how to solve them.

If you know how to do this type of conversion, try to forget for a while that you can! Work through the process and discover how to come to a logical way to solve this type of problem.

Be Clear about the Requirements

The first step to solving any problem is to make sure that you know exactly what the problems are that you are trying to solve (see Figure 8-1).

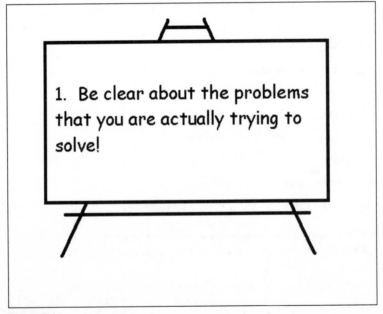

Figure 8-1

So, what are the problems that you need to solve here? Well, you might be quite surprised to find out that there are quite a few!

Before you tackle any programming problem, the first thing you need to do is make sure you know what the client (or you, if you happen to be writing an application for yourself) actually want. This is called the *client requirements* (see Figure 8-2).

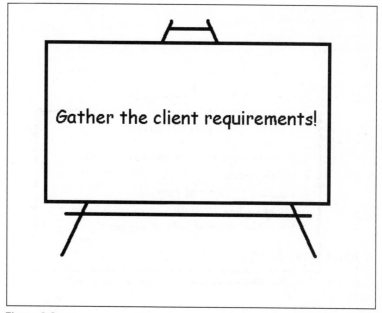

Figure 8-2

This generally involves quizzing the client about what they want the software to actually do. People can be surprisingly vague at the planning stage and only become picky and specific when you've already put in a lot of work into the project. Get the client to commit up front as to what they want the program or application to do. This can be changed later if needed but if you are charging for your time you'll be able to charge more for the work!

This stage is all about asking questions and getting back answers, questions like:

- ❑ What do you want the application to do?
- ❑ What inputs do you want the application to take?
- ❑ What outputs do you want the application to have?
- ❑ Is there anything else you want the application to do?

If you put these questions to your client you should get back answers that help you plan some more.

This stage is all about asking questions and getting back answers, questions like:

- **What will the application do?** "I want the application to convert temperatures between degrees Fahrenheit and degrees Centigrade."

- **Inputs needed?** "I want to be able to input the temperatures and have the program carry out the conversion."

- **Possible outputs.** "Numerical outputs on the screen. There is no need for the application to store the data in a file."

- **Other uses.** "Not at present."

You can now organize this feedback in a logical fashion (see Figure 8-3).

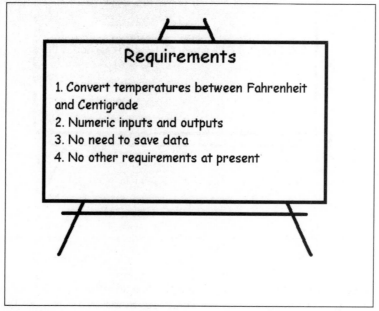

Figure 8-3

Seems clear enough, but there's one gray area that I want to clear up before progressing, and that's to do with inputs and outputs. Ask the client:

Do you want the user to be able to specify what input is being given or do you want the input to be a number that is converted to both centigrade and Fahrenheit automatically?

As you can see, I'm already beginning to think of the problem as a finished application. As far as I see, there are two simple ways that the application can work:

- The application can ask the user for the type of conversion that he or she wants carried out (see Figure 8-4) and then, based on the input, act accordingly and carry out the calculation (see Figure 8-5).

Figure 8-4

Figure 8-.5

❑ The application can ask for an input (see Figure 8-6) and output this figure in both temperature units (see Figure 8-7).

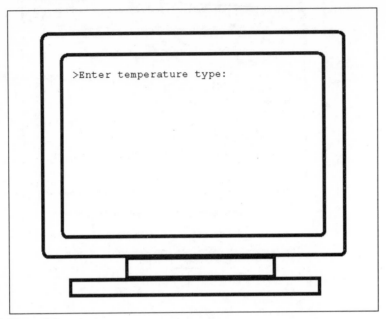

Figure 8-6

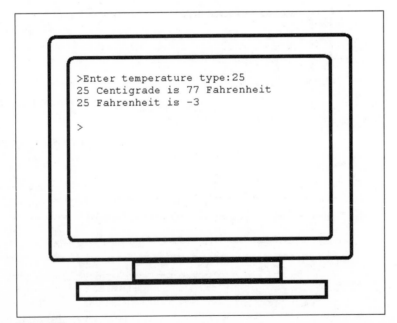

Figure 8-7

These are two ways that the program could work. The client decides that it's better if the application asks for the type of conversion to carry out and outputs values based on this input.

That significantly narrows down the requirements of the project (see Figure 8-8).

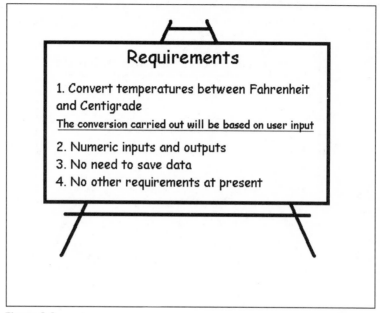

Figure 8-8

So, we now have the basic requirements of the program at hand, and you can summarize them. This will act as a blueprint in moving forward.

Research

You know how to program but do you know how to convert temperatures? Programmers are often asked to do things that they themselves might not know how to do. It is therefore the programmer's job to be good at either doing research or asking more questions.

Here we've been asked to convert between two temperature units. I know that at some point in the past I was told how to do this and wrote it down in school and probably carried out calculations based on it, but to be honest I can't remember how to do it. So I'm going to have to do some research.

There are several ways that I could carry out this research. I could ask the client but I'm pretty convinced I can find out how to do this kind of conversion on the Web, in a book, or by asking someone else. However, there are times, especially if you are working on very specific applications, when you might have to ask for access to reference materials that you can use to solve the problem at hand. For example, temperature conversions I know I can find on my own, but it would be a different matter if I were asked to write code that worked out the power outputs from different kinds of gasoline engines — I'm unlikely to easily find this kind of data on the Web, and I'd need access to calculations and figures that would be required.

OK, temperature conversions. Just how do you convert Fahrenheit to centigrade and centigrade to Fahrenheit? Fire up the browser, make a quick visit to a search engine site, and enter a few search criteria (programmers soon become good at searching the Web too!). Quickly I find the equations needed to convert from Fahrenheit to centigrade (see Figure 8-9) and from centigrade to Fahrenheit (see Figure 8-10).

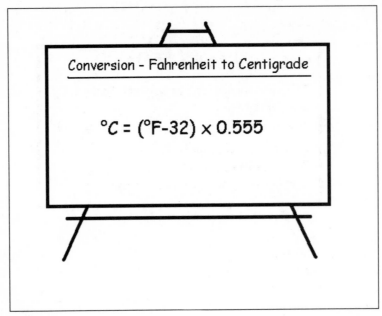

Conversion - Fahrenheit to Centigrade

$$°C = (°F-32) \times 0.555$$

Figure 8-9

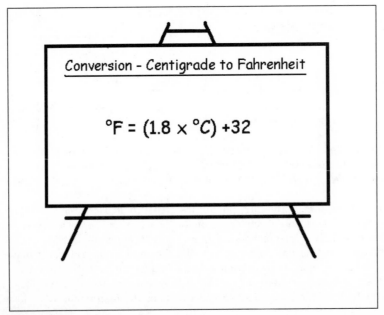

Conversion - Centigrade to Fahrenheit

$$°F = (1.8 \times °C) +32$$

Figure 8-10

It seems pretty straightforward to me. The equation itself seems quite easy to follow. However, it always helps to plug some numbers into an equation like this just so that you can familiarize yourself with how it works (see Figures 8-11 and 8-12).

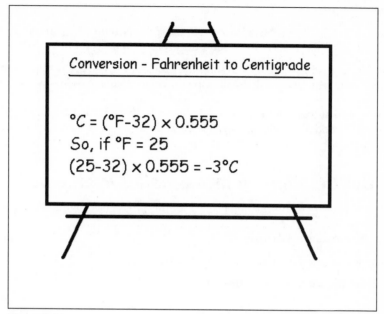

Conversion - Fahrenheit to Centigrade

$$°C = (°F-32) \times 0.555$$
So, if °F = 25
$$(25-32) \times 0.555 = -3°C$$

Figure 8-11

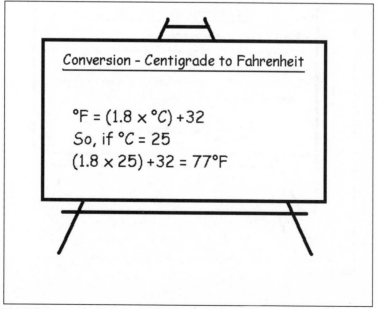

Conversion - Centigrade to Fahrenheit

$$°F = (1.8 \times °C) +32$$
So, if °C = 25
$$(1.8 \times 25) +32 = 77°F$$

Figure 8-12

This step is important because you need to have a good understanding of how any equations or principals work in real life. You need to do this for several important reasons:

❑ You can't possibly write code to solve a problem if you don't know what the code is supposed to do!

❑ If you know how the problem is solved in the real world this lets you convert this principal into working code that you can use to solve the problem in the computer world.

❑ By having a good grasp of how to solve the problem you can get an appreciation for the outputs that the code will generate that will help you know when the code is working and when it's not.

We've already looked at one input you can use in the code. I've rounded the numbers to integers but this itself will serve as a good place to start when testing code with inputs where the correct outputs are already known.

Breaking the Problem up into Smaller Problems

So far we've gathered a lot of information needed for this project (see Figure 8-13). You know:

❑ What the program needs to do

❑ What the outputs should be

❑ Equations needed to carry out these functions

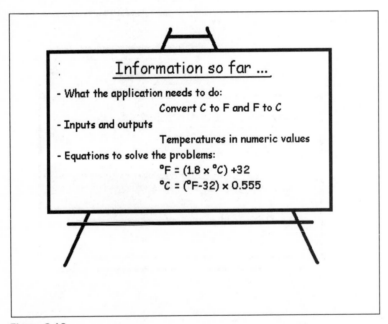

Figure 8-13

You have the information you need, but now what you need is to think about what problems (or issues) the actual program you're going to write needs to solve.

What Are the Issues That the Application Needs to Deal With?

You've written a few applications so by now you have a good idea of some of the problems or issues you are going to have to deal with in code. Some of these are just standard issues involved in programming, while others are specific to the application you are writing and the requirements of that application.

Here are the issues your application is going to have to deal with:

- **Inputs from the user.** We've already established that these are going to be numeric in nature mainly but we are also going to need a way to specify whether the temperatures inputted are centigrade or Fahrenheit.

- **Outputs to the screen.** The application is going to need to output the converted temperature to the screen. This again will be mainly numeric but we also need to add text to keep the number in context.

- **Processing.** The code needs the ability to carry out the two conversions. We need to transfer into code the equations that we detailed earlier.

- **Interface.** The application is going to need an interface of one type or another so that the program is easy to navigate and use.

This is summarized in Figure 8-14.

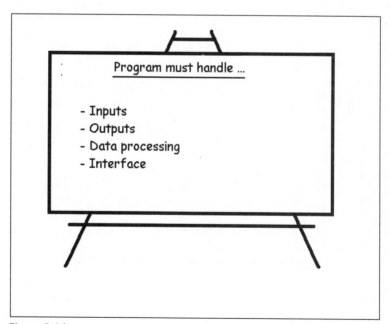

Figure 8-14

The preceding are the basics of the temperature conversion program, and this forms much of the basis of the coding that you need to write.

Moving on to the Coding Phase

So far, we've done a lot of work, asked a lot of questions, and carried out research on the theory behind the application — and we've done all this without writing a single line of code. Only now that we've done this are we ready to move on to the preliminary coding phase. Because we are going to be using C++ for this project, we can begin to create the basic layout for the temperature conversion application.

The best place to begin with any project is the basic coding template:

```
// Temperature conversion application
#include <iostream.h>
void main()
    {
        // code goes here!!!!
    }
```

Now, we know that this program is going to need to accept at least two inputs from the keyboard:

❑   The temperature needs to be converted.

❑   An input to indicate whether the conversion needs to be from centigrade to Fahrenheit or from Fahrenheit to centigrade.

So, we can start by declaring variables that are going to be needed. We already have a few decisions to make:

❑   What form will the temperature inputs be? Will they be integers (whole numbers) or floating-point numbers?

❑   How will the user indicate whether they should carry out a centigrade-to-Fahrenheit conversion or a Fahrenheit-to-centigrade conversion?

These are questions for the client — especially on the question of integers versus floating-point numbers because this has an effect on accuracy. Because the client wants the application to handle air temperatures and doesn't need high accuracy, integers will do just fine.

As for inputs to choose the type of conversion, a simple single character will do (C to carry out a centigrade-to-Fahrenheit conversion and F for Fahrenheit to centigrade).

Again, make sure that you summarize this information so that you don't forget this later (see Figure 8-15).

We can now start to integrate this into the code. First, we can declare the variables for the two inputs. These will be:

```
TempInput

ConversionType

// Temperature conversion application
#include <iostream.h>
void main()
    {
```

```
      int TempInput;
      char ConversionType;
   }
```

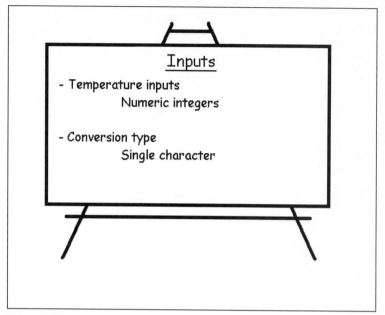

Figure 8-15

Because the program relies on an input we can use `cin` to start allowing inputs to the entered into the application. First, the temperature input:

```
// Temperature conversion application
#include <iostream.h>
void main()
    {
    int TempInput;
    char ConversionType;
    cin >> TempInput;
    }
```

We also can allow for the input for the conversion type. At this stage we don't need to be too worried about how these will be used.

```
// Temperature conversion application
#include <iostream.h>
void main()
    {
    int TempInput;
    char ConversionType;
    cin >> TempInput;
    cin >> ConversionType;
    }
```

Remember too that you need to add comments to make sure that the project stays on track and that you can remember what everything does.

```cpp
// Temperature conversion application
#include <iostream.h>
void main()
    {
    // Input temperature, numeric input
    int TempInput;

    // Input conversion type, single character
    // "C" will be used to represent C to F.
    // "F" will be used to represent F to C.
    char ConversionType;

    // Input the temperature
    cin >> TempInput;

    // Input conversion type
    cin >> ConversionType;
    }
```

Variables have been declared and inputs taken and comments added. Now we need to add some structure to the code so that it can carry out the conversion on the temperature input. Which conversion you carry out depends on the input, as summarized in Figure 8-16.

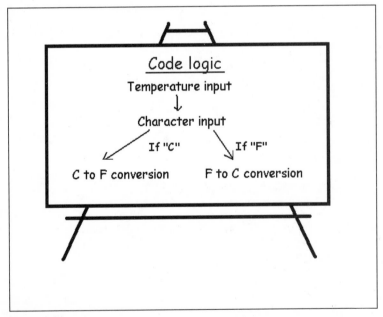

Figure 8-16

If the input is C, we need to carry out one conversion, if it's F, we need to do another. The logic here is probably best suited to the `If` statement conditional.

```
// Temperature conversion application
#include <iostream.h>
void main()
    {
    // Input temperature, numeric input
    int TempInput;

    // Input conversion type, single character
    // "C" will be used to represent C to F.
    // "F" will be used to represent F to C.
    char ConversionType;

    // Input the temperature
    cin >> TempInput;

    // Input conversion type
    cin >> ConversionType;

    // Conditionals below
    if (ConversionType == )
      // Calculation code here
    if (ConversionType == )
      // Calculation code here
    }
```

Remember that when characters are inputted we can't check for the character directly and have to test for the decimal ASCII code of that character. These are:

❑   C = 67

❑   F = 70

We can now add this to the code:

```
// Temperature conversion application
#include <iostream.h>
void main()
    {
    // Input temperature, numeric input
    int TempInput;

    // Input conversion type, single character
    // "C" will be used to represent C to F.
    // "F" will be used to represent F to C.
    char ConversionType;

    // Input the temperature
```

```
    cin >> TempInput;

    // Input conversion type
    cin >> ConversionType;

    // Conditionals below
    if (ConversionType == 67)
        // Calculation code here for C to F
    if (ConversionType == 70)
        // Calculation code here for F to C
    }
```

Now we are ready to move on to the main part of the code — this will be the code that takes the input and converts it to the appropriate temperature unit.

The first thing we need is another variable; this will be used to hold the output temperature, which will be another integer.

```
// Temperature conversion application
#include <iostream.h>
void main()
    {
    // Input temperature, numeric input
    int TempInput;

    // Output temperature, numeric output
    int TempOutput;

    // Input conversion type, single character
    // "C" will be used to represent C to F.
    // "F" will be used to represent F to C.
    char ConversionType;

    // Input the temperature
    cin >> TempInput;

    // Input conversion type
    cin >> ConversionType;

    // Conditionals below
    if (ConversionType == 67)
        // Calculation code here for C to F
    if (ConversionType == 70)
        // Calculation code here for F to C
    }
```

So, on to the conversion of the temperature input to the output. To do this, we need to refer to the conversion equations that we had earlier (see Figure 8-17).

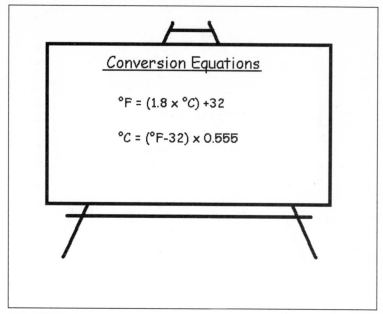

Figure 8-17

What you can now do is to take the input and output variables and integrate them into the equations. Remember, the inputs need to be inputted into the body of the equation (see Figure 8-18) and the output is the solution of the equation (see Figure 8-19).

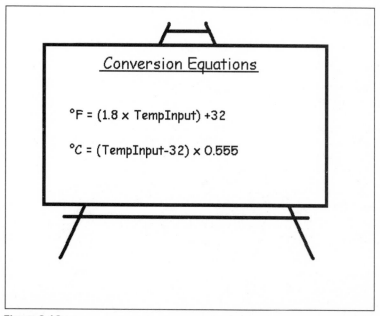

Figure 8-18

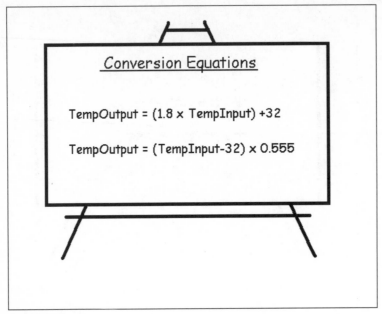

Figure 8-19

These can now be integrated into the code. Remember that * is used in the arithmetic to represent a multiplication sign, and not x.

```
// Temperature conversion application
#include <iostream.h>
void main()
    {
    // Input temperature, numeric input
    int TempInput;

    // Output temperature, numeric output
    int TempOutput;

    // Input conversion type, single character
    // "C" will be used to represent C to F.
    // "F" will be used to represent F to C.
    char ConversionType;

    // Input the temperature
    cin >> TempInput;

    // Input conversion type
    cin >> ConversionType;

    // Conditionals below
    if (ConversionType == 67)
        // Calculation code here for C to F
        TempOutput = (1.8 * TempInput) + 32;
    if (ConversionType == 70)
```

```
// Calculation code here for F to C
TempOutput = (TempInput - 32) * 0.555;


}
```

With the addition of one simple output to the screen, you can now compile the code and test it with a variety of inputs and check the outputs.

```
// Temperature conversion application
#include <iostream.h>
void main()
    {
    // Input temperature, numeric input
    int TempInput;

    // Output temperature, numeric output
    int TempOutput;

    // Input conversion type, single character
    // "C" will be used to represent C to F
    // "F" will be used to represent F to C
    char ConversionType;

    // Input the temperature
    cin >> TempInput;

    // Input conversion type
    cin >> ConversionType;

    // Conditionals below
    if (ConversionType == 67)
      // Calculation code here for C to F
      TempOutput = (1.8 * TempInput) + 32;
    if (ConversionType == 70)
      // Calculation code here for F to C
      TempOutput = (TempInput - 32) * 0.555;
    cout << TempOutput << endl;
    }
```

Save the source code, calling it `tempconv.cpp`, and you can compile it as shown in Figure 8-20.

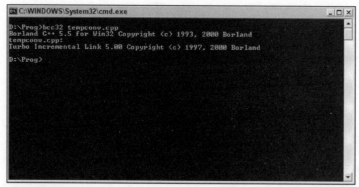

Figure 8-20

After compiling, test the code with a few inputs and check that the outputs work out properly for each conversion. Take a look at Figure 8-21 for a variety of inputs and outputs.

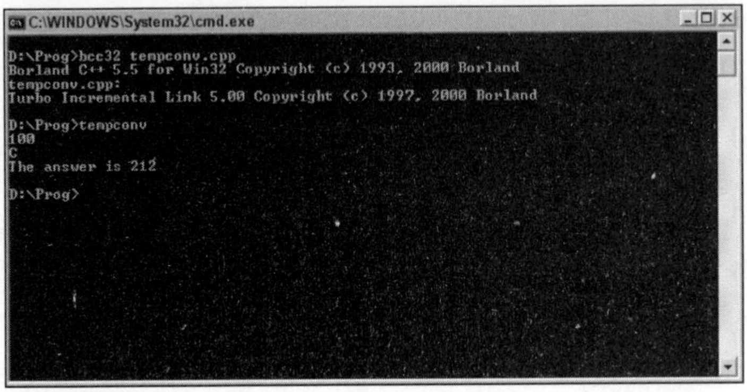

Figure 8-21

Improving the Code

You have code that works and outputs that are correct; the next thing you need to do is to make the application easier to use. Take a step back from the application and have a look at it critically. I think that as a minimum it needs the following:

❑ Text display initially to tell the user what the application is

❑ Initial instructions for use

❑ Captions for inputs

❑ Captions for outputs

```
// Temperature conversion application
#include <iostream.h>
void main()
    {
    // Input temperature, numeric input
    int TempInput;

    // Output temperature, numeric output
    int TempOutput;

    // Input conversion type, single character
    // "C" will be used to represent C to F.
    // "F" will be used to represent F to C.
    char ConversionType;

    // Welcome message
    cout << "Tempperature Converter" << endl;
    cout << "----------------------" << endl;

    // Initial instruction for use
```

```
        cout << "Enter a temperature and choose the conversion you want to carry out:"
<< endl;
     // Input the temperature
        cout << "Enter a temperature: ";
        cin >> TempInput;

     // Input conversion type
        cout << "Enter conversion type." << endl;
        cout << "Type C followed by ENTER for Centigrade to Fahrenheit conversion." <<
endl;
        cout << "Type F followed by ENTER for Fahrenheit to Centigrade conversion." <<
.endl;
        cin >> ConversionType;

     // Conditionals below
     if (ConversionType == 67)
       // Calculation code here for C to F
       TempOutput = (1.8 * TempInput) + 32;
     if (ConversionType == 70)
       // Calculation code here for F to C
       TempOutput = (TempInput - 32) * 0.555;
        cout << "Output: " << TempOutput << endl;
   }
```

It's a good idea to again compile the code and take a look at whether the code works and if the on-screen captions and instructions make sense and are accurate (see Figure 8-22).

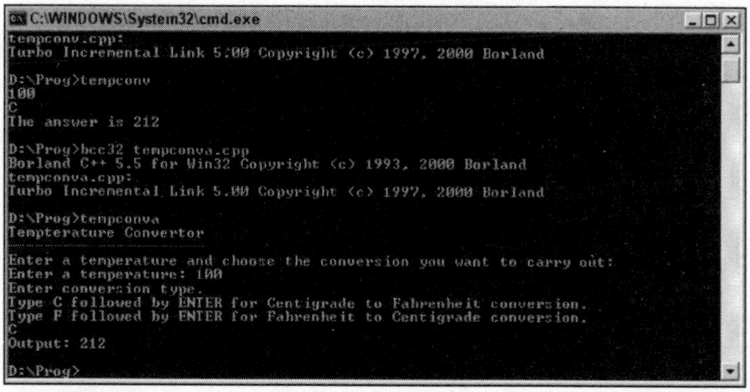

Figure 8-22

Remember that you are looking for clarity and logic in the instructions. Tell the users what to do before each step and keep them informed after each step. Also, look out for any ambiguity in the instructions or captions of outputs.

There's one aspect of this code that I think could do with improvement and that's the final output:

```
Output: 99
```

This is ambiguous, and you want to avoid this at all costs.

One improvement is to make clear that the output actually is a temperature.

```
// Temperature conversion application
#include <iostream.h>
void main()
    {
    // Input temperature, numeric input
    int TempInput;

    // Output temperature, numeric output
    int TempOutput;

    // Input conversion type, single character
    // "C" will be used to represent C to F.
    // "F" will be used to represent F to C.
    char ConversionType;

    // Welcome message
    cout << "Tempterature Converter" << endl;
    cout << "----------------------" << endl;

    // Initial instruction for use
    cout << "Enter a temperature and choose the conversion you want to carry out:"
<< endl;
    // Input the temperature
    cout << "Enter a temperature: ";
    cin >> TempInput;

    // Input conversion type
    cout << "Enter conversion type." << endl;
    cout << "Type C followed by ENTER for Centigrade to Fahrenheit conversion." <<
endl;
    cout << "Type F followed by ENTER for Fahrenheit to Centigrade conversion." <<
endl;
    cin >> ConversionType;

    // Conditionals below
    if (ConversionType == 67)
      // Calculation code here for C to F
      TempOutput = (1.8 * TempInput) + 32;
    if (ConversionType == 70)
      // Calculation code here for F to C
      TempOutput = (TempInput - 32) * 0.555;
    cout << "Temperature output: " << TempOutput << endl;
    }
```

This helps, but only partly. Take a close look at the output again:

```
D:\Prog>tempconv2
Tempterature Converter
----------------------
Enter a temperature and choose the conversion you want to carry out:
```

```
Enter a temperature: 100
Enter conversion type.
Type C followed by ENTER for Centigrade to Fahrenheit conversion.
Type F followed by ENTER for Fahrenheit to Centigrade conversion.
C
Temperature output: 212
```

There is ambiguity in the code at the end there, where it doesn't really give the user much feedback. Ideally, there should be feedback based on which choice the user made and better formatting of the output. You want the output to be as clear as possible.

When you are looking for good output, it is a good idea to prototype the output, looking at various ways that the output could be formatted. This can be done on paper, on sticky notes, or on the computer in a graphics package.

The layout that I think works best for this is shown in Figure 8-23.

Figure 8-23

Now to recreate this in code. There are several ways you could do this, but the easiest way is to make greater use of the statements run by the conditional If. To expand on these first add curly braces:

```
// Temperature conversion application
#include <iostream.h>
void main()
    {
     // Input temperature, numeric input
```

```
    int TempInput;

    // Output temperature, numeric output
    int TempOutput;

    // Input conversion type, single character
    // "C" will be used to represent C to F.
    // "F" will be used to represent F to C.
    char ConversionType;

    // Welcome message
    cout << "Tempterature Converter" << endl;
    cout << "----------------------" << endl;

    // Initial instruction for use
    cout << "Enter a temperature and choose the conversion you want to carry out:"
<< endl;
    // Input the temperature
    cout << "Enter a temperature: ";
    cin >> TempInput;

    // Input conversion type
    cout << "Enter conversion type." << endl;
    cout << "Type C followed by ENTER for Centigrade to Fahrenheit conversion." <<
endl;
    cout << "Type F followed by ENTER for Fahrenheit to Centigrade conversion." <<
endl;
    cin >> ConversionType;

    // Conditionals below
    if (ConversionType == 67)
        // Calculation code here for C to F
        {
        TempOutput = (1.8 * TempInput) + 32;
        }
    if (ConversionType == 70)
        // Calculation code here for F to C
        {
        TempOutput = (TempInput - 32) * 0.555;
        }
    cout << "Temperature output: " << TempOutput << endl;
    }
```

Now these functions can handle the appropriate outputs to the screen. First, add to each a confirmation telling the user what is going to happen:

```
// Temperature conversion application
#include <iostream.h>
void main()
    {
    // Input temperature, numeric input
```

```
        int TempInput;

        // Output temperature, numeric output
        int TempOutput;

        // Input conversion type, single character
        // "C" will be used to represent C to F.
        // "F" will be used to represent F to C.
        char ConversionType;

        // Welcome message
        cout << "Tempterature Converter" << endl;
        cout << "----------------------" << endl;

        // Initial instruction for use
        cout << "Enter a temperature and choose the conversion you want to carry out:"
<< endl;
        // Input the temperature
        cout << "Enter a temperature: ";
        cin >> TempInput;

        // Input conversion type
        cout << "Enter conversion type." << endl;
        cout << "Type C followed by ENTER for Centigrade to Fahrenheit conversion." <<
endl;
        cout << "Type F followed by ENTER for Fahrenheit to Centigrade conversion." <<
endl;
        cin >> ConversionType;

        // Conditionals below
        if (ConversionType == 67)
          // Calculation code here for C to F
          {
          cout << "Centigrade to Fahrenheit conversion:" << endl;
          TempOutput = (1.8 * TempInput) + 32;
          }
        if (ConversionType == 70)
          // Calculation code here for F to C
          {
          cout << "Fahrenheit to Centigrade conversion:" << endl;
          TempOutput = (TempInput - 32) * 0.555;
          }
        cout << "Temperature output: " << TempOutput << endl;
      }
```

After doing that, the logical thing is to take the solution output and place this inside the functions.

The proper formatting of the output can be achieved by integrating the variables with the test output to achieve the desired output, as shown in Figure 8-24.

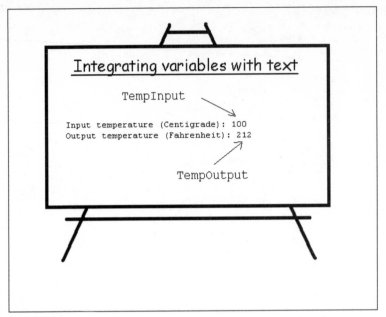

Figure 8-24

You can translate these instructions into working C++ code as follows:

```cpp
// Temperature conversion application
#include <iostream.h>
void main()
    {
    // Input temperature, numeric input
    int TempInput;

    // Output temperature, numeric output
    int TempOutput;

    // Input conversion type, single character
    // "C" will be used to represent C to F.
    // "F" will be used to represent F to C.
    char ConversionType;

    // Welcome message
    cout << "Tempterature Converter" << endl;
    cout << "----------------------" << endl;

    // Initial instruction for use
    cout << "Enter a temperature and choose the conversion you want to carry out:"
<< endl;
    // Input the temperature
    cout << "Enter a temperature: ";
    cin >> TempInput;

    // Input conversion type
```

```
      cout << "Enter conversion type." << endl;
      cout << "Type C followed by ENTER for Centigrade to Fahrenheit conversion." <<
endl;
      cout << "Type F followed by ENTER for Fahrenheit to Centigrade conversion." <<
endl;
      cin >> ConversionType;

      // Conditionals below
      if (ConversionType == 67)
        // Calculation code here for C to F
        {
        cout << "Centigrade to Fahrenheit conversion:" << endl;
        TempOutput = (1.8 * TempInput) + 32;
        cout << "Input temperature (Centigrade): " << TempInput << endl;
        cout << "Output temperature (Fahrenheit): " << TempOutput << endl;
        }
      if (ConversionType == 70)
        // Calculation code here for F to C
        {
        cout << "Fahrenheit to Centigrade conversion:" << endl;
        TempOutput = (TempInput - 32) * 0.555;
        cout << "Input temperature (Fahrenheit): " << TempInput << endl;
        cout << "Output temperature (Centigrade): " << TempOutput << endl;
        }
    }
```

You can now compile this code and take a look at it in action, as shown in Figure 8-25.

Figure 8-25

Let's now pause to look at the program we've created and see whether it fulfills the product requirements laid down at the beginning. Take a look at Figure 8-26.

So, all the requirements have been met. We took the requirements laid down initially and, by asking some simple questions, broke the problem down into smaller problems (subproblems, if you like) and then tackled each of these in turn, using programming as a tool with which to build answers. Just like the writer who uses spelling and grammar to write stories, the programmer uses the programming tool of his or her choice to build answers to the questions raised.

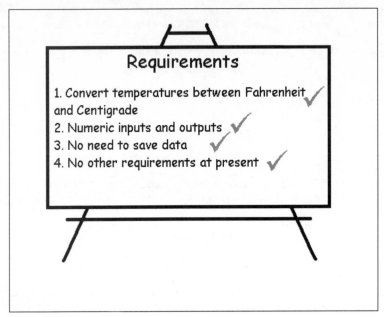

Figure 8-26

Summary

In this chapter, you've taken a look at how you should approach problem solving with regard to programming. All problems are going to be different and as such there is no "one size fits all" solution. However, by following a few basic rules, you can turn programming knowledge into a tool to solve problems and create code that produces real results.

Remember:

- Get the requirements clear.

- Break down problems into smaller problems.

- Research any aspects of the program you don't understand.

- Double-check any aspects of the program you aren't clear about with the client.

- Write code that solves the problem.

- Make sure that the application produces accurate results.

- Make sure that the application gives the user information on how to use it, as well as what the results mean.

- Remove ambiguity.

With these points in mind, your programming will be more focused and the applications you create will solve the problems they are designed to solve.

Debugging

In this chapter, we are going to be looking at errors — something which you will have probably seen quite a bit of as you've been typing in the code in the previous chapters!

Errors are a fact of life when it comes to programming. The trick is knowing how to trace them and then fixing them before other people get their hands on your program!

In this chapter, we are going to be taking a look at a variety of programming errors, what causes them, and how to fix them. We'll also look at some of the psychology behind programming errors and look at why some are more common than others.

To Err Is Human

Let me be honest with you, since it's only you and me and no one else is about.

There are many programmers who give off an aura that seems to suggest that each and every line of code and statement that they create works first time, every time, without fail, and without errors. This in turn puts a lot of stress and pressure on those new to programming to do the same. They quickly get the impression that making mistakes and getting error messages is something to be ashamed of, and that they are a sign of failure and something to be embarrassed about.

I want to clear this up with you right away — errors are a fact of life, and any programmers who tell you that they can write prefect code all the time are either lying through their teeth or don't actually do much programming — at least, much serious programming. If programmers could output perfect code then software companies would hunt down these people, give them top-paid jobs, fire all the less-than-perfect programmers, eliminate any testing and beta test stages of software releases, and save millions of dollars, releasing perfect software that didn't need service packs, maintenance releases, or patches and so save even more money. Big software companies don't do this because the "perfect programmer" is a myth generated by other programmers to boost their status.

Everyone makes mistakes. Even with basic stuff. You forget something simple or get distracted mid-statement and don't finish it right. I make mistakes and I'm happy to admit it. There have been code examples in this book where I've initially left something out or had the phone ring or an email come in mid-statement and forgotten to finish it. I've also lost track of the variables I used and then used the wrong one. That's life. It's irritating and I wish I could write perfect code all the time because this would be a major ego booster and save me a lot of time. But I'm human. I accept that, and I urge you to accept it too.

Initially, you are bound to make more errors in your coding simply because you are learning. The syntax of statements takes time to grasp, operators are unfamiliar, and basic coding practices are foreign to you: until you are comfortable with these, errors will happen. Look at mistakes as learning pointers, showing you areas that you need to pay attention to, while error-free statements are examples of things that you are doing right!

Stick with programming, and you'll notice that you make fewer and fewer errors in your code — that's good progress and something you should feel proud of. But don't worry with trying to be 100 percent error-free, leave that to the "perfect" programmers who feel they have to show off!

Errors, Errors, Errors!

Making a mistake isn't something that we think about too much in daily life. We make a mistake and hopefully we can correct it and move on. Some commonly asked questions from those starting out in programming are:

- ❑ Are errors all created the same?
- ❑ Are there different types of errors?

Both are excellent questions. The answer to this is that not all errors are made in the same way and that there are many different types of errors that can be found within computer code.

Let's take a look at the types of errors that can be present within computer code.

Different Kinds of Error

As you will see, there are many different kinds of errors that can exist within the lines of your code. Fortunately, the errors can be categorized into convenient groups so that they can be discussed easily.

There are three classes or errors that we are going to be looking at here. These are:

- ❑ Compiler errors
- ❑ Runtime errors
- ❑ Logic errors

Let's take a look at each of these types of errors in turn.

Compiler Error

A compiler error is usually the first kind of error that most programmers see. A compiler error is an error thrown up by the compiler as you are in the process or turning your source code into a standalone application.

We've already looked at compilers, and you've had some experience in taking code from source code to an executable application.

It's important to note that you will only get a compiler error if you use a compiler. So, if you are using C++, Java, or any other language that uses a compiler, you might see compiler errors. If you use a language that doesn't need compiling (such as VBScript or JavaScript), you won't see a compiler error because no compiler is involved (but that's not to say that you won't see errors thrown up when the interpreter loads the code).

Compiler errors are errors in your code that the compiler picks up on. Different compilers scrutinize the code at varying levels to look for errors, and while most pick up on some of the more common errors, it's important for you to realize right from the start that they won't pick up all of them.

Take a look at this simple block of C++ code:

```cpp
#include <iostream.h>
void main()
    (
        cout << "Hello, World!" << endl;
    }
```

Recognize it? It's the code that displays Hello, World! on the screen when run. But do you notice a problem with the code? Take a look closely at line three, where the curly brace should be:

```cpp
#include <iostream.h>
void main()
    (
        cout << "Hello, World!" << endl;
    }
```

Notice that it's not a curly brace, but an opening parenthesis or opening bracket.

What do you think the compiler will make of that if you try to compile it? Well, it won't like it for sure! Figure 9-1 shows what it had to say about it:

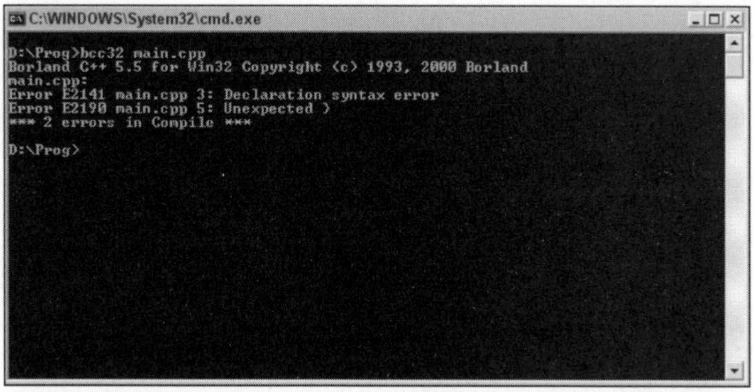

Figure 9-1

```
D:\Prog>bcc32 helloerr.cpp
Borland C++ 5.5 for Win32 Copyright (c) 1993, 2000 Borland
helloerr.cpp:
Error E2141 helloerr.cpp 3: Declaration syntax error
Error E2190 helloerr.cpp 5: Unexpected }
*** 2 errors in Compile ***
```

It says that there are two errors when there is in fact only one, but let's take a closer look at the errors it says exist. Here are the two lines where the errors are declared:

```
Error E2141 helloerr.cpp 3: Declaration syntax error
Error E2190 helloerr.cpp 5: Unexpected }
```

There are four parts to these error messages, as shown in Figure 9-2.

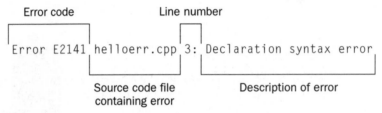

Figure 9-2

So, you have error messages telling you of two types of error on two separate lines of code. The lines of code in question are:

Line 3:

```
#include <iostream.h>
void main()
    (
        cout << "Hello, World!" << endl;
    }
```

Line 5:

```
#include <iostream.h>
void main()
    (
        cout << "Hello, World!" << endl;
    }
```

It's always a good idea to look at the first line specified with code. As you can see, in this case the compiler is right, it has spotted a *syntax error*, which is like a grammatical error in writing. We knew it was there so identifying it wasn't a huge challenge.

But what's wrong with line 5? Well, this error is a by-product of the error on line 3. Because we have made a mistake and didn't properly use the curly brace, the compiler comes to line 5 and sees the closing curly brace without a corresponding opening curly brace. This in itself is also an error, but one that arises because of an earlier error in the code.

Take a look at this code, another variation on the Hello, World! code, this time with a different error.

```
#include <iostream.h>
void main()

        cout << "Hello, World!" << endl;
    }
```

Can you spot the error?

Well, if you try to compile the code, you get the result displayed in Figure 9-3.

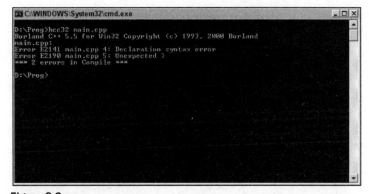

Figure 9-3

```
D:\Prog>bcc32 helloerr2.cpp
Borland C++ 5.5 for Win32 Copyright (c) 1993, 2000 Borland
helloerr2.cpp:
Error E2141 helloerr2.cpp 4: Declaration syntax error
Error E2190 helloerr2.cpp 5: Unexpected }
*** 2 errors in Compile ***
```

Again, two errors.

Line 4:

```
#include <iostream.h>
void main()

        cout << "Hello, World!" << endl;
    }
```

Line 5:

```
#include <iostream.h>
void main()

        cout << "Hello, World!" << endl;
    }
```

This time the first line declared as an error is misleading. This is a statement and the statement itself is correct. Let's move to the next line and take a look at that. This is the closing curly brace and this should give us a clue . . . take a look back at line 5. Notice something? Yes, the opening curly brace is now missing.

Sometimes the errors you get from the compiler are clear and point directly to the line that has the problem in it, whereas other times you might have to hunt around a little.

Let's look at a few more errors, so you can have some practice.

What's wrong with this code?

```
#include <iostream.h>
void main()
    {
        cout << "Hello, World!' << endl;
    }
```

Not sure? Let's compile it. The output is shown in Figure 9-4.

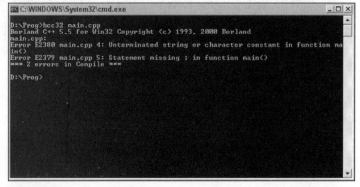

Figure 9-4

```
D:\Prog>bcc32 helloerr3.cpp
Borland C++ 5.5 for Win32 Copyright (c) 1993, 2000 Borland
helloerr3.cpp:
Error E2380 helloerr3.cpp 4: Unterminated string or character constant in function
main()
Error E2379 helloerr3.cpp 5: Statement missing ; in function main()
*** 2 errors in Compile ***
```

Errors exist on lines 4 and 5. The error on line 4 is said to be an "Unterminated string." *Unterminated string* is another term for when you forget to close a string properly using ". Can you see an example of this problem in line 4? Yes, a single quotation mark was used instead of double quotation marks.

This problem results in the second error too where the compiler expects there to be another statement in the code because the first contains problems. The rule so far is that if you get errors messages displayed, fix the first error that you find and recompile the code — the code might only contain one error, which is causing a chain of subsequent errors. Fixing that one error might cause the others to disappear.

Here is another block of code containing problems:

```
#include <iostream.h>
void main()
    {
        cout << "Hello, World!" <<< endl
    }
```

Because we've been looking at this same piece of code for a while now, chances are that the error will leap out at you! However, let's compile it anyway and see what happens. The output of the compile is shown in Figure 9-5.

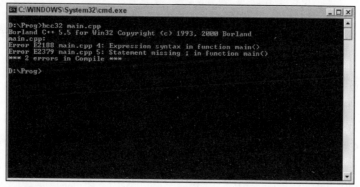

Figure 9-5

```
D:\Prog>bcc32 helloerr4.cpp
Borland C++ 5.5 for Win32 Copyright (c) 1993, 2000 Borland
helloerr4.cpp:
Error E2188 helloerr4.cpp 4: Expression syntax in function main()
Error E2379 helloerr4.cpp 5: Statement missing ; in function main()
*** 2 errors in Compile ***
```

There are two errors listed, lines 4 and 5. The compiler says that line 4 has a syntax error so that's a good place to start looking at the code.

```
#include <iostream.h>
void main()
    {
        cout << "Hello, World!" <<< endl
    }
```

Chapter 9

And there it is, just after the `"Hello, World!"`, `<<<` should in fact be `<<`. Let's fix that and recompile the code.

```
#include <iostream.h>
void main()
    {
        cout << "Hello, World!" << endl
    }
```

But there's still an error! It's still going on about that missing statement in line 5, as shown in Figure 9-6.

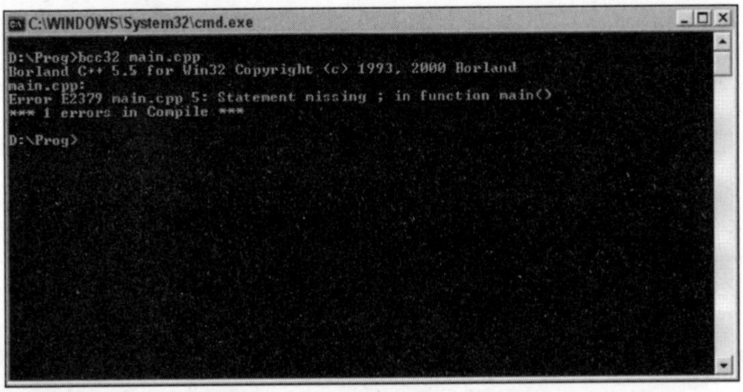

Figure 9-6

```
D:\Prog>bcc32 helloerr4.cpp
Borland C++ 5.5 for Win32 Copyright (c) 1993, 2000 Borland
helloerr4.cpp:
Error E2379 helloerr4.cpp 5: Statement missing ; in function main()
*** 1 errors in Compile ***
```

Line 5 is just the closing curly brace so the problem must be above it. Carefully work through the statement and look for the obvious. Incorrect use of quotation marks, instructions, line terminations . . . and there it is! The line-terminating semicolon is missing.

Let's add that and try again.

```
#include <iostream.h>
void main()
    {
        cout << "Hello, World!" << endl;
    }
```

Now everything works as expected (see Figure 9-7).

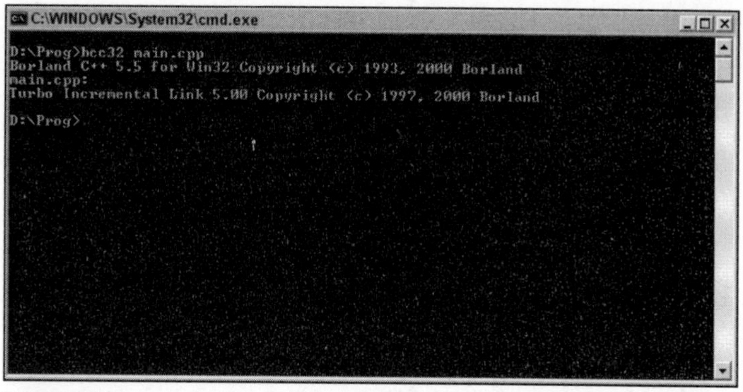

Figure 9-7

So far we've been looking at small blocks of code, code where the errors are easy to spot because you can read and review the code in a few moments. Let's now move on to look at compiler errors in larger segments of code.

Remember the calculator code from Chapter 7, "The Structure of Coding"? Here it is again, but this time the code contains an error:

```
#include <iostream.h>
void main ()
    {
    float num1;
    float num2;
    char op;
    float ans;
    cout << "Please enter a number: ";
    cin >> num1;
    cout << "Please enter another number: ";
    cin >> num2;
    cout << "Press A to add the two numbers."
        << endl
        << "Press S to subtract the two numbers."
        << endl
        << "Press M to multiply the two numbers."
        << endl
        << "Press D to divide the two numbers."
        << endl;
    cin >> op;
```

```
      if (op == 65)
        ans = num1 + num2
      if (op == 83)
        ans = num1 - num2;
      if (op == 77)
        ans = num1 * num2;
      if (op == 68)
        ans = num1 / num2;
      cout << "The answer is " << ans << endl;
    }
```

It's not so easy to spot the error this time is it! And this isn't a particularly long bit of code — it's only 30 lines long but already feels a bit unwieldy.

The best way to spot this error is to compile the code and see what you get.

The output of the compile is shown in Figure 9-8.

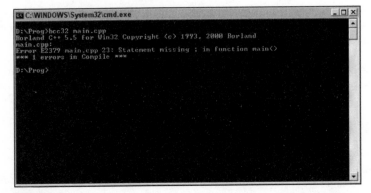

Figure 9-8

```
D:\Prog>bcc32 calcerr.cpp
Borland C++ 5.5 for Win32 Copyright (c) 1993, 2000 Borland
calcerr.cpp:
Error E2379 calcerr.cpp 23: Statement missing ; in function main()
*** 1 errors in Compile ***
```

It says that the problem is with line 23. Let's take a look at that.

```
#include <iostream.h>
void main ()
    {
      float num1;
      float num2;
      char op;
      float ans;
      cout << "Please enter a number: ";
      cin >> num1;
      cout << "Please enter another number: ";
      cin >> num2;
      cout << "Press A to add the two numbers."
```

```
                << endl
                << "Press S to subtract the two numbers."
                << endl
                << "Press M to multiply the two numbers."
                << endl
                << "Press D to divide the two numbers."
                << endl;
        cin >> op;
        if (op == 65)
           ans = num1 + num2
        if (op == 83)
           ans = num1 - num2;
        if (op == 77)
           ans = num1 * num2;
        if (op == 68)
           ans = num1 / num2;
        cout << "The answer is " << ans << endl;
    }
```

There's nothing wrong with that line because there isn't a need for a semicolon terminator there because it's not a statement. So, look around it. And then you probably see it. It's the line above that's missing the required line terminator.

One more, this time a little trickier but a very common problem with code.

```
#include <iostream.h>
void main ()
    {
        float num1;
        float num2;
        char op1;
        float ans;
        cout << "Please enter a number: ";
        cin >> num1;
        cout << "Please enter another number: ";
        cin >> num2;
        cout << "Press A to add the two numbers."
                << endl
                << "Press S to subtract the two numbers."
                << endl
                << "Press M to multiply the two numbers."
                << endl
                << "Press D to divide the two numbers."
                << endl;
        cin >> op;
        if (op == 65)
           ans = num1 + num2;
        if (op == 83)
           ans = num1 - num2;
        if (op == 77)
           ans = num1 * num2;
        if (op == 68)
           ans = num1 / num2;
        cout << "The answer is " << ans << endl;
    }
```

Any ideas? Honestly, I don't expect you to spot this problem because it is well hidden. The best way to spot this error is to compile the code (the output is shown in Figure 9-9).

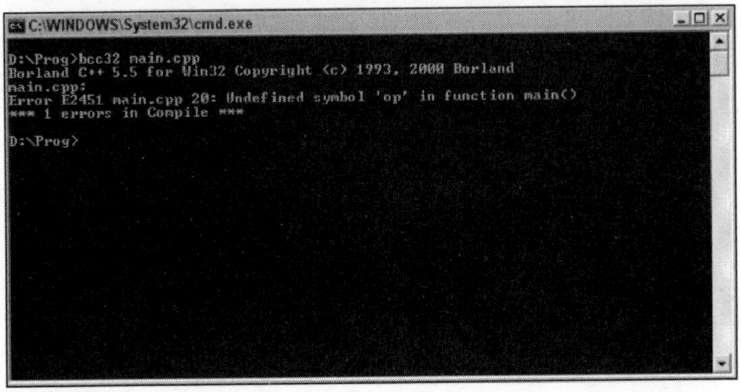

Figure 9-9

```
D:\Prog>bcc32 calcerr1.cpp
Borland C++ 5.5 for Win32 Copyright (c) 1993, 2000 Borland
calcerr1.cpp:
Error E2451 calcerr1.cpp 20: Undefined symbol 'op' in function main()
*** 1 errors in Compile ***
```

The error is described as being on line 20 of the code. Let's take a look at line 20.

```
#include <iostream.h>
void main ()
    {
      float num1;
      float num2;
      char op1;
      float ans;
      cout << "Please enter a number: ";
      cin >> num1;
      cout << "Please enter another number: ";
      cin >> num2;
      cout << "Press A to add the two numbers."
           << endl
           << "Press S to subtract the two numbers."
           << endl
           << "Press M to multiply the two numbers."
           << endl
           << "Press D to divide the two numbers."
           << endl;
      cin >> op;
      if (op == 65)
        ans = num1 + num2;
      if (op == 83)
        ans = num1 - num2;
      if (op == 77)
        ans = num1 * num2;
      if (op == 68)
```

```
        ans = num1 / num2;
        cout << "The answer is " << ans << endl;
    }
```

As you may remember, this line is used to take input from the keyboard and assign it to a variable, in this case one called `op`.

This statement seems complete, but the compiler claims that `op` is an undefined symbol. Have we declared the variable earlier in the code? Let's check:

```
#include <iostream.h>
void main ()
    {
        float num1;
        float num2;
        char op1;
        float ans;
...
```

There is the problem. We declared one variable (`op1`) and used another (`op`). This is a problem that occurs often because it's hard to keep track of the different variable names used in the code. Fortunately, the compiler picks up on it and if you understand the problem, it is easy to fix.

The code that follows contains a similar error:

```
#include <iostream.h>
void main ()
    {
        float num1;
        float num2;
        char op;
        float ans;
        cout << "Please enter a number: ";
        cin >> num1;
        cout << "Please enter another number: ";
        cin >> num2;
        cout << "Press A to add the two numbers."
             << endl
             << "Press S to subtract the two numbers."
             << endl
             << "Press M to multiply the two numbers."
             << endl
             << "Press D to divide the two numbers."
             << endl;
        cin >> op;
        if (op == 65)
          ans = num1 + num2;
        if (op == 83)
          ans = num1 - num2;
        if (op == 77)
          ans = num1 * num2;
        if (op1 == 68)
          ans = num1 / num2;
        cout << "The answer is " << ans << endl;
    }
```

If you try to compile this code you get the following error (see Figure 9-10):

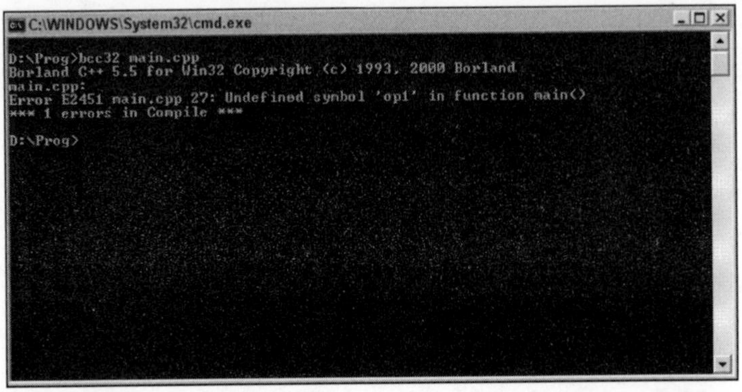

Figure 9-10

```
D:\Prog>bcc32 calcerr2.cpp
Borland C++ 5.5 for Win32 Copyright (c) 1993, 2000 Borland
calcerr2.cpp:
Error E2451 calcerr2.cpp 27: Undefined symbol 'op1' in function main()
*** 1 errors in Compile ***
```

Line 27 is now identified as being the line containing the problem. As you can see, what has happened is that we have declared op as the variable but for that statement we used op1 by mistake.

Compiling code is a great way to spot a whole host of errors with code.

But it's not only errors that you will see generated by the compiler. Compilers also can generate warnings.

Take a look at this modified code:

```
#include <iostream.h>
void main ()
    {
      float num1;
      float num2;
      char op;
      int var1;
      float ans;
      var1 = 7;
      cout << "Please enter a number: ";
      cin >> num1;
      cout << "Please enter another number: ";
      cin >> num2;
      cout << "Press A to add the two numbers."
          << endl
          << "Press S to subtract the two numbers."
          << endl
          << "Press M to multiply the two numbers."
          << endl
```

```
            << "Press D to divide the two numbers."
            << endl;
    cin >> op;
    if (op == 65)
      ans = num1 + num2;
    if (op == 83)
      ans = num1 - num2;
    if (op == 77)
      ans = num1 * num2;
    if (op == 68)
      ans = num1 / num2;
    cout << "The answer is " << ans << endl;
}
```

In this code we have declared a variable called var1 and then assigned a value to it (this can be seen on line 7).

However, if you look through the code you'll find that this isn't used anywhere in the application. The compiler could choose to ignore it but instead it gives you a warning about the problem (see Figure 9-11).

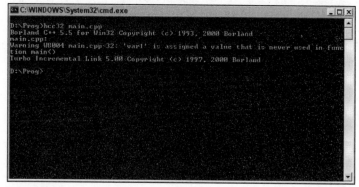

Figure 9-11

```
D:\Prog>bcc32 calcerr3.cpp
Borland C++ 5.5 for Win32 Copyright (c) 1993, 2000 Borland
calcerr3.cpp:
Warning W8004 calcerr3.cpp 32: 'var1' is assigned a value that is never used in
function main()
Turbo Incremental Link 5.00 Copyright (c) 1997, 2000 Borland
```

The other difference between an error and a warning is that when the compiler encounters an error it aborts the compile and generates the warning. With a warning, the compiler doesn't abort compiling and still builds an executable as normal. Despite containing this unused variable and assigned value, the application works normally (it can be seen in action in Figure 9-12).

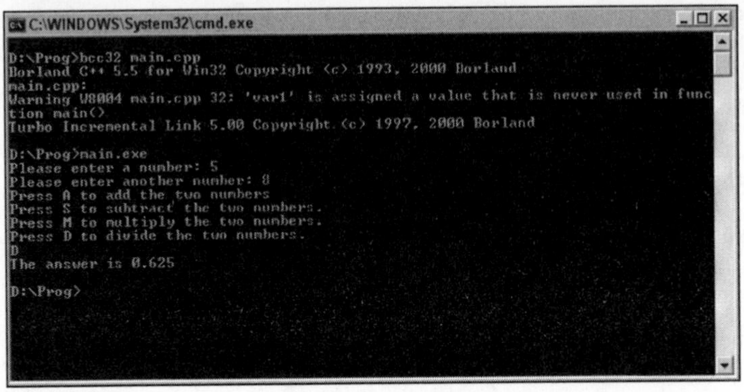

Figure 9-12

You can, if you want, choose to ignore warnings, but in the interests of tidy code it might be a good idea to correct the problems.

However, if you are just doing an interim compile and are going to be making use of the variable later, you can safely ignore the warning.

Compiler errors and warnings are your first line of defense against errors creeping into your code and causing problems.

Runtime Errors

Runtime errors are errors that appear in your program when you run it. With an application that you've compiled, such as a C++ application, runtime errors generally mean that you have to go back to the source code to discover what the problem is. With languages that are interpreted, an error like this means that you have to go back to the code and examine it.

When you are using a language that is an interpreted language as opposed to a compiled language, the errors that would normally be picked up and highlighted by the compiler will not show up until the code is run and these become runtime errors.

The types of problems that will cause runtime errors in code are similar to those that cause compiler errors. However, many of the languages that don't require a compiler aren't as strict about such things as declaring variables and rarely do they worry about unused variables.

Here is some code in VBScript that handles variables in a very haphazard way yet works without any errors being displayed.

```
dim x, y, z
x = "Hello, "
y = "Hello, World!"
zz = "World!"
msgbox(x + zz)
```

Here three variables (x, y, and z) are declared and three initialized, but the three initialized are not all the same (x, y, and zz are initialized). Then we go on only to use x and zz. The variable zz was not initially declared but nonetheless can still be used and the code works fine (as you can see from Figure 9-13).

Figure 9-13

This code doesn't generate an error either. The variable z holds no value, but it can still be used as though it does (the screen output is shown in Figure 9-14).

```
dim x, y, z
x = "Hello, "
y = "Hello, World!"
zz = "World!"
msgbox(x + z)
```

Figure 9-14

As you can see, VBScript is more forgiving of mistakes than C++ is. But that doesn't mean that you can't get it to generate errors. Try running this code:

```
dim x, y, z
x =1
y = 2
zz = 3
msgbox(zz / z)
```

When you run this code it will generate a runtime error, as you can see in Figure 9-15.

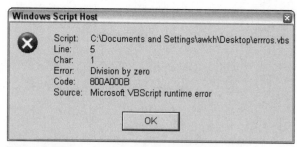

Figure 9-15

This error occurs because we are using an uninitialized variable. This contains a null value, but because we are trying to carry out a math operation with it, it is regarded as a zero.

Take a look at this C++ code:

```
#include <iostream.h>
void main ()
    {
        float num1;
        float num2;
        float ans;
        cin >> num1;
        cin >> num2;
        ans = num1 / num2;
        cout << "The answer is " << ans << endl;
    }
```

You can compile this code. When you run the application it takes in two numbers and divides them. Everything works great until you try to divide by a zero (see Figure 9-16).

Figure 9-16

What about this code, where the values are predefined, and it is inevitable that the code will end up trying to carry out a divide by zero. Does the compiler catch this?

```
#include <iostream.h>
void main ()
    {
        float num1;
        float num2;
        float ans;
        num1 = 3;
        num2 = 0;
        ans = num1 / num2;
        cout << "The answer is " << ans << endl;
    }
```

The compiler will compile this with no problems but if you try to run the application it will generate a runtime error, as shown in Figures 9-17, 9-18, and 9-19.

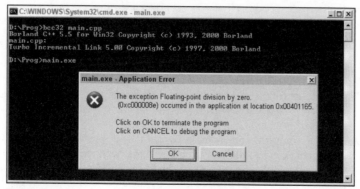

Figure 9-17

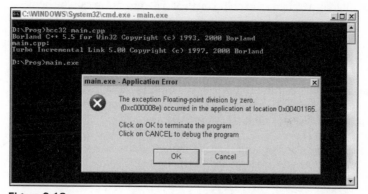

Figure 9-18

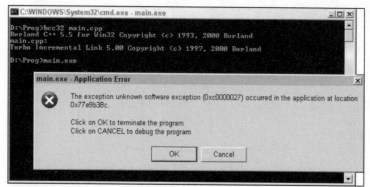

Figure 9-19

You might be beginning to notice something interesting — the error that is generated by interpreted code at runtime is far more informative than the error generated by a compiled application at runtime.

You are lucky with interpreted code in that you get given line numbers that pertain to the error generated. This line might not always take you straight to the error (just as with the line numbers given by the compiler) but they do give you a place to start looking for the errors.

> *You're probably starting to figure out by now how useful being able to go to a particular line number in the code actually is. This is one feature that doesn't exist on simple text editors such as Windows Notepad. This is the main reason why I recommend that you use a text editor that is specifically designed for programmers and that has this useful feature, among others, available.*

Tracing runtime errors in compiled code is tricky in that the application gives you a memory address and not much more. Debugging can be time-consuming and tricky. Modern development tools make life a lot easier. (Borland's full version of their software is called C++ Builder, and this comes with sophisticated debugging tools. However, because of price of the software and depth of coverage, this is beyond the scope of the discussion here.)

However, we will look at schemes to help you deal with errors later in the book.

Logic Errors

Logic errors are among the hardest errors to spot simply because they aren't errors that affect whether the code runs or compiles, but they are errors that affect how the code works. Usually, you wanted your code to do one thing, but wrote something else by mistake.

Simple example: You have an application that is supposed to add a shipping charge to an order. The code might look something like this (it's simplified to make it easier to follow):

```
Dim subtotal, shipping, ordertotal
shipping = 5
subtotal = 199
ordertotal = subtotal + shipping
msgbox("Order total is: $" & ordertotal)
```

The output from running this code is shown in Figure 9-20.

Figure 9-20

This works as you would expect. You add the shipping charge to the order total. This kind of "obvious" math is ripe for logic errors. Here's one:

```
Dim subtotal, shipping, ordertotal
shipping = 5
subtotal = 199
ordertotal = subtotal - shipping
msgbox("Order total is: $" & ordertotal)
```

The code still runs and works on the total, but the answer isn't what you expect at all (see Figure 9-21).

Figure 9-21

You might think that this kind of error is so obvious that no one would make it without spotting it. Well, you're wrong. History is full of stories of such an error. Recently in the UK when the new euro currency was launched many stores decided to program their cash registers to accept the euro along with the British pound. They built in a default exchange rate for the conversion. This is a simple calculation that took the total in one currency and converted it to another. However, the registers that were reprogrammed for some chain stores contained serious flaws that meant that the conversion was carried out incorrectly and by paying in euros customers paid far less for their purchases than they should have.

Here's some code that calculates sales tax at 7 percent (the output is shown in Figure 9-22):

```
Dim subtotal, salestax, ordertotal
salestax = 5
subtotal = 199
ordertotal = ((subtotal / 100) * salestax) + subtotal
msgbox("Order total is: $" & ordertotal)
```

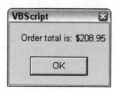

Figure 9-22

This kind of code is prone to math errors. Here are some that cost you money in lost sales (Figure 9-23):

```
Dim subtotal, salestax, ordertotal
salestax = 5
subtotal = 199
ordertotal = ((subtotal / 100) / salestax) + subtotal
msgbox("Order total is: $" & ordertotal)
```

Figure 9-23

And some that cost your customers (see Figure 9-24):

```
Dim subtotal, salestax, ordertotal
salestax = 5
subtotal = 199
ordertotal = ((subtotal * 100) * salestax) + subtotal
msgbox("Order total is: $" & ordertotal)
```

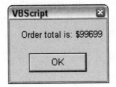

Figure 9-24

Do you notice something about the results from these three examples? Notice how the first two give answers in the range that you roughly expect and that might not draw attention to an error, while the third gives an outrageous answer that stands out as being an error. As a rule, the more outrageous the logic errors, the more the errors stand out and the more easily they are spotted.

Another type of logic error is the infinite loop. You've seen these before in Chapter 7:

```
#include <iostream.h>
void main()
  {
    int counter;

    for (counter = 20; counter <= 20; counter--)
      {
        cout << "Going loopy " << counter << endl;
      }
  }
```

Loops are used to repeat a statement or statements until a condition is met. In infinite loops, the problem is that the condition can never be met because of a logic problem, and the program carries on looping through the statements until it crashes or the program is terminated. Otherwise, the loop will carry on without end, and there is no real purpose to such a loop. However, because infinite loops are dramatic, they are usually easy to spot.

The times when infinite loops are hard to spot can be when they are controlling some function that doesn't have an obvious on-screen display. These loops will consume memory and CPU power but not be as easy to spot.

I'd suggest that no matter how simple a loop you add to your code you check it carefully to make sure that its logic is correct and that it can't possibly become infinite.

Another common logic problem, especially in a language such as C++, occurs when you use the wrong operator. Take the operators = and ==. These have different meanings (= can be used to assign a value to a variable where == is used as a comparative operator to check if the variable is equal to a value).

Below I've taken the calculator code we had earlier and made two such errors. Can you spot them?

```
#include <iostream.h>
void main ()
    {
      float num1;
      float num2;
      char op;
      float ans;
      cout << "Please enter a number: ";
      cin >> num1;
      cout << "Please enter another number: ";
      cin >> num2;
      cout << "Press A to add the two numbers."
           << endl
           << "Press S to subtract the two numbers."
           << endl
           << "Press M to multiply the two numbers."
           << endl
           << "Press D to divide the two numbers."
           << endl;
      cin >> op;
      if (op == 65)
        ans = num1 + num2;
      if (op = 83)
        ans = num1 - num2;
      if (op == 77)
        ans == num1 * num2;
      if (op == 68)
        ans = num1 / num2;
      cout << "The answer is " << ans << endl;
    }
```

The errors are on lines 23 and 28:

```
        cin >> op;
        if (op == 65)
           ans = num1 + num2;
        if (op = 83)
           ans = num1 - num2;
        if (op == 77)
           ans == num1 * num2;
        if (op == 68)
           ans = num1 / num2;
        cout << "The answer is " << ans << endl;
    }
```

Did you spot them? Not easy, is it?

The only effective ways to prevent code containing logic errors from making it out into the wide world is by thorough analysis of the code and careful, comprehensive testing of the code, using a variety of inputs and checking them against independently worked-out outputs. So, with the shipping costs calculator, you would work out the appropriate shipping for a variety of subtotals and input these, checking the outputs to make sure that they are accurate.

Spotting Errors

Spotting errors in code as you are typing out statements is probably the single most useful skill that a programmer can have.

Let's look at a few schemes that can make spotting errors easier, before it comes to compile time or runtime.

Read Each Line After You Press Enter

Seems obvious, but I'm amazed how many people don't do this.

It only takes a moment, and all you are doing it taking a quick look at the statement. Ask yourself:

❑ Does it look right?

❑ Can you spot any typos or other odd errors?

❑ Does it accomplish what you set out for it to do?

❑ Have you used the appropriate line terminator?

As you get good with code, you'll find yourself mentally translating the code you've written into English as you are reading it. This is a great way to spot errors because as code the error might not be as obvious, but when you translate it into English it may stand out a lot more.

Check the Preceding Statements

Are they in line with what you are trying to do with the code or has the focus or goals of the code changed? By reading the previous statements you are reminding yourself of what you were trying to accomplish with the code.

I'd suggest that you carry out this kind of review at least after writing a few statements, but if you can it's much better if you do the review initially after every statement because this helps you write code that moves you toward the solution you are after.

Keep the Layout Clear

Remember to keep your code layout under control. Make sure that you correctly use curly braces and parentheses in your code.

```
void functionname()
{
  // Code goes here.
}
```

You might find it easier to keep this kind of code template ready on hand so that you can copy and paste it straight into the location where you want it.

The number of hours people can waste looking for an error that has to do with their code template is staggering. Make sure that when you create a new function that you add the function name and the opening and closing curly braces as soon as you start the function.

Don't rely on remembering to add the closing curly brace! Do it as soon as you type the opening curly brace!

Comments, Comments, Comments!

Remember that when you add a comment you use the comment tag appropriate to the language you are using.

Don't:

❑ Use the wrong comment tag

❑ Forget to add the comment tag

❑ Forget to add it for subsequent lines (use tombstone comments if appropriate)

If you comment out a line of code to replace it with another or just to get rid of it, remember to add a comment detailing why you removed it and when — pretty soon you'll wonder why you removed the statement!

Remove Ambiguity in Code

Remember in Chapter 7 how I said that the following two code examples were technically the same and produced the same results:

Code 1:

```
#include <iostream.h>
void main()
    {
      int x;
      cout << "Pick an integer: ";
      cin >> x;
      if (x == 7)
      {
        cout << "You win the C++ lottery!" << endl;
        cout << "Thank you for playing the C++ lottery" << endl;
      }
      else
      {
        cout << "Thank you for playing the C++ lottery" << endl;
      }

    }
```

Code 2:

```
#include <iostream.h>
void main()
    {
      int x;
      cout << "Pick an integer: ";
      cin >> x;
      if (x == 7)
        cout << "You win the C++ lottery!" << endl;
        cout << "Thank you for playing the C++ lottery" << endl;
    }
```

Technically, both examples are identical in function but the limited use of curly braces and the absence of the else statement in the second example makes it far more complex to read and follow.

Generally, if it's a tradeoff between concise code and removing ambiguity, I'll always choose to remove ambiguity — while I might know what the code does, someone else looking at it might not. While you are learning I strongly suggest that you do the same.

Semicolons

Semicolons serve a purpose as line terminators for statements. They are not decorations or garnishes to sprinkle all over the code.

Semicolons go after complete statements. Be very careful when adding them around loops:

```
for(x = 0; x < 100; x++);
  {
    cout << "Hello, World!" << endl;
  }
```

This code block has two semicolons. The one on line three is fine:

```
for(x = 0; x < 100; x++);
  {
    cout << "Hello, World!" << endl;
  }
```

But the semicolon on the first line is wrong, and if you place a semicolon there the code will only be processed once.

```
for(x = 0; x < 100; x++);
  {
    cout << "Hello, World!" << endl;
  }
```

Get a firm grip on the use of line terminators early on in your programming career, and you'll save yourself a lot of wasted time and effort later on.

Test the Code

This seems like another really obvious point, but you'll be surprised how many beginners write lines and lines of code before taking a real look at it and seeing if it works.

If you can, break your code into functions that stand alone or at least that you can run as standalone components to test. You might have to artificially input variable values and create artificial outputs to check that everything works fine.

Keep Track of Variables

If you have code that does a lot of work with variables, then you might find it handy to periodically keep track of what they are at any point in the code.

The easiest way to do this is to have them outputted in one way or another. Output to the screen is usually OK for projects that are simple or of medium complexity. Remember the calculator code from Chapter 7 that carried out operations on numbers based on input? With code like that it might be useful to have the code output to the screen variable values used so that you can check them and see if the values are what you expect them to be.

```
#include <iostream.h>
void main ()
    {
        float num1;
        float num2;
        char op;
        float ans;
```

```
cout << "Please enter a number: ";
cin >> num1;
cout << "Please enter another number: ";
cin >> num2;
cout << "Press A to add the two numbers."
     << endl
     << "Press S to subtract the two numbers."
     << endl
     << "Press M to multiply the two numbers."
     << endl
     << "Press D to divide the two numbers."
     << endl;
cin >> op;
  cout << "------------- start test output -------------"
     << endl
     << "num1: " << num1
     << endl
     << "num2: " << num2
     << endl
     << "op: " << op
     << endl
     << "------------- end test output ---------------"
     << endl;
if (op == 65)
  ans = num1 + num2;
if (op == 83)
  ans = num1 - num2;
if (op == 77)
  ans = num1 * num2;
if (op == 68)
  ans = num1 / num2;
cout << "The answer is " << ans << endl;
}
```

The output of this code is shown in Figure 9-25.

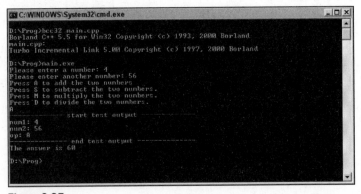

Figure 9-25

It's important to glance at the variables every so often because this can help you to spot errors. Here's another example that benefits from this treatment:

```
#include <iostream.h>
void main()
    {
      int x;
      int y;
      y = 7
      cout << "Pick an integer: ";
      cin >> x;
      if (x == y)
      {
        cout << "You win the C++ lottery!" << endl;
        cout << "Thank you for playing the C++ lottery" << endl;
      }
      else
      {
        cout << "Thank you for playing the C++ lottery" << endl;
      }
        cout << "------------- start test output -------------"
        << endl
        << "Winning condition: " << y
        << endl
        << "-------------- end test output --------------"
        << endl;
    }
```

Figure 9-26 shows this in action.

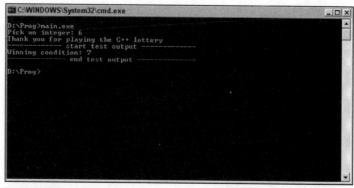

Figure 9-26

This would be particularly useful if the actual winning number were being generated randomly as opposed to being fixed as it is here.

One thing that you can do is to have this kind of output displayed based on the value of a test variable. If the variable is set to one thing, the test output is generated; if it is set to another value, it is not.

```
#include <iostream.h>
void main()
    {
      int x;
      int y;
      y = 7
```

```
      int outputvariable;
      outputvariable = 1;
      cout << "Pick an integer: ";
      cin >> x;
      if (x == y)
      {
        cout << "You win the C++ lottery!" << endl;
        cout << "Thank you for playing the C++ lottery" << endl;
      }
      else
      {
        cout << "Thank you for playing the C++ lottery" << endl;
      }
      if (outputvariable == 1)
      {
      cout << "------------- start test output -------------"
      << endl
      << "Winning condition: " << y
      << endl
      << "------------- end test output --------------"
      << endl;
      }
  }
```

If you want to prevent the output from going to the screen, just change the variable `outputvariable` to anything other than 1 (you could choose 0 because that is representative of false).

```
#include <iostream.h>
void main()
    {
        int x;
        int y;
        y = 7
        int outputvariable;
        outputvariable = 0;
        cout << "Pick an integer: ";
        cin >> x;
        if (x == y)
        {
          cout << "You win the C++ lottery!" << endl;
          cout << "Thank you for playing the C++ lottery" << endl;
        }
        else
        {
          cout << "Thank you for playing the C++ lottery" << endl;
        }
        if (outputvariable == 1)
        {
        cout << "------------- start test output -------------"
        << endl
        << "Winning condition: " << y
        << endl
        << "------------- end test output --------------"
        << endl;
        }
    }
```

This scheme can be used for multiple outputs.

```cpp
#include <iostream.h>
void main ()
    {
    int outputvariable;
    outputvariable = 1;
    float num1;
    float num2;
    char op;
    float ans;
    cout << "Please enter a number: ";
    cin >> num1;
    cout << "Please enter another number: ";
    cin >> num2;
    cout << "Press A to add the two numbers."
        << endl
        << "Press S to subtract the two numbers."
        << endl
        << "Press M to multiply the two numbers."
        << endl
        << "Press D to divide the two numbers."
        << endl;
    cin >> op;
    if (outputvariable == 1)
    {
    cout << "------------- start test output -------------"
        << endl
        << "num1: " << num1
        << endl
        << "------------- end test output --------------"
        << endl;
    }
    if (outputvariable == 1)
    {
    cout << "------------- start test output -------------"
        << endl
        << "num2: " << num2
        << endl
        << "------------- end test output --------------"
        << endl;
    }
    if (outputvariable == 1)
    {
    cout << "------------- start test output -------------"
        << endl
        << "op: " << op
        << endl
        << "------------- end test output --------------"
        << endl;
    }
    if (op == 65)
      ans = num1 + num2;
    if (op == 83)
      ans = num1 - num2;
    if (op == 77)
```

```
        ans = num1 * num2;
    if (op == 68)
        ans = num1 / num2;
    cout << "The answer is " << ans << endl;
}
```

You can see this code in action in Figure 9-27.

Figure 9-27

That code that we had earlier that calculated sales tax would have benefited from this kind of treatment:

```
Dim subtotal, salestax, ordertotal
salestax = 5
subtotal = 199
ordertotal = ((subtotal / 100) * salestax) + subtotal
msgbox("---------- test output ----------" & chr(13)
& "Salestax = " & salestax & chr(13)
& "Ordertotal = " & ordertotal & chr(13)
& "---------- test output ----------")
msgbox("Order total is: $" & ordertotal)
```

The test output is shown in Figure 9-28.

Figure 9-28

See how we use the line break character chr(13) *to format the message box. This makes it much easier to read.*

Summary

In this chapter, you've seen a lot of code — some that works and a lot that has errors in it. The purpose of this chapter has been to look at errors in programming and to give you experience handling code that has errors in it.

You might be wondering why you need to see code that has errors in it because you're capable of writing code to do this for yourself. Well, the reason is that you can control these errors, and they allow you to see where the errors are and the side effects of each type of error.

The main thing to remember with errors is that everyone makes mistakes, and the trick is to understand what causes them, to spot them, and to be able to deal with them effectively.

Also, take the time to read each and every error message you receive — I know that there is a tendency to want to get rid of them as soon as possible. This is a mistake because these error messages contain important information!

Interface

A programmer who only thinks about how a program is going to work isn't a good programmer. A good programmer not only needs to be good at writing code that makes the application work as required — he or she also needs to be able to make the application easy for the end user to use. And if your program is one of many out there that will do the same thing, it might also need to be compelling so that users choose your program over others.

This chapter looks at how to create a good interface and how not to create a bad one! It also examines the individual components of an interface and looks at how they can be brought together to make a logical and easy to use application.

What Is an Interface?

Interfaces are the bit of a program that we see. As I am typing these words, I'm looking at the complicated interface offered by Microsoft Word, as shown in Figure 10-1.

And believe me, there's a lot to the interface. There're menus and buttons for me to interact with, as shown in Figure 10-2. I have a cursor that changes depending on what it is over (see Figure 10-3), and there is a lot of information displayed on the screen about the document I'm working on (see Figure 10-4).

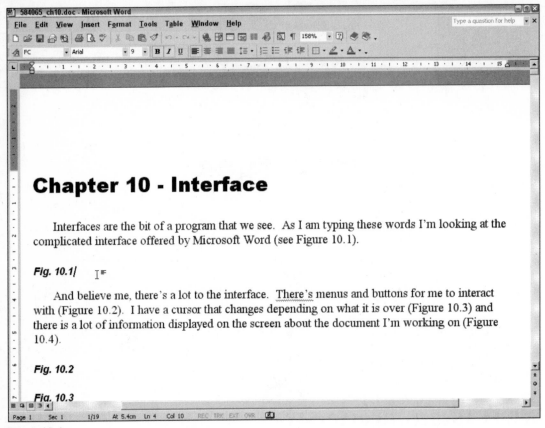

Figure 10-1

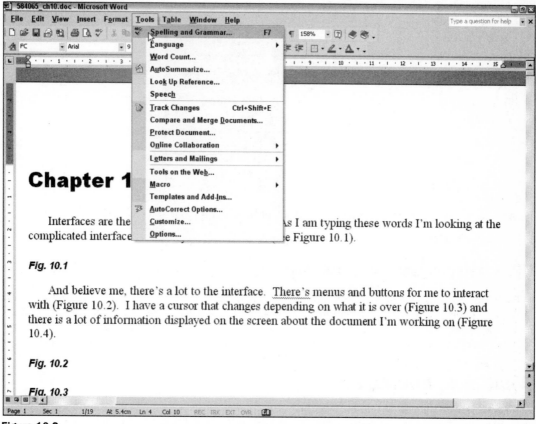

Figure 10-2

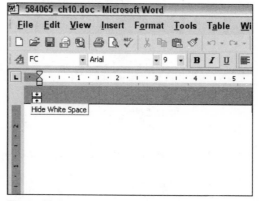

Figure 10-3

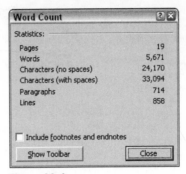

Figure 10-4

An interface is key to the user making good use of the program that you created.

The Importance of an Interface

We're so surrounded by interfaces on computer programs that we really don't give them that much thought. Whenever you are on the PC, all your interaction with the software is though the interface using either the mouse or keyboard (other input devices exist but most of these usually emulate keyboards and mice in the way that they work). To get the software to do your bidding, you pass on instructions to it in these ways.

What Is an Interface?

The interface is the part of the software that the end user sees on screen when the application is running. Figure 10-5 shows what is probably the simplest possible user interface on an application:

Figure 10-5

All that is there is one button. The button is clearly labeled and unlikely to be missed.

Nonetheless, this isn't a very good interface for reasons that we will look at later. However, it's by far not the worst possible. Figure 10-6 shows an appalling user interface.

Figure 10-6

This interface is poorly laid out and extremely difficult to navigate because the elements that go into making it are badly laid out.

We will take a look shortly at what makes a good interface and what makes a poor one.

Does All Software Have an Interface?

Most do. You might have components of a program that don't warrant having an interface, but generally an interface is useful even if all it does is pass on confirmation feedback to the users that an action that they requested by running the software has been carried out. Also, if an application has no interface, what happens when something goes wrong and the action isn't carried out?

If you believe that you have software that doesn't need any form of screen that interacts with the end user, I'd suggest that you think carefully about this and reexamine why you think the software doesn't need an interface.

Examining the Interface

Let's take a look at interfaces in action. We'll begin by taking a look at the most primitive type of interface that you are likely to encounter — the text-based interface.

Text-Based Interface

Remember the C++ calculator application you worked on in Chapter 7, "The Structure of Coding"? That application had a text-based interface.

This is the code that was used to drive that interface:

```
#include <iostream.h>
void main()
    {
        float num1;
        float num2;
        char op;
        float ans;
        cout << "Please enter a number: ";
        cin >> num1;
        cout << "Please enter another number: ";
        cin >> num2;
        cout << "Press A to add the two numbers."
             << endl
             << "Press S to subtract the two numbers."
             << endl
             << "Press M to multiply the two numbers."
             << endl
             << "Press D to divide the two numbers."
             << endl;
        cin >> op;
        if (op == 65)
          ans = num1 + num2;
        if (op == 83)
          ans = num1 - num2;
        if (op == 77)
          ans = num1 * num2;
        if (op == 68)
          ans = num1 / num2;
        cout << "The answer is " << ans << endl;
    }
```

When this program is run, the application displays instructions about how to use the application (see Figure 10-7). It tells the user what to do with the two numbers he or she has inputted.

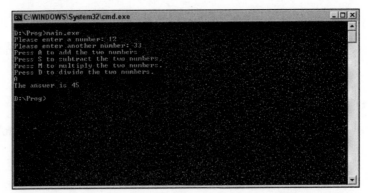

Figure 10-7

However, this isn't an example of a good user interface. Let me explain why.

To begin with, when you run the application there is no initial indication given as to what the application does or what the user is supposed to do with it. We know how the program works because we wrote it and have seen the source code and know what to expect. But put yourself in the shoes of someone who is using this program for the first time and doesn't know what to expect or what to do.

What would you make of what you see initially (see Figure 10-8)?

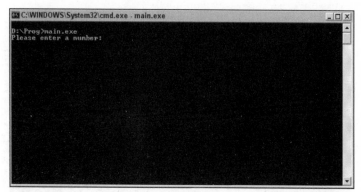

Figure 10-8

It doesn't give you much in the way of information, does it?

This is the difference between a one-off utility that you create for yourself and an application that you want others to use. As the programmers we have an insight into the application that others don't have. We programmed it and because of that we know how it works. We know what inputs it expects and what the outputs mean. Having all this information doesn't make us immune from errors in the code but it does give us a great deal of advantage over others who will use the program.

While the calculator application doesn't offer much in the way of information to the end user, it's not as bad as it could be. Take a look at this example that does exactly the same thing but without any prompts at all.

```
#include <iostream.h>
void main()
    {
        float num1;
        float num2;
        char op;
        float ans;
        cin >> num1;
        cin >> num2;
        cin >> op;
        if (op == 65)
           ans = num1 + num2;
        if (op == 83)
```

```
      ans = num1 - num2;
   if (op == 77)
      ans = num1 * num2;
   if (op == 68)
      ans = num1 / num2;
   cout << ans << endl;
 }
```

This code, when compiled, doe exactly the same as what the earlier code did, but this time there are no cues as to how to use the application (see Figure 10-9).

Figure 10-9

With the code in this condition, if you don't know when to input numbers and when to press the right keystrokes, you have no idea how to work the application and even what the output means. This is an example of an application that really leaves the user in the dark!

So, we've taken it pretty much as far as we can in the direction of keeping the user in the dark! Let's now look at ways to improve on the software and make it easier to use and more intuitive.

Program Overview

The first thing that a program needs is an overview of what it does. This sets the scene for what the users will later do and gives them the confidence that they have launched the right application and that it's ready to work.

Here's a simple example of a program overview:

```
#include <iostream.h>
void main()
   {
      float num1;
      float num2;
      char op;
      float ans;
      cout << "Simple Calculator Application" << endl;
      cout << "Enter two numbers and perform an operation." << endl;
      cout << "Enjoy!" << endl;
```

```
    cin >> num1;
    cin >> num2;
    cin >> op;
    if (op == 65)
        ans = num1 + num2;
    if (op == 83)
        ans = num1 - num2;
    if (op == 77)
        ans = num1 * num2;
    if (op == 68)
        ans = num1 / num2;
    cout << ans << endl;
}
```

The output from this code is shown in Figure 10-10. It's clear, concise, and to the point and gives the users an idea of what the application expects from them.

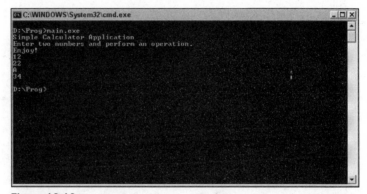

Figure 10-10

Keep the overview simple — don't give the user reams of text to read because this is discouraging and users are unlikely to read it all. Too much information!

```
#include <iostream.h>
void main()
    {
    float num1;
    float num2;
    char op;
    float ans;
    cout << "Simple Calculator Application" << endl;
    cout << "Enter two numbers and perform an operation." << endl;
    cout << "Add!" << endl;
    cout << "Subtract!" << endl;
    cout << "Multiply!" << endl;
    cout << "Divide!" << endl;
    cout << "You need to enter two numbers." << endl;
    cout << "And choose an operation to carry out on them." << endl;
    cout << "Swift and accurate!" << endl;
```

```
cout << "Tell your friends!" << endl;
cout << "Enjoy!" << endl;
cin >> num1;
cin >> num2;
cin >> op;
if (op == 65)
   ans = num1 + num2;
if (op == 83)
   ans = num1 - num2;
if (op == 77)
   ans = num1 * num2;
if (op == 68)
   ans = num1 / num2;
cout << ans << endl;
}
```

The output of this is shown in Figure 10-11. I think you'll agree that this is an example of way too much initial information.

Figure 10-11

Proper Prompting for Input

The next area of improvement that our calculator program can have is with respect to prompts for user inputs.

There prompts need to be clear. When you ask for numbers, be precise as to what you are looking for. Are you looking for integers or floating-point numbers? Are there any limits? If there are, state them.

Be careful with wording too. If you say "integers," there could be some people who are confused by that term.

If you are finding that you have to give a lot of instruction and conditions on the type of inputs that a user can enter into your program then you might have written a program that's too restrictive. For example, if your program can only take integers, is there a good reason why or is it a design limitation that really shouldn't be there?

The code that follows is a vast improvement in that it prompts for user inputs as far as the numbers go.

```
#include <iostream.h>
void main()
    {
    float num1;
    float num2;
    char op;
    float ans;
    cout << "Simple Calculator Application" << endl;
    cout << "Enter two numbers and perform an operation." << endl;
    cout << "Enjoy!" << endl;
    cout << "--------------------" << endl;
    cout << "Enter the first number and press ENTER:" << endl;
    cin >> num1;
    cout << "Enter the second number and press ENTER:" << endl;
    cin >> num2;
    cout << "--------------------" << endl;
    cin >> op;
    if (op == 65)
      ans = num1 + num2;
    if (op == 83)
      ans = num1 - num2;
    if (op == 77)
      ans = num1 * num2;
    if (op == 68)
      ans = num1 / num2;
    cout << ans << endl;
    }
```

See this in action in Figure 10-12.

Figure 10-12

That modification covers the numerical inputs; now for the input that governs the operation carried out. Again, this needs to be clear and concise.

This is what we had before:

```
#include <iostream.h>
void main()
    {
        float num1;
        float num2;
        char op;
        float ans;
        cout << "Simple Calculator Application" << endl;
        cout << "Enter two numbers and perform an operation." << endl;
        cout << "Enjoy!" << endl;
        cout << "--------------------" << endl;
        cout << "Enter the first number and press ENTER:" << endl;
        cin >> num1;
        cout << "Enter the second number and press ENTER:" << endl;
        cin >> num2;
        cout << "Press A to add the two numbers."
            << endl
            << "Press S to subtract the two numbers."
            << endl
            << "Press M to multiply the two numbers."
            << endl
            << "Press D to divide the two numbers."
            << endl;
        cout << "--------------------" << endl;
        cin >> op;
        if (op == 65)
          ans = num1 + num2;
        if (op == 83)
          ans = num1 - num2;
        if (op == 77)
          ans = num1 * num2;
        if (op == 68)
          ans = num1 / num2;
        cout << ans << endl;
    }
```

Have you noticed something odd about these instructions that we've been using? Have you noticed that they aren't truly accurate! You enter the appropriate letter and then you have to press Enter for the application to continue.

```
#include <iostream.h>
void main()
    {
        float num1;
        float num2;
        char op;
        float ans;
        cout << "Simple Calculator Application" << endl;
        cout << "Enter two numbers and perform an operation." << endl;
        cout << "Enjoy!" << endl;
        cout << "--------------------" << endl;
        cout << "Enter the first number and press ENTER:" << endl;
```

```
      cin >> num1;
      cout << "Enter the second number and press ENTER:" << endl;
      cin >> num2;
      cout << "Press A followed by ENTER to add the two numbers."
           << endl
           << "Press S followed by ENTER to subtract the two numbers."
           << endl
           << "Press M followed by ENTER to multiply the two numbers."
           << endl
           << "Press D followed by ENTER to divide the two numbers."
           << endl;
      cout << "--------------------" << endl;
      cin >> op;
      if (op == 65)
        ans = num1 + num2;
      if (op == 83)
        ans = num1 - num2;
      if (op == 77)
        ans = num1 * num2;
      if (op == 68)
        ans = num1 / num2;
      cout << ans << endl;
    }
```

Figure 10-13 shows the output from this code.

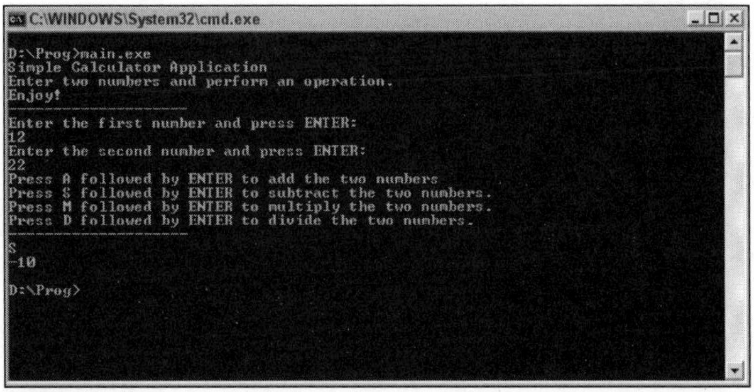

Figure 10-13

Annotating Output

Just as important as annotating inputs is annotating outputs. You don't want an output on the screen that is left as an unknown.

```
#include <iostream.h>
void main()
    {
      float num1;
      float num2;
```

```
        char op;
        float ans;
        cout << "Simple Calculator Application" << endl;
        cout << "Enter two numbers and perform an operation." << endl;
        cout << "Enjoy!" << endl;
        cout << "--------------------" << endl;
        cout << "Enter the first number and press ENTER:" << endl;
        cin >> num1;
        cout << "Enter the second number and press ENTER:" << endl;
        cin >> num2;
        cout << "Press A followed by ENTER to add the two numbers."
             << endl
             << "Press S followed by ENTER to subtract the two numbers."
             << endl
             << "Press M followed by ENTER to multiply the two numbers."
             << endl
             << "Press D followed by ENTER to divide the two numbers."
             << endl;
        cout << "--------------------" << endl;
        cin >> op;
        if (op == 65)
          ans = num1 + num2;
        if (op == 83)
          ans = num1 - num2;
        if (op == 77)
          ans = num1 * num2;
        if (op == 68)
          ans = num1 / num2;
        cout << "The answer is " << ans << endl;
      }
```

Confirming Exit

When your program is exiting, it's a good idea that it tell the user that it's done and is exiting; otherwise, the user might be wondering if he or she can still work with it.

```
#include <iostream.h>
void main()
  {
      float num1;
      float num2;
      char op;
      float ans;
      cout << "Simple Calculator Application" << endl;
      cout << "Enter two numbers and perform an operation." << endl;
      cout << "Enjoy!" << endl;
      cout << "--------------------" << endl;
      cout << "Enter the first number and press ENTER:" << endl;
      cin >> num1;
      cout << "Enter the second number and press ENTER:" << endl;
      cin >> num2;
```

```
        cout << "Press A followed by ENTER to add the two numbers."
              << endl
              << "Press S followed by ENTER to subtract the two numbers."
              << endl
              << "Press M followed by ENTER to multiply the two numbers."
              << endl
              << "Press D followed by ENTER to divide the two numbers."
              << endl;
        cout << "--------------------" << endl;
        cin >> op;
        if (op == 65)
          ans = num1 + num2;
        if (op == 83)
          ans = num1 - num2;
        if (op == 77)
          ans = num1 * num2;
        if (op == 68)
          ans = num1 / num2;
        cout << "The answer is " << ans << endl;
        cout << "Thanks for using the calculator." << endl;
        cout << "Application now exiting ... " << endl;
    }
```

The output of this is shown in Figure 10-14.

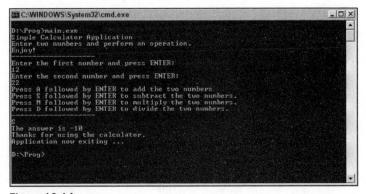

Figure 10-14

Adding Simple Help

All but the simplest programs can do with some help as to how one uses them.

With an application such as this the best way to initiate the help system is for the user to enter the ? character, which is recognized as the standard to enter a help system.

To do this though, we need to restructure the code that we have, to break up some of the code into separate functions.

```
#include <iostream.h>
void calc()
    {
      float num1;
      float num2;
      char op;
      float ans;
      cout << "Simple Calculator Application" << endl;
      cout << "Enter two numbers and perform an operation." << endl;
      cout << "Enjoy!" << endl;
      cout << "--------------------" << endl;
      cout << "Enter the first number and press ENTER:" << endl;
      cin >> num1;
      cout << "Enter the second number and press ENTER:" << endl;
      cin >> num2;
      cout << "Press A followed by ENTER to add the two numbers."
            << endl
            << "Press S followed by ENTER to subtract the two numbers."
            << endl
            << "Press M followed by ENTER to multiply the two numbers."
            << endl
            << "Press D followed by ENTER to divide the two numbers."
            << endl;
      cout << "--------------------" << endl;
      cin >> op;
      if (op == 65)
      {
        ans = num1 + num2;
      }
      if (op == 83)
      {
        ans = num1 - num2;
      }
      if (op == 77)
      {
        ans = num1 * num2;
      }
      if (op == 68)
      {
        ans = num1 / num2;
      }
      cout << "The answer is " << ans << endl;
      cout << "Thanks for using the calculator." << endl;
      cout << "Application now exiting ... " << endl;
    }

void helpsystem()
    {
      char op;
      cout << "Help System" << endl;
      cout << "Are you ready to use this application?" << endl;
      cout << "Press Y followed by ENTER to continue." << endl;
      cout << "Press N followed by ENTER to exit." << endl;
```

```
      cout << "Press ? followed by ENTER for help." << endl;
      cin >> op;
      if (op == 89)
      {
        calc();
      }
      if (op == 63)
      {
        helpsystem();
      }
      if (op == 78)
      {

      }
    }


void main()
  {
    char op;
    cout << "Simple Calculator Application" << endl;
    cout << "Enter two numbers and perform an operation." << endl;
    cout << "Enjoy!" << endl;
    cout << "Are you ready to use this application?" << endl;
    cout << "Press Y followed by ENTER to continue." << endl;
    cout << "Press N followed by ENTER to exit." << endl;
    cout << "Press ? followed by ENTER for help." << endl;
    cin >> op;
    if (op == 89)
    {
      calc();
    }
    if (op == 63)
    {
      helpsystem();
    }
    if (op == 78)
    {

    }
  }
```

A lot has happened here. Here is a quick run-through:

1. The code has been broken up into three functions called:

```
main()
calc()
helpsystem()
```

2. The `main()` function now only handles the initial text display of the application and also asks you if you are ready to use the application, you want to exit, or if you want help. The character Y is represented as 89 in decimal, while N and ? are 78 and 63, respectively.

```
void main()
    {
      char op;
      cout << "Simple Calculator Application" << endl;
      cout << "Enter two numbers and perform an operation." << endl;
      cout << "Enjoy!" << endl;
      cout << "Are you ready to use this application?" << endl;
      cout << "Press Y followed by ENTER to continue." << endl;
      cout << "Press N followed by ENTER to exit." << endl;
      cout << "Press ? followed by ENTER for help." << endl;
      cin >> op;
      if (op == 89)
      {
        calc();
      }
      if (op == 63)
      {
        helpsystem();
      }
      if (op == 78)
      {

      }
    }
```

3. Notice how we exit the application — just give the program nothing else to do in response to the N input (78) and it exits!

```
if (op == 78)
{

}
```

4. The function `calc()` is responsible for the main math done by the application. This code is similar to the code we used previously, but we have tidied up our use of curly braces in the conditionals.

```
void calc()
    {
      float num1;
      float num2;
      char op;
      float ans;
      cout << "Simple Calculator Application" << endl;
      cout << "Enter two numbers and perform an operation." << endl;
      cout << "Enjoy!" << endl;
      cout << "--------------------" << endl;
      cout << "Enter the first number and press ENTER:" << endl;
      cin >> num1;
      cout << "Enter the second number and press ENTER:" << endl;
      cin >> num2;
      cout << "Press A followed by ENTER to add the two numbers."
           << endl
           << "Press S followed by ENTER to subtract the two numbers."
           << endl
           << "Press M followed by ENTER to multiply the two numbers."
```

```
                    << endl
                    << "Press D followed by ENTER to divide the two numbers."
                    << endl;
        cout << "--------------------" << endl;
        cin >> op;
        if (op == 65)
        {
          ans = num1 + num2;
        }
        if (op == 83)
        {
          ans = num1 - num2;
        }
        if (op == 77)
        {
          ans = num1 * num2;
        }
        if (op == 68)
        {
          ans = num1 / num2;
        }
        cout << "The answer is " << ans << endl;
        cout << "Thanks for using the calculator." << endl;
        cout << "Application now exiting ... " << endl;
      }
```

5. The function `helpsystem()` handles the display of the help information we are going to provide. It also allows for the help to be redisplayed or the application used or exited.

```
void helpsystem()
  {
    char op;
    cout << "Help System" << endl;
    cout << "Are you ready to use this application?" << endl;
    cout << "Press Y followed by ENTER to continue." << endl;
    cout << "Press N followed by ENTER to exit" << endl;
    cout << "Press ? followed by ENTER for help." << endl;
    cin >> op;
    if (op == 89)
    {
      calc();
    }
    if (op == 63)
    {
      helpsystem();
    }
    if (op == 78)
    {


    }
  }
```

6. There are also a few minor changes to accommodate the reuse of variables.

We've had to do quite a bit of restructuring to accommodate the help system but that's OK because this is normal. The code is now broken up into logical components that we could build on and add more features.

In doing this, we've added a function specifically that deals with the help output that the program is capable of giving, and we can populate this with the instructions for the program.

```
void helpsystem()
   {
      char op;
      cout << "Help System" << endl;
      cout << "-----------" << endl;
      cout << "To work this application you enter two numbers and then choose" <<
endl;
      cout << "whether you want those numbers added together, subtracted, " <<
endl;
      cout << "multiplied, or divided. You choose this operation by inputting" <<
endl;
      cout << "A, S, M, or D, respectively." << endl;
      cout << "The result is displayed on-screen." << endl;
      cout << "Are you ready to use this application?" << endl;
      cout << "Press Y followed by ENTER to continue." << endl;
      cout << "Press N followed by ENTER to exit." << endl;
      cout << "Press ? followed by ENTER for help." << endl;
      cin >> op;
      if (op == 89)
      {
         calc();
      }
      if (op == 63)
      {
         helpsystem();
      }
      if (op == 78)
      {

      }
   }
```

If this code is now compiled and run you will see how much scope these three functions and a few simple inputs give us (see Figure 10-15).

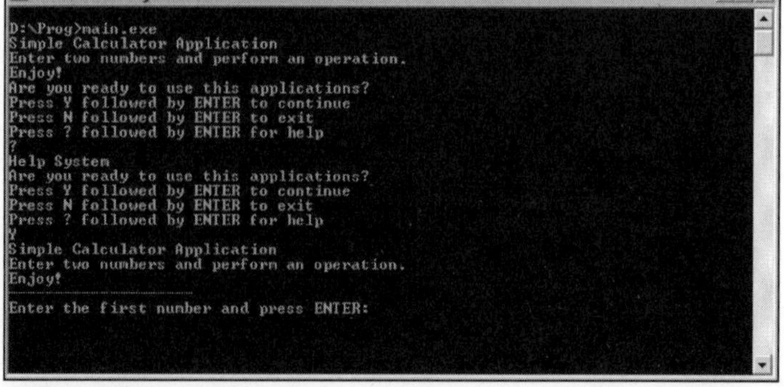

Figure 10-15

Confirmations

Another good way to make sure that the user has entered the appropriate data into an application is to show their entries to remind them what they entered (although in this example the numbers are still on-screen).

```cpp
void calc()
{
    float num1;
    float num2;
    char op;
    float ans;
    cout << "Simple Calculator Application" << endl;
    cout << "Enter two numbers and perform an operation." << endl;
    cout << "Enjoy!" << endl;
    cout << "--------------------" << endl;
    cout << "Enter the first number and press ENTER:" << endl;
    cin >> num1;
    cout << "Enter the second number and press ENTER:" << endl;
    cin >> num2;
    cout << "You entered " << num1 << " and " << num2 << endl;
    cout
        << "Press A followed by ENTER to add the two numbers."
        << endl
        << "Press S followed by ENTER to subtract the two numbers."
        << endl
        << "Press M followed by ENTER to multiply the two numbers."
        << endl
        << "Press D followed by ENTER to divide the two numbers."
        << endl;
    cout << "--------------------" << endl;
    cin >> op;
    if (op == 65)
    {
        ans = num1 + num2;
    }
    if (op == 83)
    {
        ans = num1 - num2;
    }
    if (op == 77)
    {
        ans = num1 * num2;
    }
    if (op == 68)
    {
        ans = num1 / num2;
    }
    cout << "The answer is " << ans << endl;
    cout << "Thanks for using the calculator." << endl;
    cout << "Application now exiting ... " << endl;
}
```

Moving Away from the Text-Based Interface

So far we've looked at text-based interfaces. While they are handy, most applications nowadays make use of a graphical interface system, as found within Microsoft Windows.

We don't have the time or scope here to go into details as to how you create your own graphical program interfaces in languages such as C++ — these require more coverage than we can give them here and tools that are currently beyond the scope of this book.

However, it's a good idea that you get exposed to the basic elements of an interface and look at how to best make use of them — because you can be sure that when you are ready to build graphical systems, there isn't going to be anyone around to tell you how to properly use the individual elements!

Buttons

Buttons are one of the most common and quickest input methods (see Figure 10-16).

Figure 10-16

Buttons are used to set an action in motion. Clicking the button is the start of that action. Buttons also can be a way for the program to ask for input from the user on a decision that has to be made (see Figure 10-17).

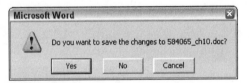

Figure 10-17

The logic behind using buttons as opposed to keystrokes is that people can use a mouse to click an object faster than they can type a letter or combination of letters on the keyboard.

While buttons were introduced to make navigating an application easier by giving the user something to click, most buttons can be operated by the keyboard too. See the underline on the letter in Figure 10-18? That shows that the button can be pressed by pressing Alt and that letter.

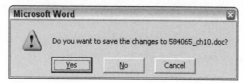

Figure 10-18

Some buttons, such as OK and Cancel, have default keyboard buttons to operate them — Enter and Esc, respectively.

Buttons are usually labelled with text (see Figure 10-19), although some buttons can be represented by an image (see Figure 10-20).

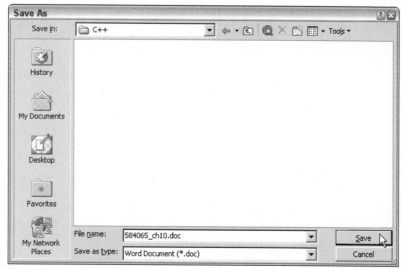

Figure 10-19

Figure 10-20

Menus

Here's something else that needs no real introduction. The menu is a pop-up that presents the user with a list of choices from which to choose (see Figure 10-21).

Figure 10-21

A menu is shown in Figure 10-22.

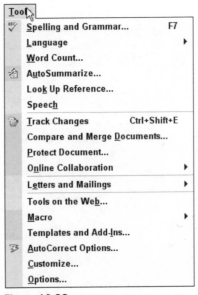

Figure 10-22

A menu item is shown in Figure 10-23.

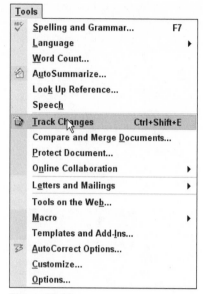

Figure 10-23

As with buttons, the idea is that it's quicker to navigate through a list using the mouse and make a choice with a click than it is to navigate through it using keystrokes. However, just as with buttons, menus have underlines on some characters — press Alt, and these characters will activate the menu or menu item (see Figure 10-24).

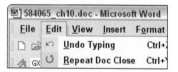

Figure 10-24

Check Box

The check box is a way for the user to make a choice. Checking the box chooses that option (see Figure 10-25).

Figure 10-25

Check boxes can come in groups where you can make multiple choices simultaneously (see Figure 10-26).

Figure 10-26

Check boxes are labeled with text (see Figure 10-27).

Figure 10-27

Radio Buttons

Radio buttons are like check boxes; the only difference is that you can only choose one at any one time (see Figure 10-28).

Figure 10-28

These are very handy when you want to give the user an exclusive option to choose from (in other words an either/or option, as shown in Figure 10-29).

Figure 10-29

These are labeled in the same way as check boxes. Make the test descriptive and make sure that there is no ambiguity.

Single-Line Text Box

The single-line text box is the most basic way for users to input alphanumeric characters into a program (see Figure 10-30).

Figure 10-30

Text boxes can come in a variety of lengths, but if they get too long they start to become unwieldy (see Figure 10-31).

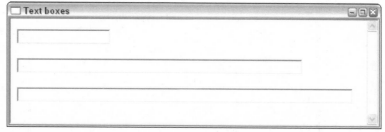

Figure 10-31

Text boxes need to be labeled clearly (see Figure 10-32).

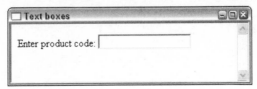

Figure 10-32

Text boxes can also have default values preprogrammed into them (see Figure 10-33).

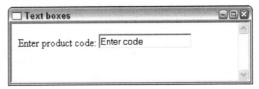

Figure 10-33

Multiline Text Box

These are similar to single-line text boxes, the difference being that they can have multiple lines of text (see Figure 10-34).

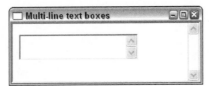

Figure 10-34

Multiline text boxes can be set to a variety of shapes and sizes (see Figure 10-35).

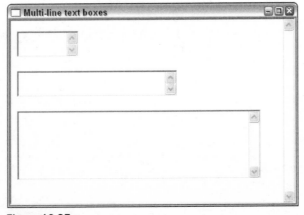

Figure 10-35

Drop-Down Menu

A drop-down menu is a menu contained within the body of the application. It enables you to give the user a quick and easy way to make a selection from a group of choices (see Figure 10-36).

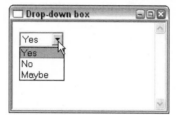

Figure 10-36

The drop-down menu in Figure 10-36 takes little space on the screen when compared to using another type of interface element, such as radio buttons (see Figure 10-37).

Figure 10-37

Putting It All Together

We've covered most of the basic elements, so now it's time to look at how to put them together effectively.

To do this, we'll examine some interfaces that might be familiar to you and see how they are used effectively.

One important thing to remember is that there is no one right way to do any of this. What you are aiming for is a logical, easy-to-use interface. You might have come across some programs that have very odd, nonstandard user interfaces and there's nothing wrong with that as long as they are easy to use, don't require a lot of specific learning to use, and don't get in the way of efficient operation of the program.

Remember, people want to use an application, not learn new interfaces!

Simple Applications

Let's take a look at a simple application — Windows Notepad (see Figure 10-38).

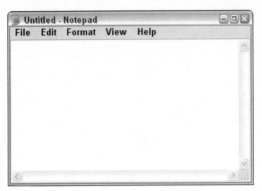

Figure 10-38

On the surface, this application is driven by menus (see Figure 10-39), and there are no buttons visible initially.

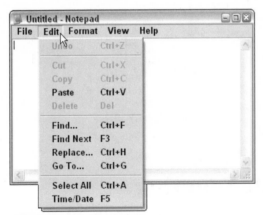

Figure 10-39

All the menus are accessible using both the mouse and keyboard.

- ❑ **File:** ALT + F
- ❑ **Edit:** ALT + E
- ❑ **Format:** ALT + O
- ❑ **View:** ALT + V
- ❑ **Help:** ALT + H

Some items in the submenus are accessible by using a combination of Ctrl and hotkeys, for example:

- ❑ **Save:** CTRL + S
- ❑ **New:** CTRL + N
- ❑ **Open:** CTRL + O

If you try to save a file, you'll get a dialog box that makes use of a variety of elements of an interface (see Figure 10-40).

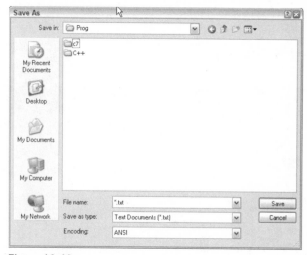

Figure 10-40

This has multiple buttons (see Figure 10-41) and multiple drop-down menus (see Figure 10-42) to help you navigate the file system and choose the location to save the file, the filename, and type.

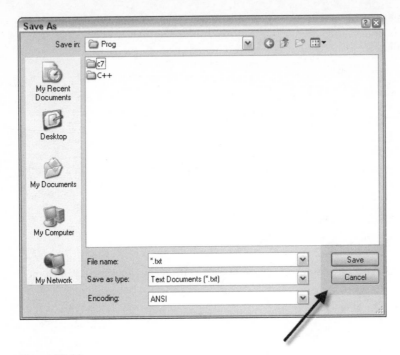

Figure 10-41

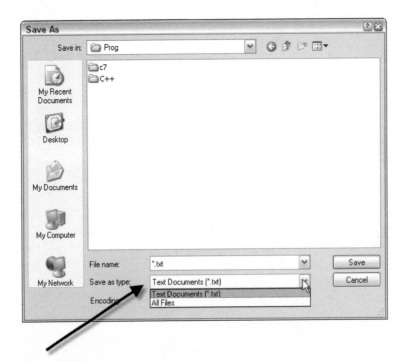

Figure 10-42

While you are in that dialog window, try pressing the Tab key and notice what happens. Notice how the focus (or element that can be used) moves from one element (such as filename — Figure 10-43) to another (file type — see Figure 10-44).

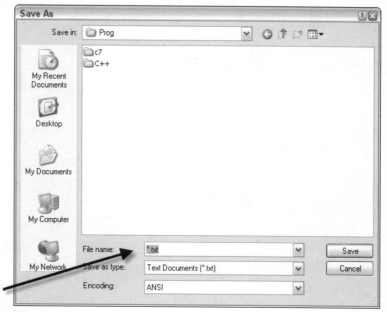

Figure 10-43

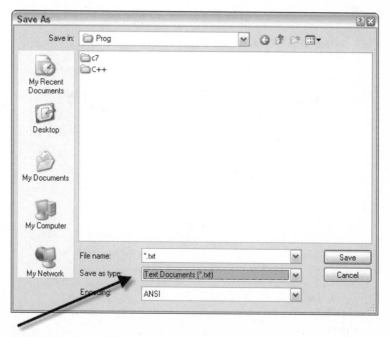

Figure 10-44

This movement from one element to another is called *tabbing*, and the order in which the focus moves from one element to another is known as *tab order*.

Different programming environments enable you to set this in different ways, but one thing you will need to be careful of is that the focus moves from one element to another in a logical way and does not leap about all over the place.

More Complicated Applications

If you want a more complicated interface, you'll have to look at a more complicated application such as Microsoft OneNote 2003 (see Figure 10-45).

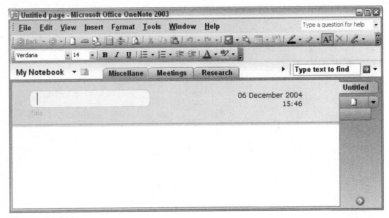

Figure 10-45

This program has masses of menus and buttons (see Figure 10-46).

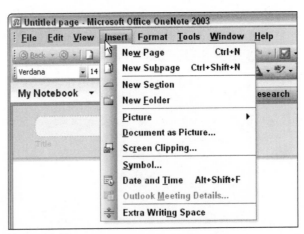

Figure 10-46

The buttons consist of images, and when you move the mouse over them there is a text pop-up (called a ToolTip) that gives you a short description of what the button does (see Figure 10-7).

Figure 10-47

Clicking Tools on the menu and then Options... brings up the options window (see Figure 10-48).

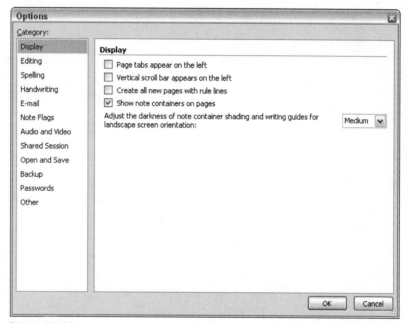

Figure 10-48

This has buttons and check boxes for you to choose the settings you want (see Figure 10-49).

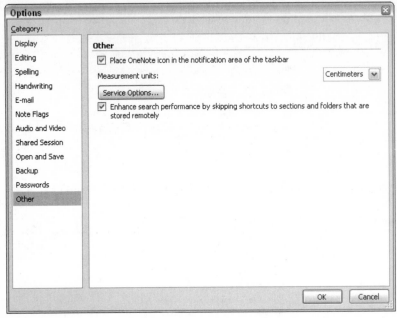

Figure 10-49

Some of the options also make use of radio buttons, used where you can only make one choice out of a few (see Figure 10-50).

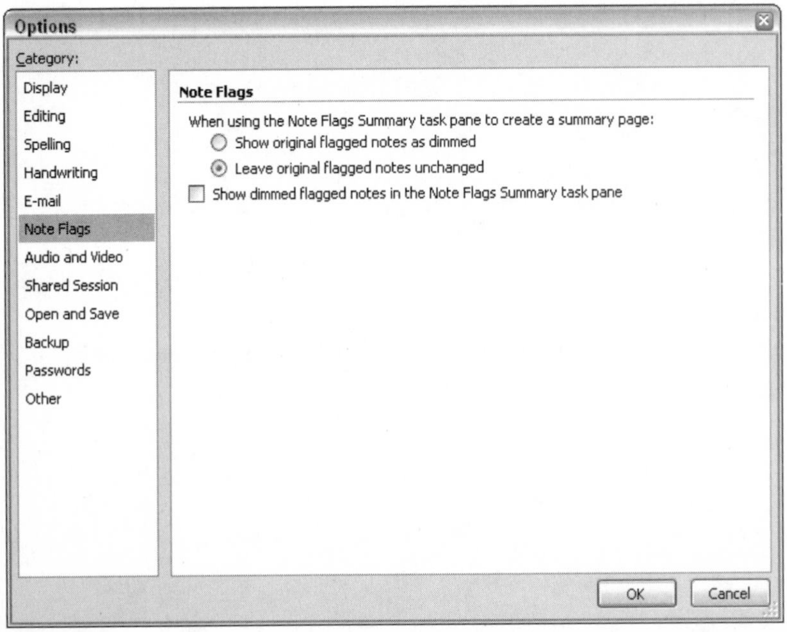

Figure 10-50

Summary

In this chapter, you've not only been exposed to more coding practice but I've also introduced you to the concept of the user interface. This is how users see your program, and as a programmer part of your job is to make your program as easy for others to use as possible. Remember, you know how your program works — others don't!

You've looked in detail at how you can add a simple interface to your C++ applications and how to make the text-based system as easy for the end user as possible, by adding prompts and confirmation screens.

You also looked at simple ways to add a help system to your C++ applications.

To close the chapter, we took a look at the elements of the user interface that form part of the Windows graphical interface. You took a tour of the elements and looked at how they are used in applications to make the user's experience as pleasant and easy as possible. Now that you know what the elements are and how they are used, you'll notice their use in other applications so that when you come to using them yourself in applications in the future, you'll be able to use them professionally right from the start.

Putting It All Together

This chapter works through the planning and execution of a programming project, from start to finish. There isn't any code in this chapter at all. Instead it concentrates on structuring, planning, and executing a medium-sized programming project.

This chapter assumes that you've followed the book closely up until this chapter and that you have probably also read a book or taken a class in the programming language that you are most interested in.

There is nothing better to stretch and test you programming muscles than to work on more challenging and complicated projects, and this chapter is intended to help you do just that.

Planning a Programming Project

When faced with a programming project, most people think that all of the work has to be done behind the keyboard, typing in code. While this might be true for some small projects, once the project is to include more than two or three features planning is a key component to the success of the project.

Without Planning

Let's take a quick look at what happens to projects that are unplanned or improperly planned at the start. From this you should hopefully get the motivation to plan your projects and also you might see some of the areas that need more attention than others when it comes to detailed planning.

More Code, Less Features

Unplanned or poorly planned projects normally are coded inefficiently. Inefficiency in the coding generally means that more code is needed to code a job than would be required if the coding were planned in advance. The reason that the code becomes bloated is that while the code carrying out the work for particular features within your project won't be any less efficient, the framework becomes clumsy as you add the features to your project in a random, ad hoc fashion.

The other reason behind the code bloat in unplanned projects is that the programmer writes duplicate functions to carry out similar or identical tasks.

All this additional, unnecessary code also hinders fast, effective debugging of your code.

More Bugs

Poorly planned projects usually result in poor applications because of the greater number and variety of bugs that the code accumulates along the way. Functions for particular features are written and created haphazardly, and the errors that usually crop up result from one set of functions relating to one feature conflicting with anther set of functions written for other features.

Proper planning eliminates these problems because you know in advance what the required features are, and you can plan how they interact with each other.

Project Takes Longer

If you are fighting with more bugs and more code because of poor planning, your coding will take more time.

Usually, an unplanned project will take substantially longer to complete than a planned program of comparable size and complexity simply because you will be programming separate features independent of the project as a whole and not planning how they are integrated from the start.

Another reason why unplanned projects take longer is that they suffer from unnecessary feature creep. *Feature creep* occurs when additional features are added to a project in the middle of coding. This can be an unnecessary use of time and effort if the only reason they need to be added is because they were left out due to a lack of planning.

Missing Features

Along with unnecessary feature creep come missing features — features that you wanted to include or you forgot to include because you didn't have a plan to follow through. This can be a huge problem, especially if you don't find out about the missing features until you enter the testing stage, because this means that you will have to go back to the code writing stage and postpone testing until the additional features are added. Either that, or you leave them out.

Planning

Now that you can see some of the drawbacks to embarking on a project that's not been properly scouted out and planned, let's take a look at how you map out a project and make the proper plans to help you get the best out of your programming.

Let's now go through the steps and stages of planning a programming project.

The Idea

A programming project starts off with an idea. Programming is partly a creative skill — you are involved in the creation of something that does something.

The idea can be one of many types:

❑ **A betterment.** You see how something is done already, and you can see how it could be accomplished much better or more easily or in less time or in fewer steps.

❑ **A new idea.** You see a gap where people want a problem solved and there is currently nothing available to help them (or if there is, it is too expansive). You see a way to change that.

❑ **Niche/market gap.** You see a gap that needs filling in the market, and you see a way to do it. Generally an idea like this starts life as a betterment or a new idea, but by the time you come to actually thinking about programming a solution it's no longer a new idea.

The first thing that you should do with an idea is document it because you can be certain that one of two things will happen to it:

❑ You'll forget about it. It is said that everyone comes up with at least one idea a year that could make them a millionaire but they don't act on it — usually because they forget about it!

❑ As you think about your idea and probably discuss it with others, the initial idea will change and it's possible at this stage in the process for the good part of the original idea to be lost.

Documenting the Idea

Here's a simple yet effective checklist that helps you document and set out your initial project ideas. This will help you record your initial idea so that you can work on it and discuss it without loosing vital aspects of the idea.

Initial Checklist

Date: ....

Time: ....

In broad terms, what is your idea?

....
....
....

What primary problem will the software meet or what need will it fulfill?

....
....
....

Will it be processing data or automating a task?

....
....
....

Is this a specialist need that you are fulfilling or one applicable to many people? If it's a specialist need, who will find it useful? If it's not for specialists, detail who might find it useful.

....
....
....

Are there any secondary needs that you think the software will meet?

....

....

Was there anything in particular that made you come up with the idea or prompted it in the first place? If yes, what was it that prompted the idea?

....

....

....

List as many key features of your ideas as you can:

....

....

....

....

....

What makes your idea different/better than existing software?

....

....

....

Are there any aspects of the program that you are unclear about?

....

....

....

Do you think that the software will be free or commercial?
Free/commercial

Why have you chosen free or commercial?

....

....

....

If commercial, what price do you think someone would pay for it? Why?

....

....

....

How do you think you will distribute the software?
On floppy disk/CD/DVD/Internet

Are you willing to offer support for the software if you release it?

....

What kind of support?
E-mail/Web- or forum-based/telephone

After completing the checklist, you should have a record of your initial idea that you can look back on to refresh your memory. As you come up with modifications, use the following checklist to make a note of those changes, and be sure to store it with your first list.

Additions/Changes Checklist

Date: ....

Time: ....

What additions/changes do you have planned?
....
....
....

What impact does this have on the initial idea?
....
....
....

Maturing Time

Once you have documented the initial idea, resist the temptation to fire up your computer and start coding away unless it is a very simple project you're undertaking. Let the idea sit with you for a while (a day at least) and mull it over. During this time, think about the idea as a whole and see if you still think it's a good idea and whether the benefits that you laid out in the initial checklist still apply. Sometimes an idea that initially seems good doesn't seem that good when you look at it later on.

Use the time to do some research. Check to see if there is software that already does what you plan. If you find some, research it as best as you can.

- ❑ How much of what you laid out in your initial checklist does the existing software appear to carry out?

- ❑ How much does it cost?

- ❑ Does it seem widely used?

- ❑ Does it seem better than your idea?

Once you have completed your research, see how this affects your initial plan. At this stage, you will probably feel one of three ways:

- ❑ You found no comparable software and so are committed to carry on.

- ❑ You found software that did what you had planned, but it is more expensive/has less features/is not as good as what you had planned.

- ❑ You've decided that it's not worth pursuing your idea.

The Requirements

If you've decided to pursue the project, then the next task for you to do is detail the requirements of the project. The requirements of the project are a detailed description of what you want the end product to do.

It is important at this stage that you be as clear and precise as you possibly can. At this stage don't be too worried about "how" the program is going to work, just concentrate on "what" it is going to do.

Here are a few questions to help you draw up a set of requirements:

Requirements

Date: ....

Time: ....

What will the primary function of your application be? Be as clear as possible.

....

....

....

What will the secondary functions of the application be? Again, be as clear as possible.

....

....

....

Will the primary and secondary function be included within one application or split into separate applications? Be as clear as possible.

....

....

....

If the application is involved in data processing, where will this data come from? (For example, will it be entered via keyboard or will a file be processed?)

....

....

....

What form does the data to be processed take?

....

....

....

If the application is going to be processing data, break the steps of the processing down into their component parts.

....

....

....

What form will the processed data (the outputted data) take?

....
....
....

How much with the end user need to interact with the software?

....
....
....

What kind of interface will the software need? Will it be very basic (command line) or modern and make use of buttons, drop-down boxes, and other advanced interface elements?

....
....
....

If yes, what elements do you see being used?

....
....
....

How will you give the user cues as to how to use the software? (A good tip here is to think about how other software provides cues and feedback to the user.)

....
....
....

Will your application need to save files?
Yes/no

If yes, what type of files, and what will they contain?

....
....
....

Will your application need to interact with other applications?
Yes/no

If yes, which ones?

....
....
....

Will your application need to print?
Yes/no

If yes, what?

....
....
....

Once you have the requirements in place you have a map detailing the function and work your software project will carry out. At this stage, you have a good idea of how the application will work and what functions it needs to carry out. If you are unclear about certain aspects of the project (for example, you know the application will need to process data but as yet you are uncertain as to the steps that the processing will take place, you can now devote time and energy to researching this and detailing it further. This is depicted in Figure 11-1.

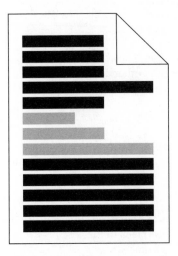

Some gray areas are inevitable early on in a project

Figure 11-1

You don't necessarily need to have the processing steps detailed until you are well into the coding of the application. This is so because it will more than likely be a function or a handful of functions that control the processing. While you are still working out what they do, you can write functions that do nothing or carry out some simple task on the data. Of course, before you can complete the coding you need all the steps detailed well enough so that you can transform the steps into code instructions, but accept for now that a few gray areas are inevitable and that you will go back to fill in the details later.

Modifying the Requirements

Just as the initial idea matures and changes, so will the requirements you initially drew up for the project. You might decide to:

- ❑   Add new features and requirements
- ❑   Modify existing requirements
- ❑   Remove requirements
- ❑   Postpone requirements for future releases

While some changes are to be expected, be careful about making significant changes — you could end up with a new project or a radically different one.

Choosing the Language

Choose the language you need to bring the project from the realms of theory to reality. A simple project might be suited to a scripting language such as JavaScript or VBScript, but anything complicated will require you to make use of a more sophisticated, versatile language such as Java or C++. In you think that your application is going to rely heavily on a professional user interface, then you may even need to make use of a "visual" language, such as Visual Basic.

Your experience levels will determine how you have to proceed now. Ask yourself if you have the skills necessary to work on the project or if you think that you need a skills upgrade. You are bound to learn something new during the course of the programming, but if you feel that you need a significant skills boost you might have to delay the project for a while.

If you feel up to it, it's time to leave the planning stage and move on to the programming stage.

Programming Stage

You have your idea documented, you have the changes and modifications to the idea, and you've documented and detailed the project requirements and refined them. You've looked at key processes within the idea and broken down processing steps. With all that done it's time to start programming!

Programming the Basics

Always start a programming project by working on the basics of the application first. The best place to start is by adding some structure to your project. Areas that might be good to concentrate on initially are:

❑ Writing code that is associated with what happens when the application is first started by the end user.

❑ Any prompts or instructions given by the application to the end user.

❑ Writing code that is associated with what happens when the application is exited, by the end user.

❑ Writing this kind of code allows you to develop a skeletal framework of code that you can attach more code to and continue to develop the application.

Testing

Test your code often as you progress. Because you will be working on specific aspects of the program, you should find it possible to run parts of the code separate to the whole (as you've been doing in the previous chapters). This will help give you confidence that you are making progress and that the code works.

Fix any problems that you come across as you test the code. Not only will this reduce your debugging workload at the end of the project, but it will also allow you to continue with coding and testing other code you write.

If you come across bugs that you choose to leave until the end of the project, make a detailed note of them (especially if they are errors in any data processing or other process) because you will no doubt not remember them all when it comes time to fix them!

Error Documenting

Date: ....

Time: ....

Describe the error that you have encountered. Be as clear as possible and describe what it affects.

....

....

....

What sections of code do you think are causing the problem?

....

....

....

Why did you decide not to fix it immediately?

....

....

....

Commenting Code

Another thing you should remember to do is comment your code well (as depicted in Figure 11-2). Do this for all functions, variables, and even for blocks of functions, and do it as you type the code.

Don't be fooled into thinking that you don't need to comment your code. Comment the code even if the code seems obvious to you as you write it. It might be obvious now, but in a few days or weeks you'll be scratching your head wondering what it all does.

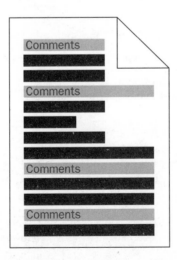

Comment your code regularly and thoroughly

Figure 11-2

One thing that beginners to programming worry about is generating too many comments for the code (as depicted in Figure 11-3). Don't be worried about this at all — you are far better off writing lots of comments that you can edit out later than not writing enough and losing track of the project. I've seen beginners write three, four, and five lines of comments for one or two lines of code, and there is absolutely nothing wrong with that.

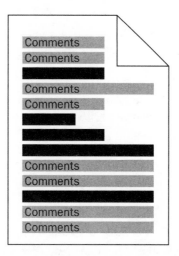

Don't worry if initially comments feel like they outweigh code sometimes – that's normal!

Figure 11-3

Commenting Tips

Here are tips to get you commenting code effectively.

❑   At the beginning of your code, add a comment detailing the project as a whole (see the depiction in Figure 11-4). To this add your name and the date. These top-of-the-page comments are commonly known as *tombstone comments* because of the way they look on the page.

Figure 11-4

❏ Detail what each function does. Do this in plain English so that you do not have to rely on deciphering the programming code to figure it out.

> **Good comment**: This function takes the final total price and adds sales tax if applicable.

> **Bad comment**: This function carried out the operations listed below. Line six is tricky!

❏ Detail what each of the variables means unless that has been detailed shortly before.

> **Good comment**: Variable x is the total value before tax, y the total value after tax.

> **Bad comment**: Variables x and y refer to the total value.

❏ Document blocks of functions.

> **Good comment**: The following three functions work on the total value of the order, adding tax and calculating the delivery charge.

> **Bad comment**: Total value, tax, and delivery.

Testing

Congratulations!

You've reached an important milestone — a project ready for full testing by others! Pat yourself on the back and feel proud of your achievement, no matter how big or small the project you undertook was.

Don't leave a thorough testing stage until the project is completed. Plan to carry out several testing sessions during the programming process. This will help to make sure that you're on track and not building up problems for later on.

Testing should consist of the following steps:

❏ **Testing for actual code errors that cause running problems.** This is actually testing the code to see whether the program operates as expected and that there are no bugs with the actual code that cause crashing or other errors.

❏ **Testing for logic errors in the code.** These errors are trickier to spot. Logic errors occur when it's the logic of the code that's at fault. A simple example of this is when you expected the code to add two numbers together, but instead it subtracts them — that's a logic error. If the logic is simple, then these types of errors can be quite easy to spot, but as the logic gets more complex, logic errors can be harder to spot and even harder to correct. Don't underestimate the devastating effect that this kind of error can have on your application — and don't underestimate how hard they can be to spot. There have been numerous cases where a commercial application (such as one involved in billing) has contained an error that cost the company or the customer extra.

> Testing with proper input and then thoroughly checking the output is by far the best way to check for these kinds of errors.

For big projects, some programmers build testbed applications that send inputs to the main programs and test the outputs to see if they are what is expected. This system dramatically reduces the scope for logic errors.

❑ **Checking for design errors.** There are problems with the way the program operates. These come to light when you use and test the application. Make detailed notes of any problems that you encounter so that you can later address them.

❑ **Missing features.** No matter how well you document your idea you are likely to find that you missed something somewhere during the course of the programming. No worries. You can go back and add it. Again, just make a note of what you left out so you don't forget again!

The Route to Better Testing

How you test is almost as important as what you test for. There is a general rule that says that a programmer is the worst person to test an application (especially an application he or she developed). This is so because the programmer has a good idea of how the program should work, what things do, and what inputs the program is expecting.

Far better than testing your application yourself is to let others test it for you by creating your own preview program and beta release.

You might have heard of the terms preview program and beta release before (probably on the Internet or in computer magazines), but just in case you haven't, let me just explain what they mean.

A *preview release* is just that — a preview. With a preview release you would let others see your program before it is fully ready. In exchange for allowing a preview, you ask for feedback on the program. The program can be nearly finished or nowhere near finished; the idea is not that you are giving people fully functional software, but instead that you let them see the progress you are making with the software. At this stage, you should be open to both bug reports and suggestions for new features and changes.

A beta release is when you release software you think is pretty much done, but you want a wider audience than just yourself to test it and give feedback, especially bug reports and problems. At this stage, you should still accept feedback about other issues, such as improvements or new features, but these are probably best left until a future release (unless they are really compelling).

The two processes are depicted in Figure 11-5.

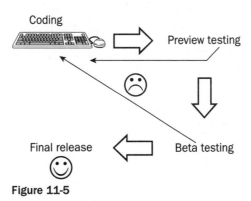

Figure 11-5

But What About . . .

You are working on some interesting software and you want some feedback on it, so you release it to others — but once they have the software why should they come back again? And if you plan on selling the software, why should you give it away for free at the beta or preview stage?

The answer to this question depends on whether you plan on selling the software or giving it away for free.

Beta and Preview Strategy for Free Software

If you are planning to release the software for free or for a donation, then you need not worry about beta or preview releases affecting later take-up of your software. In fact, people will keep coming back looking for the updates or latest release.

Beta and Preview Strategy for Commercial Software

With software that you eventually plan on asking people to pay for, you have to do things a little bit differently to stop people from simply sticking with a preview or beta version and not paying you for continued use. There are a few strategies you can use to help you ensure that the testing phase doesn't affect sales:

❑   Limit some of the features of the software — remove a vital component such as the facility to save or export files.

❑   Place an annoying feature in the software (such as a nag screen or a countdown timer that delays its launch for a few seconds).

❑   Time limit the software so that it refuses to run after a certain date or after a certain number of runs.

❑   Restrict the initial testing to a select group of users.

❑   If the software is an update, restrict the release to those that are already using your software.

❑   Place a reminder in the program that reminds the user that they are using preview or beta software.

By using a scheme like the ones detailed, you will be able to take advantage of a preview or beta release, get feedback and bug reports from others, and not affect sales.

Questions for Those Previewing Software

Here is a list of question I'd suggest that you ask people who agree to review and test your software.

Some people might not be able to answer all the questions presented, but no one will if you don't ask them in the first place!

PC System Questions

PC brand

CPU/processor

RAM

Amount of hard drive free space

Operating system (listing any service packs installed)

Problems

Did you encounter any problems?

If yes, describe the problem in as much detail as possible.

Were you using any other applications at the time?

Usability

How easy did you find the software to use?

Were there some areas that you found confusing?

If yes, why?

How do you think they could be improved upon?

Suggestions

How would you improve the software?

What additional features would you add?

Are there any features that you would remove?

General questions

Do you find the software useful?

Would you buy the software?

If yes, how much would you be willing to pay?

If no, why not?

If you are unsure, why?

Additional Features

If you were at the preview stage, you can now think about additional features to your software.

The first thing I suggest that you do now is to make and keep a backup of the code as it stands at this stage. If you are working with a language that requires you to compile, keep a copy of the executable as well as the source code. You should have been keeping backups of your source code along the way anyway (at least once a day), but this is especially important now because it represents a milestone in your project. It is important to keep all the materials at this stage in case any future changes break anything — if that happens, early on at least, you can go back to where you were.

Once you have a backup safe, you can then go to work on the code yet again and set about making changes based on your feedback.

Now you need to correct any flaws, defects, and bugs that exist in the code. Check carefully that the corrections you've made actually correct the problem.

> It's an excellent idea to try to reproduce the error, bug, or defect in the code before trying to fix it because this allows you to later see clearly if you actually have fixed it!

This stage of the coding shouldn't take as long as the first step (unless you have to add some really tough feature). As you add a feature, test it and move on. Keep a checklist of what the changes you make are and which you choose to leave until a future version of the software.

Once you've fixed all the bugs that were found in testing and added any new features, you need to go back to another testing phase because as you've been working on the code you've undoubtedly added newer bugs to the code. These need to be hunted down and eliminated, so you need help from others again!

So it's almost time to go back to the testing stage — this time a beta test! However, before you do that, it's time to tweak the code a bit.

Tweak the Code

The code is now pretty near being complete (bar the removal of any bugs it contains), so it's an excellent time to tweak the code to streamline it a bit.

The first thing to do is look for functions or code that are unused within the program. This can be a laborious task, but it may well reduce the size of the final application you create quite dramatically, and that in turn will reduce the amount of system resources the application will consume while in use. Go through your code function by function and see if you can follow the overall logic of it, and remember to look for anything out of place and see if it is used.

While you are going through the code, you might also see lines of code that can be condensed or compressed (especially the early code you wrote — no doubt your coding will have improved over the course of the project). This will streamline the code, as well as improve speed and performance.

If you are using a language that is interpreted rather than compiled (such as VBScript or JavaScript), now is a good time to remove all the comments that you have in the beta code (but keep a copy for your reference of course). This also will help streamline things and improve loading times and performance.

You're now ready to move onto the final testing stage so that any remaining bugs can be found and destroyed.

Final Testing

This final testing stage is only concerned with finding and destroying bugs. At this stage, don't be concerned with new features or new ideas. Those will wait and can be included in the next version you release!

Get the final feedback from your testers (preferably the same testers you had for the preview) and make any final adjustments to the code. Do your own testing too just for your piece of mind. Then, if possible, put the application on one side for a few days before you come back to it and test it again.

When you are sure that the bugs are out, you are then in a position to think about doing a full release (unless that is that you want to create help file documentation before release — that's optional).

Some programmers start work on help files and instructions early on for their applications, but I tend to think that this is a bad idea because the program can change but the documentation remains static, causing confusion. It is best to leave creating the help files until the application is nearing completion.

Then all that's left to do is unleash your application onto the waiting world!

Summary

In this chapter, you've taken a tour through the process of creating an application, starting from the point of the initial idea, building on that and taking it through to a final application. I've concentrated not on code but the process you need to follow and also how to document what you are doing so that you always know what you are currently doing, what you've done, and what you have left to do.

I've tried to be as detailed as possible, while keeping the process generic and applicable to whatever kind of project you might have. You may need to customize the steps based upon what you are doing because not all of the steps will be relevant to all kinds of projects. Not only that, but you should also stay within what you feel comfortable with. All this is just fine and quite normal. As long as you plan ahead and don't rush, you'll be just fine!

Interacting with Files

This chapter explores ways to interact with the file system on your PC. You will learn to use some simple programming principles to begin creating sample applications that will actually save data to the hard drive for later retrieval.

The process of saving and retrieving data is normally an advanced feature that most beginners never get to touch, but it is an important aspect of modern computing. Because of that I have decided that in this book you will get a chance to work with code that will save information and later retrieve it.

The Principles of Saving Data

As I am typing out this page (using Microsoft Word), I am occasionally saving the data to the hard drive. When most people save files they don't really think about what they are actually doing — they are just saving a file because they want access to that data later on and it's too much work to type it all out again. Or maybe they want to send that data to someone else. That's what I'm going to be doing. I'll be sending this to my editor, who will pass it along to other people where it eventually will end up at the printers. At that point the file will be transformed from being digital to an analog form. Eventually you'll pick up the book and read it. All that's possible because I typed out the chapter, then saved it.

Saving files is all about what is being saved. When I save a word processor file, I'm saving a lot more than just the text. Some of the other things I'm saving are:

- The formatting of the words, paragraphs, and pages
- Inclusion of any images on the page
- Author information
- Information about when the file was last saved
- Language information
- Custom templates

You're probably starting to see that the more complicated your application, the more complicated the file it will have to save.

However, you have to start somewhere and a word processor isn't the place I'd recommend! Let's begin by working with text-based files and build up from there.

We'll also take a look at some simple applications and use those as a platform to build on and look at how something simple, such as saving a text file, can be a good place to start for saving files with a more complicated structure.

The File Life Cycle

Before we look at code to work with files it is a good idea to start off by looking at the life cycle of a file and how different files have different life cycles.

If you think about it for a while, I'm sure that you will agree that most files have a life cycle that consists of four stages:

❑   File creation

❑   File editing

❑   Distribution

❑   Archival/deletion

This is the normal path for most files, and while the beginning and end are fixed, what happens between file creation and archival or deletion can be either simple or complicated.

Let's look at a few examples. Figure 12-1 shows a typical life cycle of a simple note file that you might create to remind you of something. The file is created, and then might not have any edits done to it at all, and goes straight to the deletion stage.

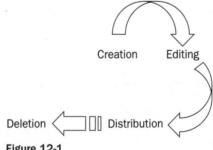

Creation   Editing

Deletion ⟵ ⬚⬚ Distribution

Figure 12-1

Figure 12-2 shows a more complicated life cycle — this time a word processor file or maybe a spreadsheet or a graphic you are working on. This file undergoes multiple edits and possibly multiple distributions (maybe it's printed out several times or distributed by e-mail to others to read). Usually these files, just like the files from the notes example, outlive their useful life and are either deleted (no longer required) or archived in case they need to be referred to at some point in the future.

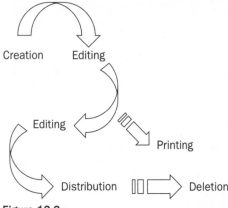

Creation   Editing

Editing   Printing

Distribution   Deletion

Figure 12-2

In Figure 12-3 I've depicted the life cycle of a file such as a database file. These kinds of files undergo countless updates once they have been created and have an extremely long lifespan. Many database files are never archived or deleted as such, but certain aspects of the data may be deleted or archived as time goes on.

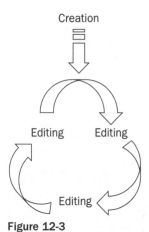

Creation

Editing   Editing

Editing

Figure 12-3

Complex file structures are way beyond the scope of this book because of the skill you need, not only to write applications that use them, but also to plan the actual internal workings of the file format. In this chapter, we are going to concentrate on simple file formats based on text files. However, as you will see shortly, even simple file formats offer huge potential without your having to do too much work — which is something that the programmer is always on the lookout for!

Working with Files

I'm simplifying things here a little, but by doing this we can start to write code that turns the three distinct stages of creation, editing, and deletion from theory into reality.

The Tools

Each programming language handles files in different ways, some simple and some complicated. Some hide working with files behind "black boxes" of code, which you have to hand over whenever you want to create and work with files. One of the easiest and clearest programming languages for handling files is Visual Basic, but because that's a commercial product we'll have to use the next best freely available language — VBScript. VBScript is a scripting language, but by running it through a utility called Windows Script Host (a feature available in all modern incarnations of Microsoft Windows), we can leverage this language and get it to work like a programming language.

There are several advantages to using this language:

❑   **Free.** Always a great reason!

❑   **Nothing to set up.** All you need to do is write code, save it, and run it and you will see results instantly. There are no applications to install.

❑   **No complicated program to learn.** Half the battle with a new programming language is working your way around the actual programming environment — to work with VBScript you need only know how to use a text editor! This is quick and simple.

❑   **No compiling.** Because you do not need to compile your code before it runs, you can see the results of your code more quickly and easily.

❑   **Easier to fix errors.** Because you don't have to keep flipping between source code and compiled code the whole time, you can spot and correct errors a lot more quickly.

So, as a Windows user, all you need is a text editor and you're ready to start programming!

Getting Started

Since the file life cycle begins normally with file creation, we'll start there. A program doesn't always have to create the files that it works with though — a utility that you write to work with the Windows registry (see Chapter 13, "The Windows Registry") works with a file that already exists. You might want to write a utility that searches your hard drives for useless temporary files to delete, in which case your utility needn't be bothered by file creation and editing and can just delete files. But we'll start at the beginning and take a look at the process involved in creating a file.

Creating a File with VBScript

When you are running VBScript code through the Windows Script Host system (that is, running it on your system directly rather than across the Internet in a browser), it is surprisingly easy to create your own files.

Basics

You will probably be surprised just how little code you need. In fact you only need five lines of code!

```
Dim fso, TestFile
Set fso = CreateObject("Scripting.FileSystemObject")
Set TestFile = fso.CreateTextFile("c:\hello.txt", True)
TestFile.WriteLine("Hello, World!")
TestFile.Close
```

Five lines. Take this code, place it into a text editor such as Windows Notepad and save it with a .vbs file extension (the filename doesn't matter), then double-click the file to run it and it will silently create a file called hello.txt in the root of C: drive (see Figure 12-4).

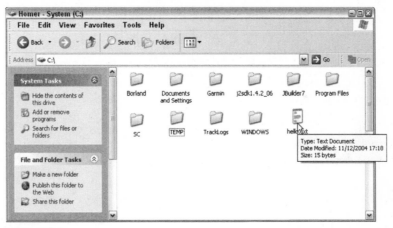

Figure 12-4

Take a closer look at this file (open it), and you'll notice that it contains the line "Hello, World!" (see Figure 12-5).

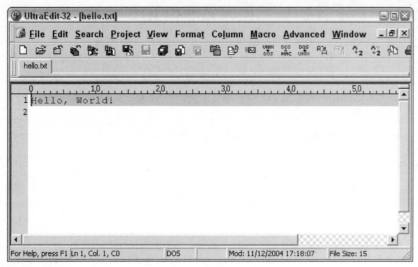

Figure 12-5

Let's take a trip through the code and look at how it works.

```
Dim fso, TestFile
Set fso = CreateObject("Scripting.FileSystemObject")
Set TestFile = fso.CreateTextFile("c:\hello.txt", True)
TestFile.WriteLine("Hello, World!")
TestFile.Close
```

The first line of the code purely declares variables that we are going to use later. Technically, this isn't needed and could be dispensed with but by clearly declaring the variables we reduce the risk of misspelling the variables later on.

```
Dim fso, TestFile
Set fso = CreateObject("Scripting.FileSystemObject")
Set TestFile = fso.CreateTextFile("c:\hello.txt", True)
TestFile.WriteLine("Hello, World!")
TestFile.Close
```

This line is the powerhouse of the code and introduces the object that enables us to access the file system; this line too is not really necessary but it allows us to write less code later on.

```
Dim fso, TestFile
Set fso = CreateObject("Scripting.FileSystemObject")
Set TestFile = fso.CreateTextFile("c:\hello.txt", True)
TestFile.WriteLine("Hello, World!")
TestFile.Close
```

In this case, later on is the next line. This line uses the object from line 2 to create a test file. The test file is assigned to the variable `TestFile`. The Windows Registry we have declared the location and name of the file.

You could, if you wanted to, choose a different filename and location. Let's say that you want to create the file on another drive or in a different folder or give it a different name, then that's just a case of changing the path used:

```
...
Set TestFile = fso.CreateTextFile("d:\hello\hello.txt", True)
...
```

One thing that you must have in place is the folder — this statement cannot create folders for the file, so if you declare a path that doesn't exist, you will get an error when you try to run the code, as shown in Figure 12-6.

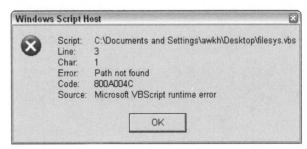

Figure 12-6

If the file already exists, this statement will cause it to be overwritten. If you wanted to prevent that you would change the `True` at the end to `False`:

```
...
Set TestFile = fso.CreateTextFile("c: \hello.txt", False)
...
```

If the file is already in existence, the code will generate an error message.

```
Dim fso, TestFile
Set fso = CreateObject("Scripting.FileSystemObject")
Set TestFile = fso.CreateTextFile("c:\hello.txt", True)
TestFile.WriteLine("Hello, World!")
TestFile.Close
```

The next line is the line that populates the file that was created with the text that you want it to contain. This is written a line at a time using the `WriteLine` method. This can be repeated as needed.

```
Dim fso, TestFile
Set fso = CreateObject("Scripting.FileSystemObject")
Set TestFile = fso.CreateTextFile("c:\hello.txt", True)
TestFile.WriteLine("Hello, World!")
TestFile.WriteLine("Another line")
TestFile.WriteLine("This is getting boring now.")
TestFile.WriteLine("That's it, I'm outta here. . . .")
TestFile.Close
```

Finally, the code closes by closing the file. This is the way that the code saves the updates to the file.

Creating a Folder

I said earlier that the code so far doesn't enable you to create a folder to put files into, but fortunately writing code to do that is not difficult to accomplish.

To create folders, use the `CreateFolder` method. The following is an example that lets you create a folder:

```
Dim fso, fld
Set fso = CreateObject("Scripting.FileSystemObject")
Set fld = fso.CreateFolder("c:\New Test Folder")
```

The main part of this code is the third line, which is the statement that creates the folder.

If the folder exists, an error will be displayed, as shown in Figure 12-7.

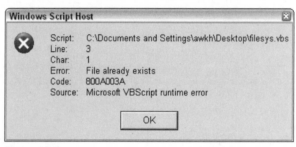

Figure 12-7

Incorporating the two code snippets, we can write code that creates a folder then places a file in the newly created folder.

```
Dim fso, fld, TestFile
Set fso = CreateObject("Scripting.FileSystemObject")
Set fld = fso.CreateFolder("c:\New Test Folder")
Set fso = CreateObject("Scripting.FileSystemObject")
Set TestFile = fso.CreateTextFile("c:\New Test Folder\hello.txt", True)
TestFile.WriteLine("Hello, World!")
TestFile.Close
```

Save this code in a file with the `.vbs` file extension and run it and check to see if the folder and file are created properly. Here I check my system and find everything in order (see Figure 12-8).

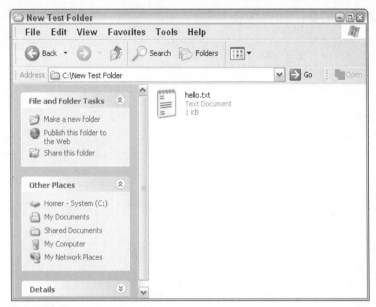

Figure 12-8

Creating Multiple Files

The code can be modified to create multiple files in the same folder in the same code.

```
Dim fso, fld, TestFile, TestFile2, TestFile3
Set fso = CreateObject("Scripting.FileSystemObject")
Set fld = fso.CreateFolder("c:\Folder2")
Set fso = CreateObject("Scripting.FileSystemObject")
Set TestFile = fso.CreateTextFile("c:\Folder2\hello.txt", True)
TestFile.WriteLine("Hello, World!")
TestFile.Close
Set TestFile2 = fso.CreateTextFile("c:\Folder2\another file.txt", True)
TestFile2.WriteLine("I don't have anything to say any more!")
TestFile2.Close
Set TestFile3 = fso.CreateTextFile("c:\Folder2\and another.txt", True)
TestFile3.WriteLine("D'oh!")
TestFile3.Close
```

The code is starting to become complex, but it's also prone to errors such trying to create a folder where one already exists. It's a good idea to modify the code to first check for the existence of the folder and only try to create it if it doesn't exist.

Making Use of Conditionals

Here we are going to need a conditional to check for the folder and make a choice based on whether the conditional resolves to true or false.

```
Dim fso
Set fso = CreateObject("Scripting.FileSystemObject")

If (fso.FolderExists("c:\Folder")) Then
    msgbox("Folder exists.")
Else
    msgbox("Folder doesn't exist.")
End If
```

This code checks for the existence of the folder c:\folder. If it exists one message is displayed (see Figure 12-9).

Figure 12-9

And a different message is displayed if the folder doesn't exist (see Figure 12-10).

Figure 12-10

Displaying messages is one thing, but you can now get the code to create the folder if it doesn't already exist, which is far more useful than generating error messages or dialog boxes.

```
Dim fso, fld
Set fso = CreateObject("Scripting.FileSystemObject")

If (fso.FolderExists("c:\Folder")) Then
    msgbox("Folder exists.")
Else
    Set fld = fso.CreateFolder("c:\Folder")
End If
```

This code does just that, but because it doesn't use variables for the folder name, there is scope for an error like this one to creep into the code:

```
Dim fso, fld
Set fso = CreateObject("Scripting.FileSystemObject")

If (fso.FolderExists("c:\Folder")) Then
    msgbox("Folder exists.")
Else
    Set fld = fso.CreateFolder("c:\Folder2")
End If
```

Making Use of Variables

Presently the code checks for the existence of one folder, but creates one with a different name — a troublesome and potentially hard-to-spot error.

Using a variable to hold the folder name dramatically reduces the scope for error:

```
Dim fso, fld, fldName, drvName
drvName = "c:\"
fldName = "folder"
Set fso = CreateObject("Scripting.FileSystemObject")

If (fso.FolderExists(drvName & fldName)) Then
    msgbox("Folder exists.")
Else
    Set fld = fso.CreateFolder(drvName & fldName)
End If
```

This code is now beginning to operate in a clever and professional way. It's intelligent enough to check for the folder before trying to create it and is coded in such a way that the scope for errors is reduced to a minimum.

We can now take this code and apply it to the earlier example that creates files.

```
Dim fso, fld, fldName, drvName, TestFile
drvName = "c:\"
fldName = "folder"
Set fso = CreateObject("Scripting.FileSystemObject")

If (fso.FolderExists(drvName & fldName)) Then
    msgbox("Folder exists.")
Else
    Set fld = fso.CreateFolder(drvName & fldName)
End If

Set TestFile = fso.CreateTextFile(drvName & fldName & "\hello.txt", True)
TestFile.WriteLine("File contents here")
TestFile.Close
```

Adding Flexibility — Prompt for File and Folder Names

This works great but the only problem is that folder names, filenames, and the file contents are fixed. This is an awkward situation as it generally makes the code inflexible and greatly restricts functionality.

A better scheme therefore is to use inputs for the folder and filenames. Here the code is modified to ask for input as to the name of the file to save.

```
Dim fso, fld, fldName, drvName, TestFile, fileName
drvName = "c:\"
fldName = "folder"
fileName = inputbox("Enter the name of the file:", "Filename")
Set fso = CreateObject("Scripting.FileSystemObject")

If (fso.FolderExists(drvName & fldName)) Then
    msgbox("Folder exists.")
Else
    Set fld = fso.CreateFolder(drvName & fldName)
End If

Set TestFile = fso.CreateTextFile(drvName & fldName & "\" & fileName & ".txt",
True)
TestFile.WriteLine("File contents here")
TestFile.Close
```

You can now take this idea and apply it to the drive and the folder names:

```
Dim fso, fld, fldName, drvName, TestFile, fileName
drvName = inputbox("Enter the drive to save to:", "Drive letter")
fldName = inputbox("Enter the folder name:", "Folder name")
fileName = inputbox("Enter the name of the file:", "Filename")
Set fso = CreateObject("Scripting.FileSystemObject")

If (fso.FolderExists(drvName & fldName)) Then
    msgbox("Folder exists.")
Else
    Set fld = fso.CreateFolder(drvName & fldName)
End If

Set TestFile = fso.CreateTextFile(drvName & fldName & "\" & fileName & ".txt",
True)
TestFile.WriteLine("File contents here")
TestFile.Close
```

Let's save the file (again, name it anything as long as it has the .vbs extension) and run it.

The first thing you'll see is a prompt asking you for the drive name where the file is going to be saved (see Figure 12-11).

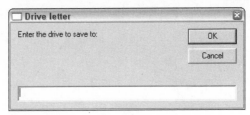

Figure 12-11

This is generated by this line of code:

```
Dim fso, fld, fldName, drvName, TestFile, fileName
drvName = inputbox("Enter the drive to save to:", "Drive letter")
fldName = inputbox("Enter the folder name:", "Folder name")
fileName = inputbox("Enter the name of the file:", "Filename")
Set fso = CreateObject("Scripting.FileSystemObject")

...
```

Enter the drive name where the file is going to be saved, for example:

```
c:\
d:\
```

Then you get another prompt asking for a folder name (see Figure 12-12).

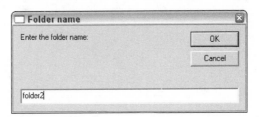

Figure 12-12

```
Dim fso, fld, fldName, drvName, TestFile, fileName
drvName = inputbox("Enter the drive to save to:", "Drive letter")
fldName = inputbox("Enter the folder name:", "Folder name")
fileName = inputbox("Enter the name of the file:", "Filename")
Set fso = CreateObject("Scripting.FileSystemObject")
...
```

Then, another prompt asking for the filename (see Figure 12-13).

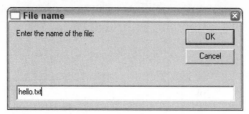

Figure 12-13

```
Dim fso, fld, fldName, drvName, TestFile, fileName
drvName = inputbox("Enter the drive to save to:", "Drive letter")
fldName = inputbox("Enter the folder name:", "Folder name")
fileName = inputbox("Enter the name of the file:", "Filename")
Set fso = CreateObject("Scripting.FileSystemObject")

...
```

Now with all the variables sorted out, the conditional is run to check to see if the specified folder exists:

```
...
If (fso.FolderExists(drvName & fldName)) Then
    msgbox("Folder exists.")
Else
    Set fld = fso.CreateFolder(drvName & fldName)
End If
...
```

If the folder doesn't exist, it's created:

```
...
If (fso.FolderExists(drvName & fldName)) Then
    msgbox("Folder exists.")
Else
    Set fld = fso.CreateFolder(drvName & fldName)
End If
...
```

While if it does already exist, a prompt is displayed instead (see Figure 12-14):

```
...
If (fso.FolderExists(drvName & fldName)) Then
    msgbox("Folder exists.")
Else
    Set fld = fso.CreateFolder(drvName & fldName)
End If
...
```

Figure 12-14

Check for Duplicate Files

We can modify the code a little more to check whether the file specified by the filename already exists.

```
Dim fso, fld, fldName, drvName, TestFile, fileName
drvName = inputbox("Enter the drive to save to:", "Drive letter")
fldName = inputbox("Enter the folder name:", "Folder name")
fileName = inputbox("Enter the name of the file:", "Filename")
Set fso = CreateObject("Scripting.FileSystemObject")

If (fso.FolderExists(drvName & fldName)) Then
    msgbox("Folder exists.")
Else
    Set fld = fso.CreateFolder(drvName & fldName)
End If
```

```
If (fso.FileExists(drvName & fldName & "\" & fileName & ".txt")) Then
    msgbox("File already exists.")
Else
    Set TestFile = fso.CreateTextFile(drvName & fldName & "\" & fileName & ".txt",
True)
    TestFile.WriteLine("File contents here")
    TestFile.Close

End If
```

Editing an Existing File

We now have code that effectively creates a file in the location where we want it saved. Now that we have this file, we can write code that will be capable of opening files that already exist.

```
Dim fso, opnFile
Set fso = CreateObject("Scripting.FileSystemObject")
Set opnFile = fso.OpenTextFile("c:\test.txt", 2, True)
opnFile.Write "Hello world!"
opnFile.Close
```

Again, five lines of code are all that are needed.

```
Dim fso, opnFile
Set fso = CreateObject("Scripting.FileSystemObject")
Set opnFile = fso.OpenTextFile("c:\test.txt", 2, True)
opnFile.Write "Hello world!"

opnFile.Close
```

The first line of the code declares all the variables that will be needed. They're not required, but it does make the code easier to follow and less prone to error.

```
Dim fso, opnFile
Set fso = CreateObject("Scripting.FileSystemObject")
Set opnFile = fso.OpenTextFile("c:\test.txt", 2, True)
opnFile.Write "Hello world!"

opnFile.Close
```

The second line is there simply to use a variable to shorten the third line for convenience and to reduce possible errors in the code later.

```
Dim fso, opnFile
Set fso = CreateObject("Scripting.FileSystemObject")
Set opnFile = fso.OpenTextFile("c:\test.txt", 2, True)
opnFile.Write "Hello world!"

opnFile.Close
```

The third line defines the method needed to open the file. The statement also defines the file to open. There's a bit more to this statement. Near the end notice the number 2. This sets one of three options for the statement:

❑   Opens a file for reading only. You can't write to this file.

❑   Opens a file for writing to.

❑   Opens a file and writes to the end of the file (in other words it appends the file).

The True *defines how the file should be opened.* True *specifies Unicode;* False, *ASCII, and* UseDefault, *the system default.*

In this example, we are choosing to write to the file.

```
Dim fso, opnFile
Set fso = CreateObject("Scripting.FileSystemObject")
Set opnFile = fso.OpenTextFile("c:\test.txt", 2, True)
opnFile.Write "Hello world!"

opnFile.Close
```

The next line is the line that will be written to the file.

```
Dim fso, opnFile
Set fso = CreateObject("Scripting.FileSystemObject")
Set opnFile = fso.OpenTextFile("c:\test.txt", 2, True)
opnFile.Write "Hello world!"
opnFile.Close
```

Finally, the file is closed.

In Action

First, create a file in the root of `c:\` called `test.txt`. Inside this file put whatever text you want. I've just added a few lines as you can see in Figure 12-15.

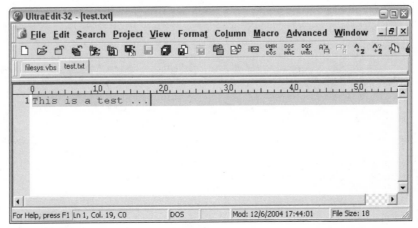

Figure 12-15

Now, with this code saved in a file with the `.vbs` extension, run it. It should run invisibly, but if you take a look at the file `test.txt`, you should notice that the contents of the file have been changed by the code (as shown in Figure 12-16).

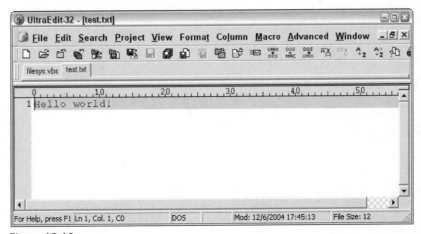

Figure 12-16

Appending a File

One small change to the code will mean that instead of updating the file, the file is appended and has text added to the end of it.

```
Dim fso, opnFile
Set fso = CreateObject("Scripting.FileSystemObject")
Set opnFile = fso.OpenTextFile("c:\test.txt", 8, True)
opnFile.Write "Hello world!"
opnFile.Close
```

By running this, the existing copy of test.txt is opened and the text Hello world! added to the end, as shown in Figure 12-17.

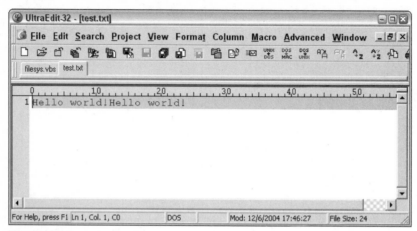

Figure 12-17

Open File for Reading

If you just wanted to open a file for reading, you would use the following code:

```
Dim fso, opnFile
Set fso = CreateObject("Scripting.FileSystemObject")
Set opnFile = fso.OpenTextFile("c:\test.txt", 1, True)
```

However, do bear in mind that trying to write to a file that you opened for reading only, by writing code such as the snippet that follows, will result in an error being generated (as shown in Figure 12-18).

```
Dim fso, opnFile
Set fso = CreateObject("Scripting.FileSystemObject")
Set opnFile = fso.OpenTextFile("c:\test.txt", 1, True)
opnFile.Write "Hello world!"
opnFile.Close
```

ReadAll, ReadLine, and Read Methods

You can choose how to read a file too. For this, let's create a file that has a little content, something like what I've done in Figure 12-19.

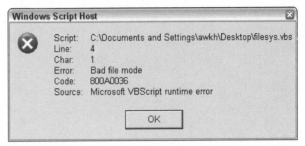

Figure 12-18

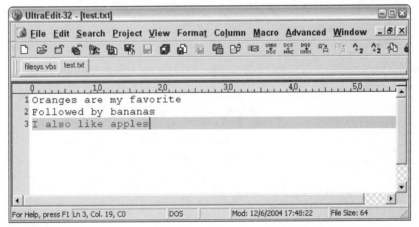

Figure 12-19

Using this, we can examine the difference between the ReadAll method and the ReadLine method.

ReadAll

Here is an example of code that uses the ReadAll method.

```
Dim fso, opnFile
Set fso = CreateObject("Scripting.FileSystemObject")
Set opnFile = fso.OpenTextFile("c:\test.txt", 1, True)
MsgBox(opnFile.ReadAll)
```

Running this file causes the content of the file to be displayed in a pop-up message box, as shown in Figure 12-20.

Figure 12-20

ReadLine

ReadLine is similar to ReadAll, except that one line is read instead of the whole of the file:

```
Dim fso, opnFile
Set fso = CreateObject("Scripting.FileSystemObject")
Set opnFile = fso.OpenTextFile("c:\test.txt", 1, True)
MsgBox(opnFile.ReadLine())
```

Running this file causes the first line of the file to be displayed in a pop-up message box, as shown in Figure 12-21.

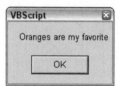

Figure 12-21

To read a progression of lines, add more ReadLine statements to the end of the code. The following will read three lines from the text file:

```
Dim fso, opnFile
Set fso = CreateObject("Scripting.FileSystemObject")
Set opnFile = fso.OpenTextFile("c:\test.txt", 1, True)
MsgBox(opnFile.ReadLine())
MsgBox(opnFile.ReadLine())
MsgBox(opnFile.ReadLine())
```

This code generates a progression of message boxes, each showing a line at a time. Figure 12-22 shows the third one generated.

Figure 12-22

If you add more `ReadLine` statements than you have lines, that will result in an error being generated.

```
Dim fso, opnFile
Set fso = CreateObject("Scripting.FileSystemObject")
Set opnFile = fso.OpenTextFile("c:\test.txt", 1, True)
MsgBox(opnFile.ReadLine())
MsgBox(opnFile.ReadLine())
MsgBox(opnFile.ReadLine())
MsgBox(opnFile.ReadLine())
MsgBox(opnFile.ReadLine())
MsgBox(opnFile.ReadLine())
MsgBox(opnFile.ReadLine())
MsgBox(opnFile.ReadLine())
MsgBox(opnFile.ReadLine())
```

The error message (shown in Figure 12-23) shows the line number that causes the error and halts the running of the script.

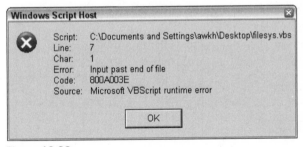

Figure 12-23

Read

The `Read` method enables you to specify the number of characters that should be read from the file.

The following code snippet will read one character from the file (the output of the code is shown in Figure 12-24).

```
Dim fso, opnFile
Set fso = CreateObject("Scripting.FileSystemObject")
Set opnFile = fso.OpenTextFile("c:\test.txt", 1, True)
MsgBox(opnFile.Read(1))
```

Figure 12-24

While this will read 20 characters (the output of the code is shown in Figure 12-25).

```
Dim fso, opnFile
Set fso = CreateObject("Scripting.FileSystemObject")
Set opnFile = fso.OpenTextFile("c:\test.txt", 1, True)
MsgBox(opnFile.Read(20))
```

Figure 12-25

This code reads 2,000 characters and goes beyond the length of the file, but that doesn't generate any errors; it just displays the entire contents of the file (see Figure 12-26).

```
Dim fso, opnFile
Set fso = CreateObject("Scripting.FileSystemObject")
Set opnFile = fso.OpenTextFile("c:\test.txt", 1, True)
MsgBox(opnFile.Read(2000))
```

Figure 12-26

That covers a lot to do with reading and creating files and folders.

324

Deleting Files and Folders

Finally, let's take a look at how to accomplish the final step in the file life cycle — deleting files and folders using code. First, let's look at how to delete files.

Delete Files

Deleting files only takes three lines of code (less than is needed to create files!). Files are deleted using the DeleteFile method.

```
Dim fso
Set fso = CreateObject("Scripting.FileSystemObject")
fso.DeleteFile("c:\test.txt")
```

The last line of code is the line that does the actual deleting, and it is here that we specify the file that is required for deletion.

This statement has to contain the complete path to the file to be deleted (unless the file to be deleted is in the same folder as the script), and the filename must contain the file extension if it is used.

The code can be modified to accept filenames through the use of a prompt.

```
Dim fso, fileDel
fileDel = InputBox("Enter filename to Delete:", "File deletion")
Set fso = CreateObject("Scripting.FileSystemObject")
fso.DeleteFile(fileDel)
```

Remember to include the full path to the file and the file extension, as shown in Figure 12-27.

Figure 12-27

Delete Folders

Deleting folders is similar to deleting files. Folder deletion is carried out by making use of the DeleteFolder method. The code is similar to the code used to delete files.

```
Dim fso
Set fso = CreateObject("Scripting.FileSystemObject")
fso.DeleteFolder("c:\testfolder")
```

This method does not discriminate between folders that have content and those that don't and will delete either.

Summary

In this chapter, you've looked at code that can be used to access the file system. You've looked at the life cycle of typical files and used this as a template to categorize the skills needed to effectively work with files in the file system.

You saw how to use VBScript through the Windows Script Host to:

- ❑ Create files
- ❑ Create folders
- ❑ Edit files
- ❑ Delete files
- ❑ Delete folders

Each of these is a key skill to experiment with and master, and once you have worked through the examples in this chapter, I suggest that you experiment, modify, and combine the code from the examples provided and work on your own mini-projects to improve your skills and confidence — just take care when it comes to editing and deleting!

The Windows Registry

This chapter looks at one of the mysteries of the Windows operating system: The Windows registry. Getting the basics on this repository of information contained within the operating system will give you a head start in programming, especially if you are going to end up programming in one of the "visual" programming languages designed to make applications for Windows.

The Windows Registry

Before we move on to look at the Windows registry, let's just make it clear here that we are talking about something that only applies to Windows operating systems. None of this applies to other operating systems such as Mac, Unix, or Linux.

The Windows operating systems that use a registry are:

- Windows 95
- Windows 98
- Windows Me
- Windows NT 4
- Windows 2000
- Windows XP
- Windows CE
- All Pocket PC operating systems

The registry does not apply to the DOS operating system.

What Is the Windows Registry?

The registry has been around for a while now, having been first introduced in Windows 95, but it's surprising just how many people are either unaware of it or only aware of its existence because of the problems that it has given them.

This section takes a close look at what the registry actually does.

Definition

The Windows registry is a central database used by the Windows operating system to store a broad range of information about the operating system itself.

There are three main types of information that the registry holds:

- ❏ **Applications.** The registry is used to hold a vast amount of information about applications. This includes, but is not limited to:
  - ❏ Initial default settings
  - ❏ User customizable setting
  - ❏ Configuration information
  - ❏ File type information
- ❏ **Hardware.** The registry is also key to controlling most of the hardware that users have access to through Windows. There is a lot of information here.
- ❏ **User information.** You can have multiple profiles on Windows operating systems because all the information relating to user profiles is stored in the registry. This makes creating new profiles, modifying existing ones, and deleting old ones much easier.

The registry contains a lot of information that the operating system continually has to refer to — general settings for how Windows looks and operates, user profiles, application data, what applications to use to open particular files, the hardware that exists on the system, and even what icons are used where. This is a lot of diverse information that has to be accessed on the fly, and it is because of the database format used by the registry that this process is fast.

Prior to the Windows registry, all this information and these settings were stored in text-based files, many known as *initialization files* (with the extension .ini). Most applications had their own initialization files scattered about the system all over the place (some would be in the folders of the application in question, but in reality they could be anywhere). These were a nightmare to administer and keep track of and the cause of much grief when it came to updating applications or making changes.

There might still be a few .ini files on a modern PC but the vast amount of what they used to do is now done by the registry.

The registry also replaces other system files present on earlier operating systems, including:

```
autoexec.bat

config.sys

system.ini

win.ini
```

If you perform a search on your system, you might still find some of these files but they remain only as a last resort for applications that truly cannot operate without them.

The Windows registry is stored in binary files that cannot directly be edited without using specific applications. Also, even though all versions of Windows since Windows 95 have used a registry, the format that they take is not identical, although there are commonalities.

The Layout of the Windows Registry

As well as being a database, the registry is organized in a hierarchical format. This means that the registry follows a logical layout. When you look at and navigate through the registry (as we will shortly), notice that it is similar to navigating the file system, where you have folders, subfolders, and files.

The data that the registry contains is ordered logically. You can use a few signposts you to find your way around quite easily.

The easiest way to become familiar with the registry is to take a look at it. To do this you need to familiarize yourself with viewing and editing it.

Regedit and Regedit32

You edit the registry all the time and probably don't know that you are even doing it. Every time you make a change to an application, install or uninstall an application, or modify your user profile you are making changes to the registry.

It is accepted that the safest way to make changes to the registry is to a allow applications installed on the PC to carry out the changes rather than editing it manually. For most people that's good advice, but as a programmer you are eventually going to find that you want to store some information about your product or its user, and you might come to the conclusion that the registry is the place to store this information. To do this, you need to be familiar with the basics of the registry, and to do that you need to use it hands-on.

There are two programs that can be used to view and modify the registry and they are probably both already installed on your PC. These are called Regedit and Regedit32.

The easiest way to access these applications is to use the Run function of the Start Menu. Click Start followed by Run. In the box that is then displayed (shown in Figure 13-1) either type:

```
Regedit
```

and click OK for Regedit, or type:

```
regedt32
```

and click OK for Regedit32.

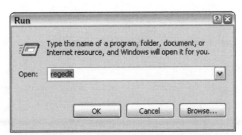

Figure 13-1

The loaded application is shown in Figure 13-2. On Windows XP, it doesn't matter whether you type `regedit` or `regedt32` because `regedt32.exe` is just a small file that loads up `regedit.exe`. However, on Windows NT and Windows 2000 I recommend that you use `regedt32`. Refer to Figure 13-2.

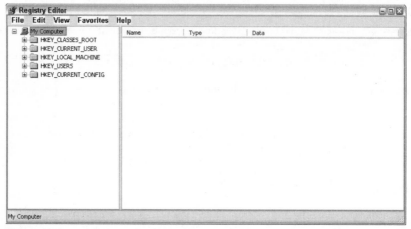

Figure 13-2

On Windows 95, 98, and Windows Me only use Regedit.

Using the registry editor you can navigate around the registry by expanding and collapsing the branches. However, before looking at that, it's a good idea to know how to back up the registry.

Backing Up the Registry

Because the registry is a key to the proper running of the Windows operating system, it is important to take care of it and protect if from accidental damage. The best way to do this is to keep a backup of the registry. Let's quickly take a look at how to back up the registry for a variety of operating systems.

Windows XP

When you back up the registry in Windows XP, you have two choices available to you:

❑ **Back up specific entries (known as *subkeys*).** This creates a small, specific backup file that is easy to replace.

❑ **Back up the whole registry.** This creates a larger file containing the whole registry. Replacing this is a longer, more involved process.

Back up Subkeys

You can use the following steps to export a registry subkey before you edit it.

1. Click Start, and then click Run.

2. In the Open box, type:

```
regedit
```

Then click OK.

3. Navigate through the registry by clicking on keys and subkeys (see Figure 13-3).

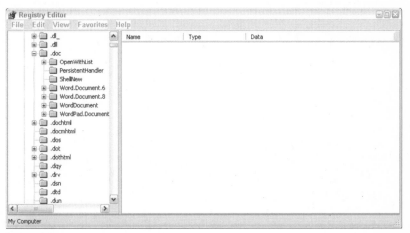

Figure 13-3

4. Locate and then click the subkey that contains the value that you want to edit.

5. On the File menu, click Export (see Figure 13-4).

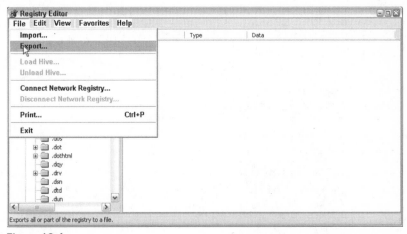

Figure 13-4

6. In the Save in box, select a location where you want to save the registration entries (.reg) file, type a filename in the File name box, then click Save (see Figure 13-5).

Figure 13-5

Don't use this method to back up the whole registry — it is likely to fail.

Back Up the Whole Registry

To back up the whole registry, use the Backup utility to back up the system state.

You must have permissions as an administrator or as a backup operator on your computer to back up files and folders.

1. Click Start, point to All Programs, point to Accessories, point to System Tools, and then click Backup. The Backup or Restore Wizard starts (see Figure 13-6).

Figure 13-6

2. Next, click Advanced Mode (see Figure 13-7).

Figure 13-7

3. Click the Backup tab (see Figure 13-8).

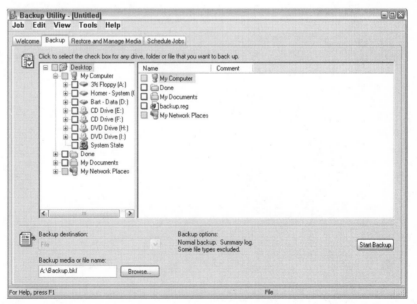

Figure 13-8

4. On the Job menu, click New (see Figure 13-9).

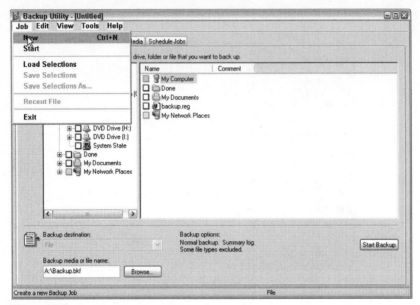

Figure 13-9

5. Check the System State check box to select it (see Figure 13-10).

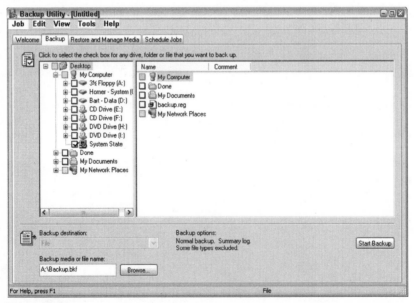

Figure 13-10

The system state data includes such items such as the Windows registry, the COM+ class registration database, files under Windows File Protection, and boot files.

6. In the Backup destination list, click the backup destination that you want to use (see Figure 13-11).

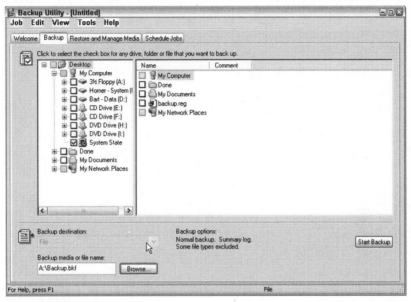

Figure 13-11

7. If you clicked File in the previous step, type the full path and filename that you want in the Backup media or filename box (see Figure 13-12).

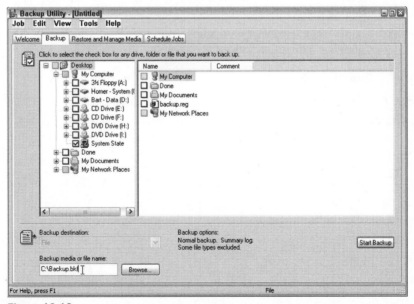

Figure 13-12

8. Click Start Backup. Doing this will cause the Backup Job Information dialog box to appear, as shown in Figure 13-13.

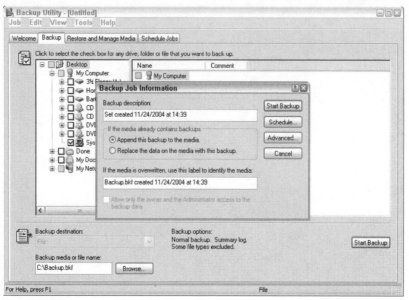

Figure 13-13

9. Under If the media already contains backups, use one of the following steps:

❑ If you want to append this backup to previous backups, click Append this backup to the media.

❑ If you want to overwrite previous backups with this backup, click Replace the data on the media with this backup.

10. Click Advanced (see Figure 13-14).

11. Select the Verify data after backup check box (Figure 13-15).

12. In the Backup Type box, click the type of backup that you want. When you click a backup type, a description of that backup type appears under Description (see Figure 13-16). The choices available to you are:

❑ Normal

❑ Copy

❑ Differential

❑ Incremental

❑ Daily

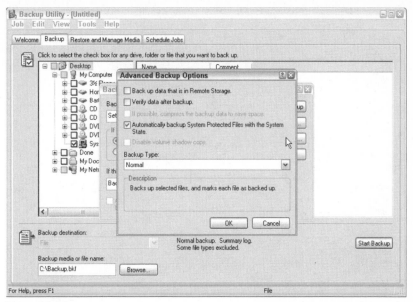

Figure 13-14

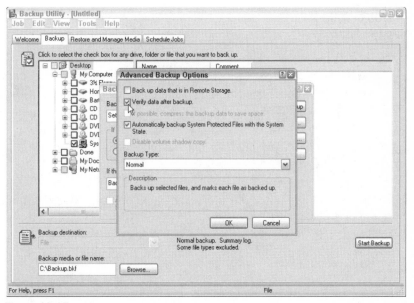

Figure 13-15

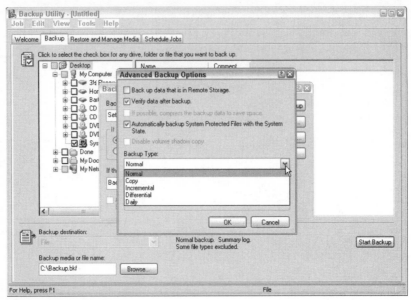

Figure 13-16

13. Click OK, and then click Start Backup. A Backup Progress dialog box appears, and the backup starts (see Figure 13-17).

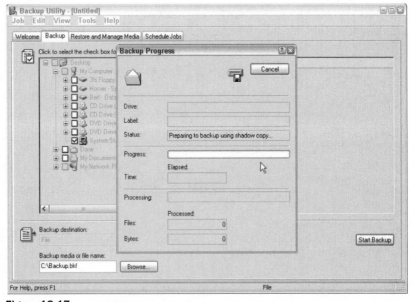

Figure 13-17

14. When the backup is complete, click Close.

Restoring the Registry

How you restore the registry depends on what method you chose to back it up.

Restoring Subkeys

To restore registry subkeys that you exported, double-click the registration entries (.reg) file that you saved. A conformation dialog box will be displayed, and you need to click OK to complete the restoration process, as shown in Figure 13-18.

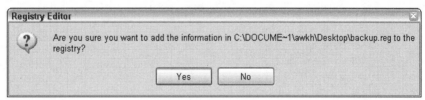

Figure 13-18

Restoring the Whole Registry

Here is a step-by-step guide to recovering the registry.

1. Click Start, point to All Programs, point to Accessories, point to System Tools, and then click Backup. The Backup or Restore Wizard starts.

2. Click Advanced Mode.

3. Click the Restore and Manage Media tab (see Figure 13-19).

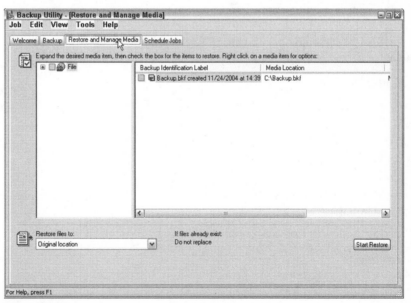

Figure 13-19

4. Use one of the following steps:

    ❏ If you want to restore from a backup file, expand File, and then expand the backup file that you want to use (see Figure 13-20).

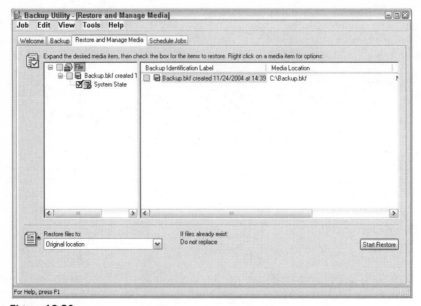

Figure 13-20

    ❏ If you want to restore from a tape backup, expand the tape device that you want, and then expand the media name that you want to use.

5. Since you are restoring registry, select the System State check box (see Figure 13-21).

6. In the Restore files to box, choose Original location.

7. Click Start Restore.

8. You will receive the following message, and you will need to click OK because you want to restore the System State information with the selected backup:

```
Warning
Restoring System State will always overwrite current System State unless restoring
to an alternative location.
```

9. At the Confirm Restore prompt, click OK. A Restore Progress dialog box appears and the restore operation starts.

10. When the restore operation is completed, click Close. When you are prompted to restart the computer, remember to click Yes.

Having a backup of the registry is recommended before exploring it. Experienced users might feel that this is unnecessary, but if you have any doubts or uncertainties, make a backup!

Working with the Registry

Working with the Windows registry involves the following six types of procedures. Each is discussed in detail in the following pages:

- ❑ Finding a subtree, key, subkey, or value
- ❑ Adding a new subkey
- ❑ Adding a new value
- ❑ Changing an existing value
- ❑ Renaming an existing subkey or a value
- ❑ Deleting an existing subkey or a value

Finding a Subtree, Key, Subkey, or Value

There are five top-level registry subtrees, and each one of them starts with the prefix HKEY. In the example that follows (shown in Figure 13-21), HKEY_LOCAL_MACHINE is the subtree, SOFTWARE is the key, and Microsoft is the subkey.

```
HKEY_LOCAL_MACHINE\SOFTWARE\Microsoft
```

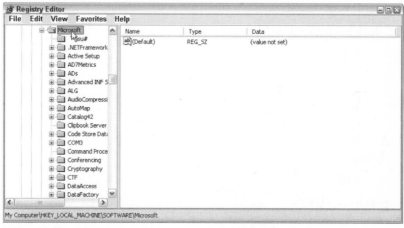

Figure 13-21

In Registry Editor, you can search through the keys and subkeys in much the same way that you search through your folders and files in Windows Explorer.

The keys and the subkeys are listed in the folder tree in the left pane of Registry Editor (see Figure 13-22). If you click a key or a subkey in the left pane, information about the value name, the value type, and the value data appears in the right pane (see Figure 13-23).

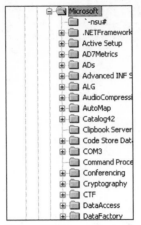

Figure 13-22

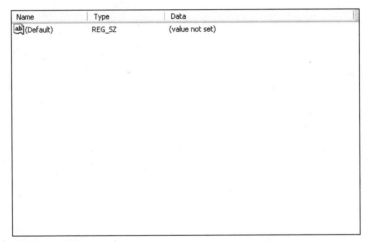

Figure 13-23

Just as in Windows Explorer, each folder may be expanded by clicking the plus sign (+) that is next to it. After a folder is expanded, the plus sign changes to a minus sign (-). Clicking this will collapse it.

When I say you should expand an item, I mean that you should click the plus sign next to that item.

To locate the Microsoft subkey that I mentioned earlier, follow these simple steps:

1. Click Start, click Run, type regedit, and then click OK.

2. Expand HKEY_LOCAL_MACHINE.

3. Expand SOFTWARE.

4. Click Microsoft.

When you click the Microsoft subkey, the values for it appear in the right pane. If you want to view the next lower level of subkeys, then you need to expand the Microsoft subkey. If you want to locate a value, click the subkey that contains the value, then view the contents of the right pane.

Adding a New subkey

Now we are going to add a new subkey. This will be a new subkey called NewTestSubkey, and we will add it to the Microsoft subkey.

To do this, follow these steps:

1. Expand HKEY_LOCAL_MACHINE.

2. Expand SOFTWARE.

3. Click the Microsoft subkey.

4. On the Edit menu, point to New, and then click Key (see Figure 13-24).

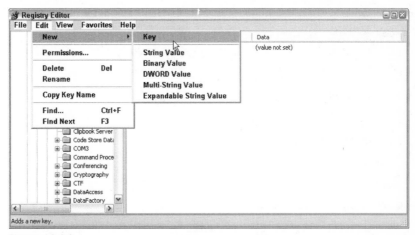

Figure 13-24

5. Type NewTestSubkey, and then press Enter (see Figure 13-25). The new key will now be created.

There is no Save feature within Regedit — all changes are carried out immediately. This is one feature that makes it so dangerous!

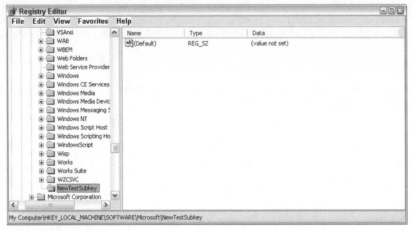

Figure 13-25

Adding a New Value

Now you are going to add a new value. This will be a new DWORD value named NewTestDWORD and to set its value data to 1 in the NewTestSubkey key that you just created.

DWORD stands for double word, which means a bit of data that is 4 bytes long. This is reserved for numbers in the registry.

1. Expand HKEY_LOCAL_MACHINE.
2. Expand SOFTWARE.
3. Expand Microsoft.
4. Click the NewTestSubkey subkey.
5. On the Edit menu, point to New, and then click DWORD Value (see Figure 13-26).

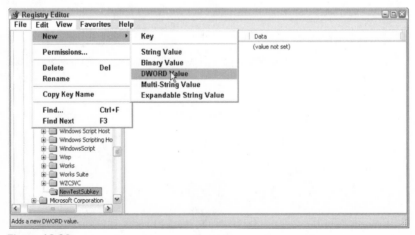

Figure 13-26

6. Type NewTestDWORD, and then press Enter (see Figure 13-27).

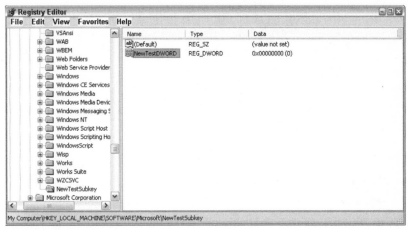

Figure 13-27

7. Right-click NewTestDWORD, and then click Modify (see Figure 13-28).

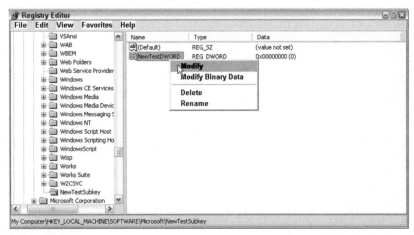

Figure 13-28

8. Type 1, and then click OK (see Figure 13-29).

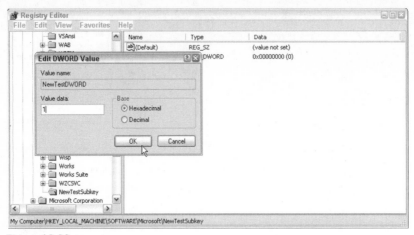

Figure 13-29

Changing an Existing Value

Now let's look at how you go about changing exiting registry values. To change the value data for the NewTestDWORD DWORD value to 0 in the NewTestSubkey key, follow these steps:

1. Expand HKEY_LOCAL_MACHINE.

2. Expand SOFTWARE.

3. Expand Microsoft.

4. Click the NewTestSubkey subkey.

5. Right-click the NewTestDWORD DWORD value, and then click Modify (see Figure 13-30).

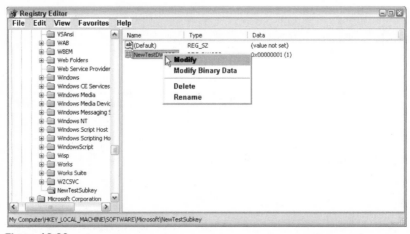

Figure 13-30

6. Type 0, and then click OK (see Figure 13-31).

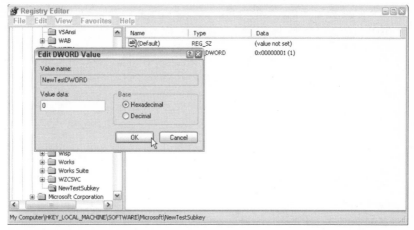

Figure 13-31

Renaming an Existing Subkey or a Value

Let's now take a look at how to rename the NewTestSubkey subkey to OldTestSubkey. To do this, follow these steps:

1. Expand HKEY_LOCAL_MACHINE.

2. Expand SOFTWARE.

3. Expand Microsoft.

4. Right-click the NewTestSubkey key, and then click Rename (see Figure 13-32).

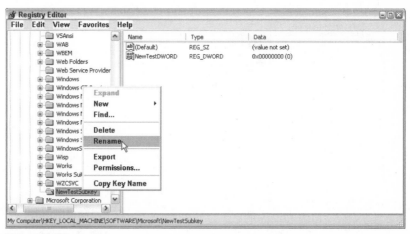

Figure 13-32

5. Type OldTestSubkey, and then press Enter (see Figure 13-33).

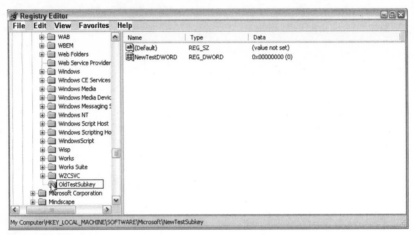

Figure 13-33

Deleting an Existing Subkey or a Value

Finally, let's take a look at how to delete the NewTestDWORD DWORD value in the OldTestSubkey subkey.

1. Expand HKEY_LOCAL_MACHINE.

2. Expand SOFTWARE.

3. Expand Microsoft.

4. Click the OldTestSubkeysubkey.

5. Right-click the NewTestDWORD DWORD value, and then click Delete (see Figure 13-34).

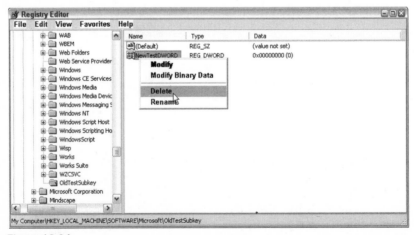

Figure 13-34

6.   Click Yes to confirm that you want to delete the value (see Figure 13-35).

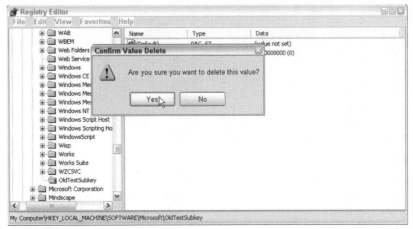

Figure 13-35

7.   That's it — the value is gone! You can now do the same with the `OldTestSubkey` subkey.

Manipulating the Windows Registry Using Programming

It's all very well and good making manual edits to the registry through Regedit, but as a programmer you can't afford the time to go to all your user's PCs and make edits manually! A far better idea would be to use code to carry out these tasks.

To do this we will use VBScript and some JScript code (that's Microsoft's implementation of JavaScript, and it's virtually identical to JavaScript). To run this code, we will use a programming tool know as Windows Script Host that enables you to run VBScript and JScript as a programming language from within Windows.

What we are going to do here is write some code that adds a subkey to the Windows registry, read that subkey, then delete it. For clarity and practice, we will use both VBScript and JScript for the job.

VBScript Registry Editing

Fire up your favorite text editor and create a new, blank document. Once you have this, you can start to write the code you will need.

The first thing that is needed is to declare the variable that you are going to use. This is `WshShell`.

```
Dim WshShell
```

Chapter 13

Now you need to define the WshShell variable as follows:

```
Dim WshShell
```

```
Set WshShell = WScript.CreateObject("WScript.Shell")
```

This enables you to create an instance of the WScript.Shell object, which enables you to run the code on the operating system itself. The purpose of WScript.Shell is predefined and you are merely using this to enable access to the registry through the Windows operating system.

By using variables like this you provide yourself with a good shortcut for writing the code, as you will see shortly.

Now you can start to create the subkeys.

There are a few rules to creating subkeys. The first rule is that subkeys higher up in the hierarchy have to be created before those below. If you try to break this rule, errors will occur.

Another important rule is that you have to talk to the operating system in a way that it understands. This means that you have to do things a certain way. One such rule is that you have to refer to the root keys (the top-level keys in the registry) using abbreviations. The abbreviations for the root keys are as follows:

Root key name	Abbreviation
HKEY_CURRENT_USER	HKCU
HKEY_LOCAL_MACHINE	HKLM
HKEY_CLASSES_ROOT	HKCR
HKEY_USERS	HKEY_USERS
HKEY_CURRENT_CONFIG	HKEY_CURRENT_CONFIG

You must use these abbreviations in your code — using anything else, such as full names, will result in the code not working as expected.

You want to add keys to HKEY_CURRENT_USER/Software, so you need to abbreviate this as follows:

```
HKCU\Software
```

First you want to add a subkey called TestKey under Software. The line of code to do this is this:

```
Dim WshShell
Set WshShell = WScript.CreateObject("WScript.Shell")
```

```
WshShell.RegWrite "HKCU\Software\TestKey\", 0, "REG_BINARY"
```

There are four parts to this single statement that you need to look at.

First, notice the use of the variable `WshShell` at the beginning. This is done to reduce the amount of code you need to write. Without this, the line of code would be:

```
WScript.CreateObject("WScript.Shell").RegWrite "HKCU\Software\TestKey\", 0,
"REG_BINARY"
```

I think you'll agree that that is unwieldy, long, and a lot to type (especially more than once) and that the code as we have it is much easier to follow.

The next part to look at is `RegWrite`. This is a method that allows you to create a new key, adds another value name to an existing key (and assigns it a value), or changes the value of an existing value.

The `RegWrite` method has a specific syntax that you need to follow.

```
object.RegWrite(strName, anyValue [,strType])
```

❑ **Object.** This is the `WshShell` object that is required for it to work.

❑ **StrName.** This is a string value indicating the key name, value name, or value you want to create, add, or change.

❑ **AnyValue.** This is the name of the new key you want to create, the name of the value you want to add to an existing key, or the new value you want to assign to an existing value name.

❑ **StrType.** This is an optional string value that indicates data type (although we will always use it).

This syntax is used to specify a key name by ending `strName` with a final backslash. Don't include a final backslash if you are specifying a value name.

There are four possible data types you can specify with `strType`, and I've listed these in the following table.

Type	Description	Form
REG_SZ	A string	A string
REG_DWORD	A number	An integer
REG_BINARY	A binary value	An integer
REG_EXPAND_SZ	An expandable string (For example, `"%windir%\\paint.exe"`, which would resolve out the folder that Windows is installed into and find the appropriate application)	A string

You actually need to create three subkeys, and you will do that using the following code:

```
Dim WshShell
Set WshShell = WScript.CreateObject("WScript.Shell")

WshShell.RegWrite "HKCU\Software\TestKey\", 0, "REG_BINARY"
```

```
WshShell.RegWrite "HKCU\Software\TestKey\TestSubKey\", 1, "REG_BINARY"
WshShell.RegWrite "HKCU\Software\TestKey\TestSubKey\Test", "A value", "REG_SZ"
```

At this point you can save this file. You can call it whatever you want but it needs to have the .vbs file extension to denote that it is a VBScript file. In Figure 13-36, I've saved the file as reg.vbs. Notice the icon for the file has changed.

reg.vbs

Figure 13-36

You can now run this file. Double-click it. Visually, you should see nothing, but if you open up Regedit and examine it you'll see that the keys and values have been created. The created keys are shown in Figure 13-37.

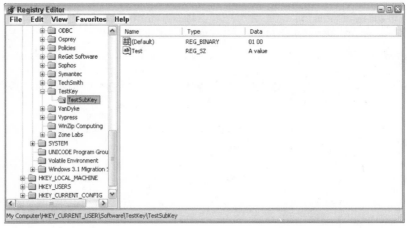

Figure 13-37

Now you can look at the code necessary for the reading of the registry keys.

To do this you use a different method — the RegRead method.

This line of code might seem big but it's actually quite an easy statement to follow.

```
Dim WshShell
Set WshShell = WScript.CreateObject("WScript.Shell")

WshShell.RegWrite "HKCU\Software\TestKey\", 0, "REG_BINARY"
WshShell.RegWrite "HKCU\Software\TestKey\TestSubKey\", 1, "REG_BINARY"
```

```
WshShell.RegWrite "HKCU\Software\TestKey\TestSubKey\Test", "A value", "REG_SZ"
```

```
WScript.Echo WshShell.RegRead("HKCU\Software\TestKey\TestSubKey\Test")
```

There are two parts to this statement. The following causes what has been read from the registry to be displayed on screen:

```
WScript.Echo
```

This is the part of the statement that reads the appropriate registry key:

```
WshShell.RegRead("HKCU\Software\TestKey\TestSubKey\Test")
```

Save the file and run it. This time the process won't go without you noticing something — a dialog box is displayed (see Figure 13-38).

Figure 13-38

You also can check the actual registry to prove to yourself that the process actually worked — as I've done in Figure 13-39.

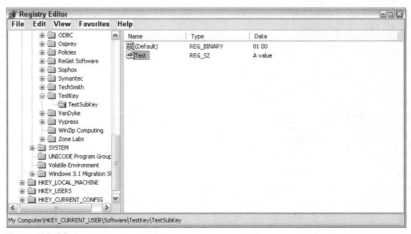

Figure 13-39

Finally, you need to clean up after yourself. This is done using the RegDelete method. This is easy to use, and you can easily delete all the subkeys you created.

```
Dim WshShell
Set WshShell = WScript.CreateObject("WScript.Shell")

WshShell.RegWrite "HKCU\Software\TestKey\", 0, "REG_BINARY"
WshShell.RegWrite "HKCU\Software\TestKey\TestSubKey\", 1, "REG_BINARY"
WshShell.RegWrite "HKCU\Software\TestKey\TestSubKey\Test", "A value", "REG_SZ"

WScript.Echo WshShell.RegRead("HKCU\Software\TestKey\TestSubKey\Test")

WshShell.RegDelete "HKCU\Software\TestKey\TestSubKey\Test"
WshShell.RegDelete "HKCU\Software\TestKey\TestSubKey\"
WshShell.RegDelete "HKCU\Software\TestKey\"
```

Save the file and run it again. This will create the registry keys, read them and then clear up after itself and leave things just as they were before you ran the code.

If you check the registry, you will notice that all the keys that you created are now gone. Heady power indeed!

But as with any heady power, you do need to be very careful when you are deleting registry keys because it is so easy to cripple your machine by deleting something that you need!

JScript Registry Editing

The code to do the same thing in JScript is surprisingly similar to the code for VBScript. There are a few differences, but nothing major:

```
var WshShell = WScript.CreateObject("WScript.Shell");

WshShell.RegWrite ("HKCU\\Software\\TestKey\\", 0, "REG_BINARY");
WshShell.RegWrite ("HKCU\\Software\\TestKey\\TestSubKey\\", 1, "REG_BINARY");
WshShell.RegWrite ("HKCU\\Software\\TestKey\\TestSubKey\\Test", "A value",
"REG_SZ");

WScript.Echo (WshShell.RegRead ("HKCU\\Software\\TestKey\\TestSubKey\\Test"));

WshShell.RegDelete ("HKCU\\Software\\TestKey\\TestSubKey\\Test");
WshShell.RegDelete ("HKCU\\Software\\TestKey\\TestSubKey\\");
WshShell.RegDelete ("HKCU\\Software\\TestKey\\");
```

A few differences that you will notice are:

❑　First, each statement ends with a semicolon (;). This is standard for both JScript and JavaScript but is optional. It does, however, make the code easier to follow. The following code will work just as well:

```
var WshShell = WScript.CreateObject("WScript.Shell")

WshShell.RegWrite ("HKCU\\Software\\TestKey\\", 0, "REG_BINARY")
WshShell.RegWrite ("HKCU\\Software\\TestKey\\TestSubKey\\", 1, "REG_BINARY")
WshShell.RegWrite ("HKCU\\Software\\TestKey\\TestSubKey\\Test", "A value",
"REG_SZ")

WScript.Echo (WshShell.RegRead ("HKCU\\Software\\TestKey\\TestSubKey\\Test"))

WshShell.RegDelete ("HKCU\\Software\\TestKey\\TestSubKey\\Test")
WshShell.RegDelete ("HKCU\\Software\\TestKey\\TestSubKey\\")
WshShell.RegDelete ("HKCU\\Software\\TestKey\\")
```

❏ Second, declaring variables is different — but you knew that already!

❏ Third, the backslashes in the strings require two — this is because a single backslash is used to represent an escape character that varies depending on what follows. Trying to use one would cause errors.

❏ Finally, notice the use of parentheses. Again, standard JavaScript/JScript stuff.

As an aside, here is a list of JavaScript and JScript escape characters:

\b	*Backspace*
\f	*Formfeed*
\n	*New line*
\r	*Carriage return*
\t	*Horizontal tab*
\ '	*Single quote*
\ "	*Double quote*
\uHHHH	*Unicode encoded character (where HHHH is character code)*
\###	*Latin encoded character (where ### is character code)*

Another difference is the file extension — instead of .vbs , you use .js. The icon is the same though (as you can see in Figure 13-40).

reg.js

Figure 13-40

Possible Uses for the Windows Registry

Before we close let's take a look at what kind of information you can store in the Windows registry.

It should be apparent to you that lengthy info is not something suited to the registry. That's not to say that the registry can't hold lengthy information, take a look at `HKEY_LOCAL_MACHINE\SOFTWARE\Microsoft\Windows\Current Version\explorer\tips\` and you will see that some of the tips here are very lengthy indeed (see Figure 13-41).

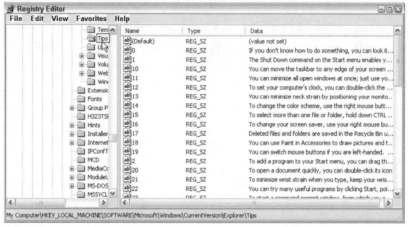

Figure 13-41

But these are settings, not files, and one thing you shouldn't use the registry for is to store files. That is what the file system is for.

Here are a few types of information that the registry is useful for. This isn't a definitive list but there just to give you an idea:

❑ Storing user licensing information

❑ Storing menu/option defaults

❑ Storing specific file paths relating to your application

❑ Storing version information

❑ Storing information on when the application was last run

In Closing

There are countless other uses for the registry that will be application-specific — it all depends on what you are doing. However, let me leave you with a few thoughts about the registry and its use.

❑ Use of the registry is potentially dangerous and can cause severe damage to a system — yours during the programming stage and others during testing. Make sure that you take precautions against such damage and test thoroughly before letting others try your software.

❑ Don't use the registry for frivolous things!

❑ Many programming tools, especially free ones, don't allow you easy access to the registry. Generally, the more expensive the programming tool, the easier access it gives you to the Windows registry (except for Windows Script Host, which is free and allows you good access to the registry!).

❑ One great use for the registry, especially in combination with Windows Script Host, is to create simple tools to make quick modifications to the system (if you know what you are doing). For example, you can use what we have done here today and easily modify the code that you worked with to change the Windows tips contained in the registry, or even to delete them completely.

❑ Finally, don't worry too much about using the registry — if you are worried about causing problems on your system or other systems, leave it alone!

Summary

In this chapter, you've taken a tour of the Windows registry and looked at how it stores data relating to your Windows operating system. Knowing how the data is stored is key to getting access to it.

You also looked at how you can take steps to protect your registry from harm by backing it up — just in case things go wrong!

Finally, you moved on to look at some programming and looked at simple, yet powerful ways to access the data stored in the registry and also ways to add, modify, and remove data from it.

Organizing, Planning, and Version Control

It's a fact of life nowadays that as computer users we generate loads of files in our day-to-day interactions with computers. It's also a fact of life that as a programmer (or an active programmer at least) the more you write code the more code you end up with.

If you aren't careful to take the right steps early on, you'll find yourself searching though what could be hundreds or thousands of files trying to look for that one particular file you're after. As you can imagine, this can be quite a task, requiring time and effort and producing both boredom and frustration. It is needless and unnecessary and might even result in the loss of good code.

There's another related problem, one that happens far too frequently: saving over your old code with new, untested, code. This causes problems down the line when you want to revert to the old code.

Getting into any kind of source code mess usually spells trouble down the line, so in this chapter I show you how to take control of your code and keep it under control, so you can find the files that you want when you want them!

Organize, Organize, Organize!

The first item on the agenda for version control is to get yourself organized. This means organizing yourself, your workspace, and your PC for the job.

Organize Yourself

The best place to begin is by organizing yourself. Don't worry though — there's nothing enormously life changing you will have to do here!

The first element to organizing yourself is to get a plan of the overall project and the direction that you think it will take. Refer to Chapter 11, "Putting it All Together," for details about how to plan a programming project. Go through this carefully and plan the project as best you can. The clearer your plan, the better things will go for you!

Stages of Planning

The planning is a multistep process. The main steps are:

- ❑ **The idea.** Document the idea that you have thoroughly. This is the seed from which your project will grow, so make sure that you've documented this clearly. It's easy for the idea to change and get lost as you develop it.

- ❑ **The requirements.** This is a listing of what you think the software should do. Your list of features is likely to grow and shrink as you go through the planning stage and compare your dreams to your actual programming skill but that's normal and nothing to worry about. Remember, you can always add features to a program you've already written, whereas if you burden yourself with too big a project at the beginning you might never complete it.

Plan Your Time

Another critical issue is time. We've all been warned about taking on too much, of having eyes bigger than our stomachs or biting off more than we can chew. This can adversely affect the outcome of your project.

The key to success is to be honest about your skills and the time that you have available. Start off by working on small projects and build up gradually. This way, you can build up your programming muscles so that you can take on bigger projects, while also improving your planning skills!

Organize Your Workspace

The next thing you need to do is organize your workspace. Different people can work in different kinds of areas, and while some people think a cluttered workspace encourages disorganized, erratic thinking, others have little problem in working in such conditions and find tidiness too sterile and artificial.

You know better than I what kind of person you are and I'm not going to ask you to change or tell you that you have to be one particular sort of person to be a programmer. What I will say is that you need a workspace that enables you to work for extended periods and do that in comfort.

The minimum I'd say you need is:

- ❑ **A comfortable workspace.** This includes a chair that is comfortable and set at the right height (roughly so that your feet are flat on the floor when you sit in it), and a keyboard at the appropriate height (roughly so that your forearms are parallel to the floor). The room should be warm, but not too warm.

- ❑ **A place for books and notes.** You are likely to have books, papers, and notes around you to which you will refer. I suggest that even if you aren't the type of person who likes a clear desk that you have enough space for these basics. Also keep a pen or pencil and notepad nearby to jot notes down.

- ❑ **Minimal distraction.** Try to work in a spot where you have the minimal of distraction from others. Use music if you find that helps to create a sphere of personal space around you. If possible, try to be away from phones (turn them off or lower their volume), and switch off e-mail applications and other sources of distraction.

Other things that can help but aren't essential for your workspace are:

❏ **Large monitor.** The bigger your monitor, the more you can fit on the screen. When you are programming you might find that you're either in one application for a long time (such as a text editor) or you are shifting from application to application often (such as between a text editor, a compiler, and the compiled application). The bigger your monitor, the more you can fit onto it while still keeping text sizes comfortable.

The minimum screen resolution I'd recommend for programming is 1024 x 768. Anything below this I find to be unworkable. In Figures 14-1, 14-2, and 14-3, I have included two schematics showing the relative sizes of different screen elements at 800 x 600, 1024 x 768, and 1200 x 1024 screen resolutions.

Figure 14-1

Figure 14-2

Figure 14-3

❑ **Customized keyboards/mice.** There are a number of mice and keyboards on the market that have a variety of buttons and scroll wheels on them designed so that you can customize their functions to a specific action (such as cut, paste, switch application or whatever). For some good peripherals that have features handy for programmers, take a look at www.microsoft.com/hardware and www.logitech.com.

These can be really useful for programming because you can program tasks into them that would otherwise take large mouse movements or several key presses.

The main drawback to these systems is that it normally takes a while to get used to them. I have buttons on my mouse and keyboard for functions such as cut, copy, paste, switch applications, scrolling down the page, and much more but I still occasionally forget they are there and revert to the less efficient but more established way of doing things. The other drawback to these is that if you get really used to using them and then have to switch systems, you will really miss them and your productivity will drop dramatically.

The Main Event — Organize Your PC

You've gotten yourself organized, and you have your workspace the way you want it (or at least somewhere near to how you want it — most things involve a compromise). Now it's time for the main event which is looking at ways to organize your PC for programming.

Create a Workspace

Just as you create a workspace around yourself, create a digital workspace for yourself too. One good place to start is to create for yourself a programming profile on your PC. Microsoft Windows gives you the ability to create profiles on your PC that have different configurations, and having one specific for programming might be a good idea. There you could locate programs and applications specific to programming in the Start menu and remove unnecessary and distracting applications (games, e-mail applications, and so on).

Figure 14-4 shows such a customized Start menu that I created.

Doing this also gives you other advantages. First, removing unnecessary applications and clutter provides you with more memory to devote to required applications. This means that your PC will work more smoothly and faster — and so will you! Fewer applications running also means fewer conflicts and crashes — something you will want to avoid when programming as a crash means lost work.

No matter how stable and secure your system is, get in the habit of saving your work frequently. If the text editor or development environment you are using supports an autosave feature to periodically save a copy of your work, take advantage of it. There is nothing more discouraging and annoying than losing a whole afternoon's work!

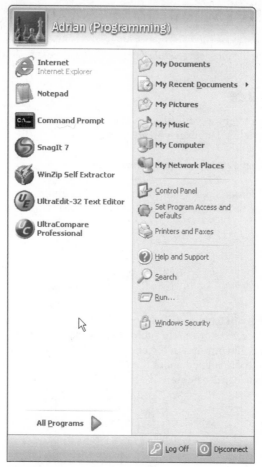

Figure 14-4

Another advantage is having a ready-made workspace for your project. You can use the Windows desktop to save files (see Figure 14-5).

Figure 14-5

Don't just save files directly onto the Windows desktop because that will result in a lot of clutter and soon become impossible to navigate. You need to spend some time organizing a little more.

Folders, Folders, Folders

One of the key components to keeping your work organized is folders. There are many ways that you can approach this but some of the most successful schemes I have found are described in the following sections.

Group by Language

One of the simplest ways to group your files, and one that works very well in the beginning, is grouping your files by the programming language you are using.

This is a very simple scheme and works as follows:

1.   You create a folder for a particular programming language, say, in this example, VBScript. Give this folder a clear, but concise name that summarizes the language you are using (see Figure 14-6).

Figure 14-6

2.   Inside this folder you have one of two options. You can group all your files in the one folder (see Figure 14-7) or organize them into subfolders for clarity (see Figure 14-8). You will probably find that if you group all your files in the one folder, they soon become hard to manage unless you are very clear and disciplined about filenames, as I have been in Figure 14-9, where I have given all the files a clear, concise name.

Figure 14-7

Figure 14-8

Figure 14-9

3. When you have finished a project or just want to create a backup, you can copy or move the relevant files to a compressed archive such as a .zip archive (see Figure 14-10). You can either keep these archives on your hard drive or move them onto a media such as CD or DVD.

Figure 14-10

Group by Project

Grouping by language might be a good way for the beginner to work, but pretty soon you're going to find that you have a preference for one language over another and once this happens it's time to start organizing files based on projects. I generally start off with a one folder per project approach, but often this becomes restrictive or too big to manage, and then I tend to either remove and archive old backup files to another folder (as shown in Figure 14-11), which is always a good idea anyway, or to break the project up into subproject folders (see Figure 14-12), which means that I have fewer files in the folder.

Figure 14-11

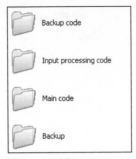

Figure 14-12

Folder Contents Note

Another good tip I can extend to you is to make a text file in the folders you work from, and in that file list what each file does and which project it relates to. I tend to call this file something like `Project_Details.txt` (see Figure 14-13) and keep it plain text so that it can be opened and edited quickly, easily, and with any text editor.

Figure 14-13

Word processor files might enable you to have fancy formatting in the document, but they require specific programs to be installed to run. The end choice as to whether to use plain text or a specific word processor format is entirely up to you, but I find that the speed and simplicity of plain text always wins with me!

Generally, the layout for the document I use tends to follow this format:

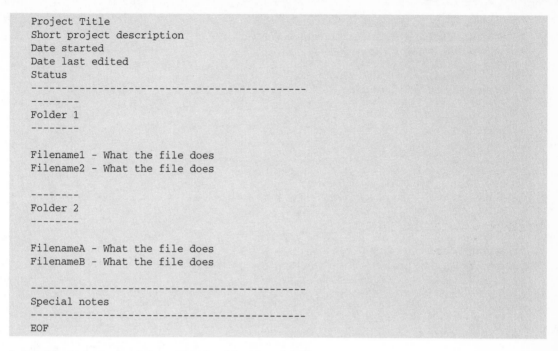

```
Project Title
Short project description
Date started
Date last edited
Status
------------------------------------------------
--------
Folder 1
--------


Filename1 - What the file does
Filename2 - What the file does


--------
Folder 2
--------


FilenameA - What the file does
FilenameB - What the file does


-----------------------------------------------
Special notes
-----------------------------------------------
EOF
```

Let's take a look at what information should go into this file:

❑ **Project title.** The title of the project that you are working on.

❑ **Short project description.** Give a short description of the project here. Keep it short. If you have any other files created that refer to the project, list them here so that they can be found if needed. This is a good place to list the programming language used and target operating systems (if known).

❑ **Date started.** The date that you started work on the project.

❑ **Date last edited.** The date that you last edited the folder contents note.

❑ **Status.** Status of the project. For example, Not started, In progress, Undergoing testing, and Completed.

❑ **Folder1, Folder 2, and so forth.** A listing of folder names, below which you list the filenames (Filename1, Filename2, FilenameA, and so on) along with a description of what each of the files actually does.

❑ **Special notes.** Any other notes relevant to the project.

❑ **EOF.** This stands for end of file, and while it might seem like an odd thing to have in the file, it's important because it lets you know as you are reading and editing the file where it ends. This one simple addition makes reading the file easier.

Here is a sample notes file.

```
"Hello, World!" application
A simple "Hello, World!" application written in C++. This should work on all the
latest version of Microsoft Windows.
Date started - 11/04/2004
Date last edited - 11/05/2004
Status - Undergoing testing
---------------------------------------------
--------
Working_Files
--------


folder_info.txt - This file
hello.cpp - Main C++ source code file
hello.cpp.bak - Current backup C++ source code file
hello.exe - Compiled code


--------
Backup_Folder
--------


hello_110504.cpp - Backup of C++ source code file
hello_110404.exe - Executable file. Does not display message
hello _110404_old.cpp - Backup of C++ source code file


---------------------------------------------
Program tested on Windows XP and 2000. Undergoing testing on Windows Me.
---------------------------------------------
EOF
```

That provides you with the basic information about the files contained in the folder. Notice that I also include the name of the folder information file in the listing. This is done for completeness and so that the listing is complete and shows all files.

Figure 14-14 shows the folder structure and files represented by the folder information file.

Figure 14-14

Filename Control

Along with effective folder naming, it is important to use effective file naming. I tend to find the following file-naming convention helps to keep things in order.

❑ **`filename.ext`.** I use this for standard filenames. The extension of the file is determined by the language being used. Try to keep the filename quite short and to the point. It need not be descriptive as long as you keep a folder information file.

❑ **`filename_mmddyy.ext`.** A backup of the file (say from the previous day or before making any major changes. *mmddyy* represents the date of the file. If you make more than one in a day, then you can add a letter or number to the end to give you more scope, for example: `filename_mmddyyA.ext` or `filename_mmddyy01.ext`.

❑ **`filename_mmddyy.ext.bak`.** Notice the double extension here. This is a current work-in-progress backup. This is done as you work and is the previously saved copy of the file. Applications such as UltraEdit can do this for you automatically. If you make more than one in a day, then you can add a letter or number to the end to give you more scope, for example: `filename_mmddyyA.ext.bak` or `filename_mmddyy01.ext.bak`.

❑ **`filename_mmddyy_old.ext`.** An old version of a backup. These are kept just in case they might be useful. They are only worth keeping if they are *working* examples of code; if not, they are best deleted. If you make more than one in a day, then you can add a letter or number to the end to give you more scope, for example: `filename_mmddyyA_old.ext` or `filename_mmddyy01_old.ext`.

Be disciplined and methodical about filenames. It might take you some time to actually get working, but in the long run this will save you time and reduce problems and errors.

One thing that this system relies on is your not using underscores (_) in your filenames generally. The underscore is so rarely used in filenames by most people that this is not a problem. However, if you currently have a file naming convention that uses underscores, feel free to substitute another symbol.

Some examples include:

```
filename-mmddyy.ext
filename$mmddyy.ext
filename+mmddyy.ext
filename#mmddyy.ext
```

All of these examples will work just fine if you already use the underscore in filenames in your file system.

Figure 14-15 shows the different file-naming conventions in action.

Figure 14-15

If you must, or if you feel that it adds clarity to your file system, you can happily mix the conventions in the same folder. You also could give different meanings to different symbols, as I have done in Figure 14-16. As long as you remember to document this in the folder information file, you will be fine and won't forget the meanings or run into problems.

Figure 14-16

More Version Control Tips

Let's look at a few other tips and tricks to help you keep track of your source code and make it easier to find, and help guard against loss.

Add Version Information to the Tombstone Comment Block

This is a simple trick that many new to programming forget to do.

Remember that you can add version information to the tombstone comments of code. This means that not only do you have a file of versions and version changes but you also have a listing of these changes in the actual source code.

How simple or detailed the version control comments you add are depends on how you feel. Here is an example of simple comments:

```
// Tombstone comments
// Widget 1.0.2
// Author: A. N. Other
// 22-10-04
//
// Code starts below.
```

Here are more detailed comments in the tombstone comment block:

```
// Tombstone comments
// Widget 1.0.2
// Author: A. N. Other
// Simple application that displays random messages on-screen
```

```
// Started: 22-10-04
// Last revision: 04-11-04
// Last revision by: A. N. Other
// Project status: In progress
//
// Code starts below.
```

There are both advantages and disadvantages to using comments in this way. The main advantage is that you keep the information right where you need it — with the file that contains the source code. That way there is little chance that the information will be separated from the code. This can be a huge advantage if you accidentally save the file somewhere unexpected (or you move the files by accident).

A disadvantage is that you have to maintain the information within the actual file as opposed to in a separate file. If you are maintaining the separate folder information file, then this can seem like hard work but in reality it's mostly a case of cutting and pasting information from one file to another.

There is another beneficial side effect of keeping version information in with the actual source code, and that is if the file is accidentally moved or saved in the wrong location you can use the search facility provided by Windows to help you look for it.

Using Windows Search

Let's say that you are looking for a file containing C++ source code that you've somehow lost on your hard drive. You know that this file has the file extension .cpp, so you could just do a search for that (see Figure 14-17).

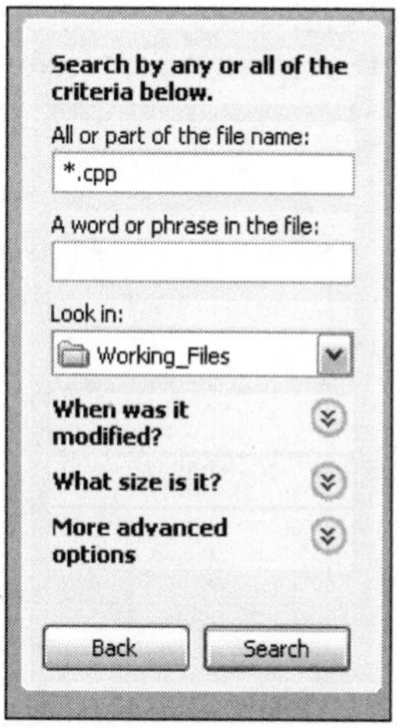

Search by any or all of the criteria below.

All or part of the file name:

`*.cpp`

A word or phrase in the file:

Look in:

Working_Files

When was it modified?

What size is it?

More advanced options

Back   Search

Figure 14-17

This will pull up all the files with the appropriate file extension (see Figure 14-18).

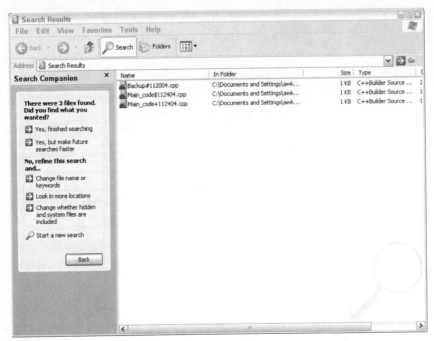

Figure 14-18

This is useful but if you have a lot of files on your system, then even narrowing down to just the files with the appropriate file extensions might not be much help. However, if you have added comments to the actual source code, you can search for these as part of searching for what the file contains (see Figure 14-19).

Figure 14-19

This can be a big help and enables you to really narrow down the search criteria, helping you to uncover the actual file you're after. You might have to be creative with the search parameters, but if you can still find the relevant folder information file then you can use the information it contains to narrow down the search criteria for you and reduce the files found during the search to something manageable (hopefully, down to just one — the right one!).

Add Summary Information to the File

When you right-click a file in Windows XP or 2000, you might notice a tab at the top of the Properties screen titled Summary, like the one shown in Figures 14-20 (Windows XP) and 14-21 (Windows 2000).

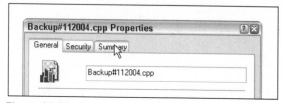

Figure 14-20

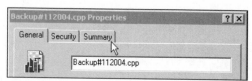

Figure 14-21

If you click on the Summary tab, you will see that it contains several text box fields that you can fill in (see Figure 14-22).

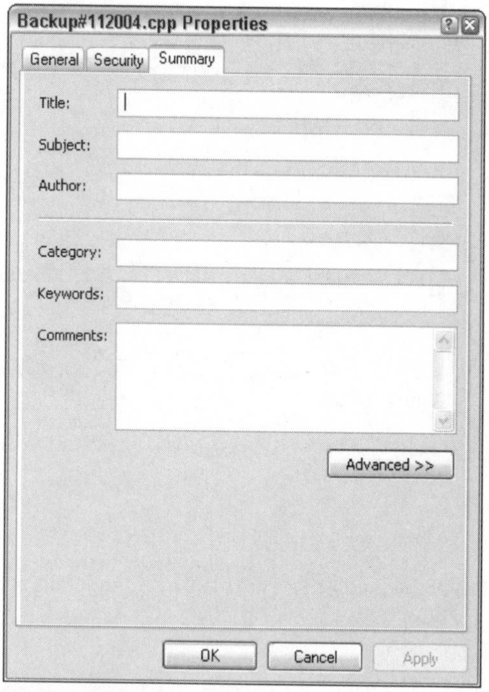

Figure 14-22

These fields are:

- ❑ Title
- ❑ Subject
- ❑ Author
- ❑ Category
- ❑ Keywords
- ❑ Comments

You will also notice a button marked Advanced >>. Clicking this button changes the properties box (see Figure 14-23) and adds more fields for you to fill in.

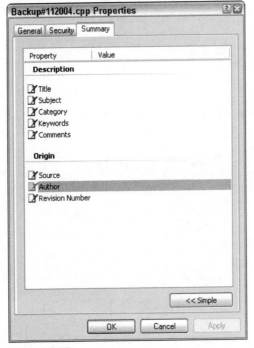

Figure 14-23

- ❑ Source
- ❑ Revision number

As you can tell from the titles of the fields, these are ideal to enter details about your source code. Figure 14-24 shows a completed summary box.

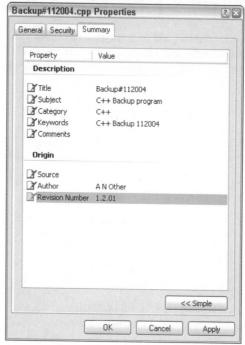

Figure 14-24

When you are done filling out the fields, click OK, and the information is automatically saved and is available for review and editing at a later stage.

You can search for information stored in the summary pane in much the same way as you'd search for any other text that the file contains. If we add the word Bimbamboozle to the summary pane, we'd search for it by looking for the same text string (see Figure 14-25).

Figure 14-25

If you choose to use the summary pane for details, you can either choose to duplicate the information here or use only one. Which approach you choose is up to you but using the summary means you keep the code cleaner.

Version Control — Looking Beyond Release

Remember that version control doesn't end with the first release of your software. If anything, your workload increases because not only will you have to control the changes made to your source code, but you will also need to keep track of different versions of the final code (whether that be interpreted code or compiled code).

The two best ways to keep track of the versions of compiled code are:

❑ Add it to the filename (see Figure 14-26) of the executable and the compressed file if you choose to compress the executable.

Backup1.20.3.exe

Figure 14-26

❑ Add it to the summary panel (see Figure 14-27). If you do this, remember to zip up the file, especially if you upload files to the Internet, because the summary information might not survive the process.

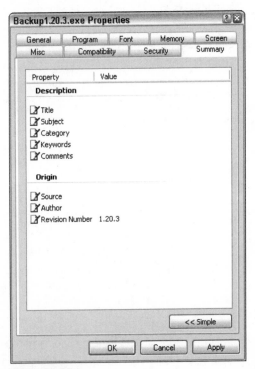

Figure 14-27

A third option is available if the compiler or program that you use to create a setup application enables you to add specific version information to the file when it is being created. If this is possible, use this in preference to the summary pane.

As well as keeping track of the version of the source and executable files, make sure that you add the version information to the actual application so that people running it know what version they have!

Software Version Control

Believe it or not, there are software applications that can help you to keep track of all the code and executables that you create while programming. Better still, there is free software that lets you do this!

Here is a quick listing of some of the best available.

- ❑ **GNU Revision Control System, `ftp://ftp.gnu.org/pub/gnu`.** A powerful, yet easy-to-use version control system, this program is unique in the fact that instead of storing complete versions of your code, it keeps track of the changes and stores only them. This is a very convenient way to keep track of your code, and it works on Windows and older DOS systems.

- ❑ **JediVCS (Version Control System), `http://www.freevcs.de`.** Previously known as FreeVCS, JediVCS is a freeware open-source version control system that comes either as a standalone version that works with any language or as versions specific for Delphi, BCB, and VC++ Expert.

- ❑ **SourceJammer, `http://sourcejammer.org`.** SourceJammer is a version control system that has been written in Java, so it should run on any system that has the Java VM (Virtual Machine).

- ❑ **Arch, `http://wiki.gnuarch.org`.** This is another version control system that is available for a variety of operating systems.

- ❑ **TortoiseCVS, `http://www.tortoisecvs.org`.** TortoiseCVS lets you perform version control actions from within the Windows Explorer file manager. You work with files directly, usually through the right-click context menu. This offers a huge advantage in that it is easy to use, but it can be slow because it is heavily integrated into the operating system. Still, it's free and easy to use and well worth checking out.

Summary

In this chapter, you've looked at how to organize yourself and your system ready for programming and also how to keep track of the different versions of the code and executables you are going to generate as you do more and more programming.

While organizing yourself is optional, organizing your PC is important if you are going to write effective code. Disorganized coding is a sure path to problems, so avoid the headaches early and prepare in advance for all the files that you will create.

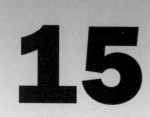

Compiling Code and Alternatives to Compiling

Compiling the source code that you spend days, weeks, or even months slaving over is generally seen as important because it not only enables the code to be tested as an application, but also acts as a milestone — each compile of source code you do means that you are getting closer to finishing.

In this chapter, we take a closer look at the process of compiling and examine the advantages and disadvantages of the process as well as look at ways to tweak and optimize the compiling process.

In addition, we also examine the alternatives to compiling that are available to you if you choose to use a scripting language instead.

Compiling Code

We've already looked at how to compile C++ code using the free Borland C++ command-line compiler. The process is relatively simple and straightforward.

1. You type the source code into a text editor.

2. The file containing the source code is saved with an appropriate file extension.

3. The compiler takes the file and the source code and processes it, creating an executable file. The file created is a standalone application that can be run on other systems.

While all compilers create an executable file that can be run, not all create an executable file that is genuinely "standalone." Some compilers, such as the one that is included with Visual Basic or the ones shipped with Borland compilers for Windows, create executable files that rely on additional files being installed on the system running the executable. An executable created by these means requires a runtime library to be installed on the system running it. The discussion of these types of libraries is beyond us here, but it's important for you to be aware that not all executables are truly standalone.

In other words, the compiling process is a process that takes code in plain-text form that is typed in by a human and is human readable (or at least, readable to some) and then converts it into a form that the computer understands.

So, you take code such as that which appears in Figure 15-1

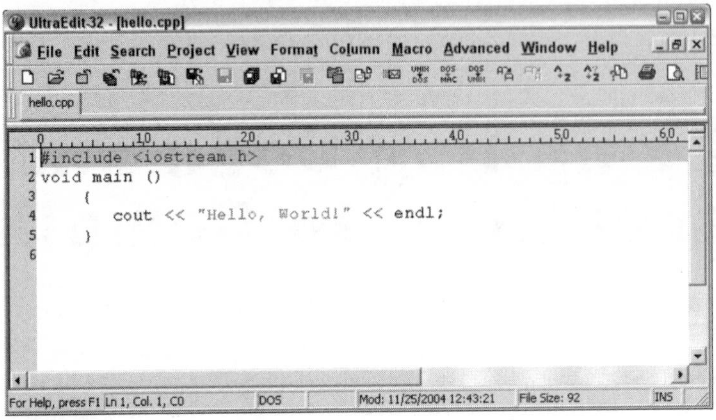

Figure 15-1

and convert it into code that looks like the code shown in Figure 15-2.

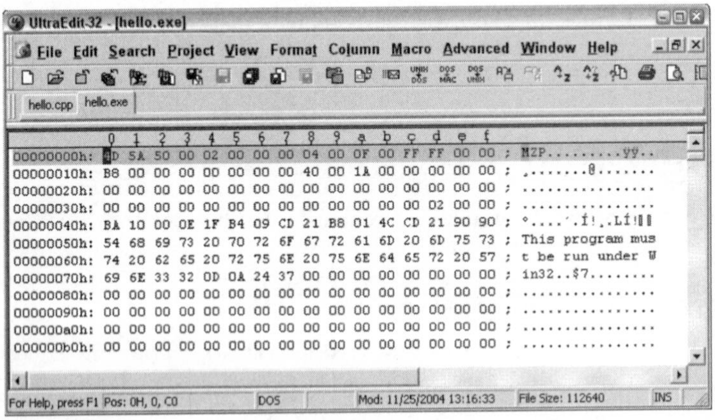

Figure 15-2

The compiler turns the source code that you typed in into code that the computer understands.

But there's more to it than that. Notice how a few lines of source code translates into many, many lines of instructions in the end application. Five lines of code (and that's including the curly braces) such as this:

```
#include <iostream.h>
void main()
    {
    cout << "Hello, World!" << endl;
    }
```

is translated into hundreds of lines of instructions in the final output. The obvious question that this leads to is "Why?"

Well, the answer is that below the surface things are far more complicated than they initially appear. Even complicated languages such as C++ in fact shield the programmer from the even harsher realities of how complex the instructions are when it gets down to a language that PCs understand. So even just writing code that outputs a line of text to the screen actually involves a lot of work behind the scenes that really isn't covered in the few lines of code you typed.

Take the instruction `cout`. This is the command used in C++ to take some data and output it to the screen. But what `cout` actually stands for is a shorthand way to represent a lot of code. You type `cout` in the source code and the compiler knows what you want to do, in this case output something to the screen, and then writes for you the code to handle this.

So, most of the code that you type just consists of shorthand notation for the compiler to create code and insert it in the application. This stops you from having to write the code yourself — so in a way it means that you don't have to keep on reinventing the wheel each time you want to do something.

This leads on to some interesting questions that need answering.

Are All Compilers the Same?

Interesting question! Let's consider for a second just the C++ language. If you do a search on the Internet, you will come across a lot of different compilers that you can use (many of which are free).

Here are a couple of alternatives to the Borland C++ compiler we've been using thus far in this book.

❑ Digital Mars, www.digitalmars.com

❑ DJGPP, www.delorie.com/djgpp

But the question is, are compilers all the same? Well, there's only one way to find out and that's to take a look.

To do this I'm going to compile some simple C++ code using the Borland compiler and the Digital Mars compiler and see if there are any differences.

The installation of these two programs is very different. With the Digital Mars compiler all you need to do is extract the files from a download into a folder, and they are ready to use. With the DJGPP compiler the setup is more complicated, and you need to carefully follow the instructions provided. I warn you now that DJGPP is not for the faint-hearted and is much stricter than either of the others, thus making it less tolerant of your code. It's a good compiler, but I don't recommend it for beginners.

The first code example we will use is a simple one based on the standard Hello, World! example (the file containing the C++ source code for this application is called `c-test.cpp`).

```
#include <iostream.h>
void main ()
   {
      cout << "This is a compiler test." << endl;
   }
```

You know how to compile this using the Borland compiler (see Figure 15-3).

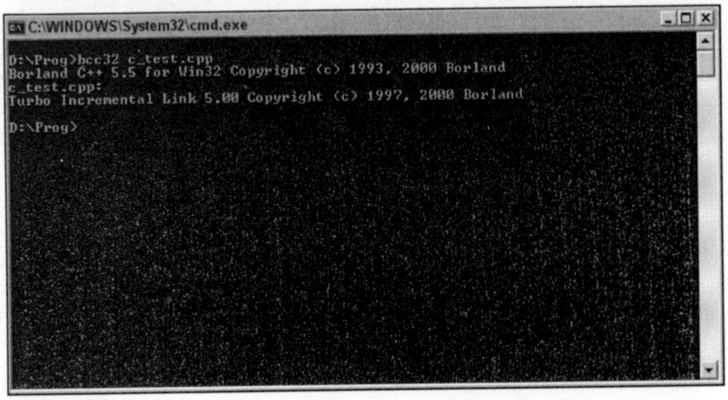

Figure 15-3

This creates a file that is 110 KB.

Now to compile this code using the Digital Mars compiler: On my system, I've installed the compiler into a folder called dm on the D: drive. The easiest way to get the compiler to work is to copy the source code into the bin folder within dm. Then you can open a command prompt and navigate to it.

Change to the D: drive (see Figure 15-4).

Figure 15-4

Change to the appropriate folder and subfolder (see Figure 15-5).

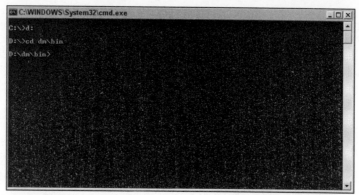

Figure 15-5

Now you can run the compiler with the following command (see Figure 15-6).

```
dmc c_test.cpp
```

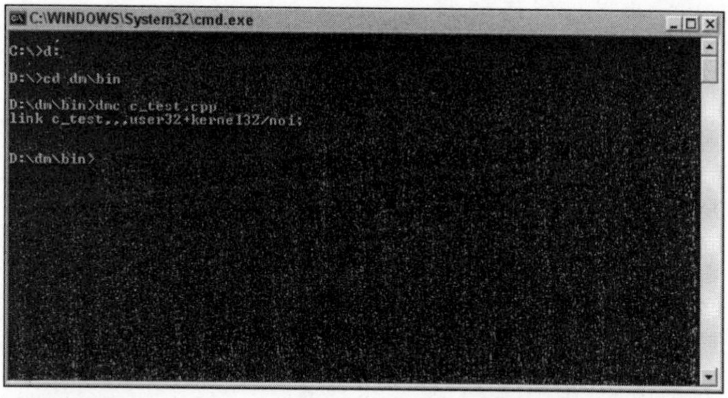

Figure 15-6

This also creates an executable file, but there are two differences you might have noticed:

❑ The Digital Mars compiler is a really fast compiler, and you should have noticed that it compiles the source code a lot more quickly than the Borland compiler.

❑ The executable is a lot smaller than the executable created by the Borland compiler, in this case 47K.

So, you can immediately see that to produce the same result (in this case, a simple result), the two compilers create different output files.

For more information about using the Digital Mars compiler, type dmc *at the command prompt and read the on-screen instructions.*

If you have a suspicious mind, you're probably thinking that the files are both the same and that the Borland compiler just adds additional information to the file somewhere. I can assure you that the files are quite different. Figure 15-7 shows the executable files made by both compilers loaded in UltraCompare (www.ultradeit.com), which is a program that can highlight the differences in the files. I've chosen a random location in the file. Differences are shown by colored blocks, while the identical points are shown uncolored. As you can see, there are quite significant differences in the files.

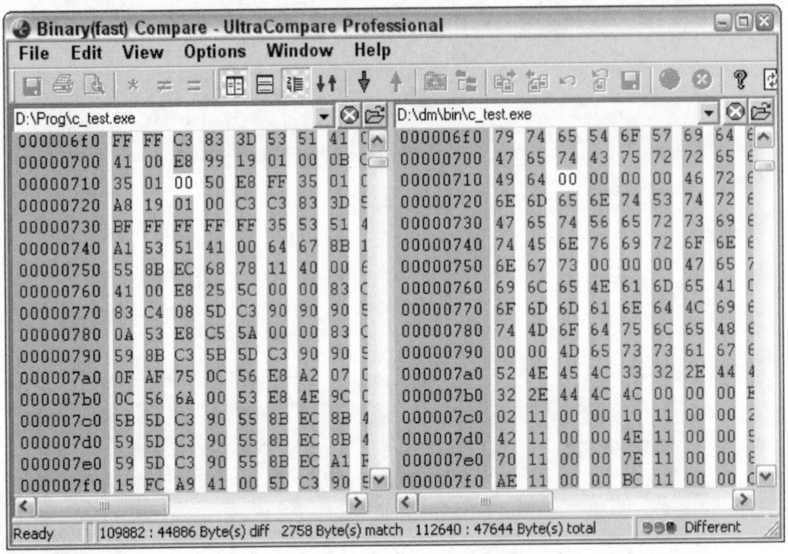

Figure 15-7

However, there are patterns of similarities within the files, as is clearly shown in Figure 15-8. The files are different, but also in some respects similar.

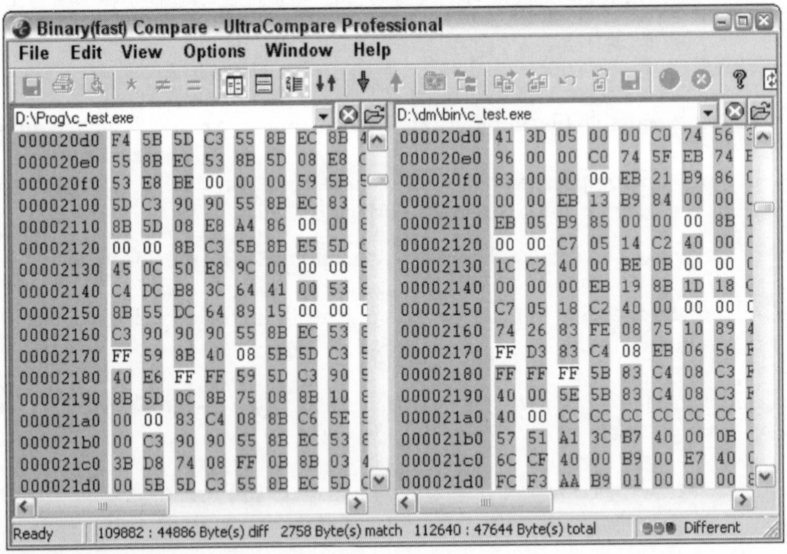

Figure 15-8

So, even though the files are definitely not the same, they're not completely dissimilar either.

Let's take a look at what happens when we compile something that's a little bit bigger with the Digital Mars compiler. Let's see if there are any differences.

For this experiment, we will use the code for the simple calculator that has the full interface.

```
#include <iostream.h>
void calc()
    {
      float num1;
      float num2;
      char op;
      float ans;
      cout << "Simple Calculator Application" << endl;
      cout << "Enter two numbers and perform an operation." << endl;
      cout << "Enjoy!" << endl;
      cout << "--------------------" << endl;
      cout << "Enter the first number and press ENTER:" << endl;
      cin >> num1;
      cout << "Enter the second number and press ENTER:" << endl;
      cin >> num2;
      cout << "You entered " << num1 << " and " << num2 << endl;
      cout
            << "Press A followed by ENTER to add the two numbers."
            << endl
            << "Press S followed by ENTER to subtract the two numbers."
            << endl
            << "Press M followed by ENTER to multiply the two numbers."
            << endl
            << "Press D followed by ENTER to divide the two numbers."
            << endl;
      cout << "--------------------" << endl;
      cin >> op;
      if (op == 65)
      {
        ans = num1 + num2;
      }
      if (op == 83)
      {
        ans = num1 - num2;
      }
      if (op == 77)
      {
        ans = num1 * num2;
      }
      if (op == 68)
      {
        ans = num1 / num2;
      }
      cout << "The answer is " << ans << endl;
      cout << "Thanks for using the calculator." << endl;
      cout << "Application now exiting ... " << endl;
    }

void helpsystem()
```

```
    {
        char op;
        cout << "Help System" << endl;
        cout << "-----------" << endl;
        cout << "To work this application you enter two numbers and then choose" <<
endl;
        cout << "whether you want those numbers added together, subtracted, " <<
endl;
        cout << "multiplied, or divided. You choose this operation by inputting" <<
endl;
        cout << "A, S, M, or D respectively." << endl;
        cout << "The result is displayed on-screen." << endl;
        cout << "Are you ready to use this applications?" << endl;
        cout << "Press Y followed by ENTER to continue." << endl;
        cout << "Press N followed by ENTER to exit." << endl;
        cout << "Press ? followed by ENTER for help." << endl;
        cin >> op;
        if (op == 89)
        {
            calc();
        }
        if (op == 63)
        {
            helpsystem();
        }
        if (op == 78)
        {

        }
    }


void main()
    {
        char op;
        cout << "Simple Calculator Application" << endl;
        cout << "Enter two numbers and perform an operation." << endl;
        cout << "Enjoy!" << endl;
        cout << "Are you ready to use this applications?" << endl;
        cout << "Press Y followed by ENTER to continue." << endl;
        cout << "Press N followed by ENTER to exit." << endl;
        cout << "Press ? followed by ENTER for help." << endl;
        cin >> op;
        if (op == 89)
        {
            calc();
        }
        if (op == 63)
        {
            helpsystem();
        }
        if (op == 78)
        {

        }
    }
```

When this code is compiled with the Borland compiler the final application is 148 KB. When we compile this code with the Digital Mars compiler the final output is 70 KB. This is nearly 80 KB smaller. Smaller applications compile faster, take up less storage space, load more quickly, and use less system resources while running.

So, in answer to the question of whether all compilers are the same, I think we can safely say that while the actual applications work in the same way, the manner in which this is achieved by the two compilers is quite different.

Error Handling

What about error handling? Do compilers treat errors in the same way?

Because errors are something that the compiler encounters that it doesn't really expect to come across it's a safe bet that the compilers aren't going to output the same error message word for word. After all, each compiler is programmed to issue error messages specific to itself and to also give error codes that help the user discover the sources of the errors for themselves.

Let's revisit this code from Chapter 9, "Debugging."

```cpp
#include <iostream.h>
void main ()
    {
        float num1;
        float num2;
        char op;
        float ans;
        cout << "Please enter a number: ";
        cin >> num1;
        cout << "Please enter another number: ";
        cin >> num2;
        cout << "Press A to add the two numbers."
              << endl
              << "Press S to subtract the two numbers."
              << endl
              << "Press M to multiply the two numbers."
              << endl
              << "Press D to divide the two numbers."
              << endl;
        cin >> op;
        if (op == 65)
          ans = num1 + num2
        if (op == 83)
          ans = num1 - num2;
        if (op == 77)
          ans = num1 * num2;
        if (op == 68)
          ans = num1 / num2;
        cout << "The answer is " << ans << endl;
    }
```

This code contains an error (as a matter if interest, can you spot it?). What you can do is to compile the code and that will give you some insight into the cause of the error.

First, compile it with the Borland compiler and remind yourself of the error that you get from that compiler (see Figure 15-9).

Figure 15-9

```
D:\Prog>bcc32 calcerr.cpp
Borland C++ 5.5 for Win32 Copyright (c) 1993, 2000 Borland
calcerr.cpp:
Error E2379 calcerr.cpp 23: Statement missing ; in function main()
*** 1 errors in Compile ***
```

There's one error on line 23. Remember what it is yet?

Before taking a look, let's compile the same code using the Digital Mars compiler. The output that you get is shown in Figure 15-10.

Figure 15-10

```
D:\dm\bin>dmc calcerr.cpp
        if (op == 83)
        ^
```

```
calcerr.cpp(23) : Error: ';' expected following declaration of struct member
--- errorlevel 1
```

Immediately you should see that this compiler gives different output. As well as giving a line number and a description of the error (the description of the error isn't as meaningful to the beginner as the one given by the Borland compiler I think), it also gives us a snippet of code — line 23 in the code.

Can you see the error yet? Let's focus on the code on either side of the error:

```
   ...
   cin >> op;
   if (op == 65)
      ans = num1 + num2
   if (op == 83)
      ans = num1 - num2;
   if (op == 77)
      ans = num1 * num2;
   ...
```

Notice where the missing semicolon is now? It's in the statement preceding line 23:

```
   ...
   cin >> op;
   if (op == 65)
      ans = num1 + num2
   if (op == 83)
      ans = num1 - num2;
   if (op == 77)
      ans = num1 * num2;
   ...
```

Remember the warning that this code gave with the Borland compiler because there is a variable declared initially that's not used?

```
#include <iostream.h>
void main ()
   {
      float num1;
      float num2;
      char op;
      int var1;
      float ans;
      var1 = 7;
      cout << "Please enter a number: ";
      cin >> num1;
      cout << "Please enter another number: ";
      cin >> num2;
      cout << "Press A to add the two numbers."
           << endl
           << "Press S to subtract the two numbers."
           << endl
           << "Press M to multiply the two numbers."
           << endl
```

```
                    << "Press D to divide the two numbers."
                    << endl;
          cin >> op;
          if (op == 65)
            ans = num1 + num2;
          if (op == 83)
            ans = num1 - num2;
          if (op == 77)
            ans = num1 * num2;
          if (op == 68)
            ans = num1 / num2;
          cout << "The answer is " << ans << endl;
      }
```

The Borland compiler gives this message (Figure 15-11).

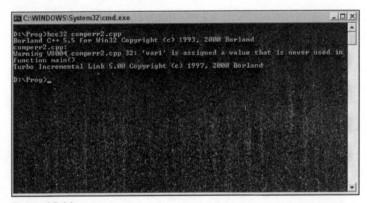

Figure 15-11

```
D:\Prog>bcc32 calcerr3.cpp
Borland C++ 5.5 for Win32 Copyright (c) 1993, 2000 Borland
calcerr3.cpp:
Warning W8004 calcerr3.cpp 32: 'var1' is assigned a value that is never used in
function main()
Turbo Incremental Link 5.00 Copyright (c) 1997, 2000 Borland
```

The code is still compiled and a working executable is created, it's just that the compiler warns you of the unused variable.

The Digital Mars compiler chooses to ignore the issue altogether and just creates the executable normally (see Figure 15-12).

```
D:\dm\bin>dmc calcerr3.cpp
link calcerr3,,,user32+kernel32/noi;
```

Figure 15-12

What about Different Languages?

Compilers for different languages require different source code as the input for the compiler. This means that the outputs are bound to be different.

Take, for example, the Java language. If you were to create a simple Hello, World! application in this language the source code you would need would look something like this:

```
public class HelloWorld
{
    public static void main(String args[])
    {
        System.out.println("Hello, World!");
    }
}
```

If you save this in the `bin` folder of the Java installation you have on your system, give it the name `HelloWorld` (to match the name of the public class), and make sure that you save it with the `.java` file extension. This means that if you changed the name of the public class, the name of the file would have to change. So, in the example that follows the name of the file would have to be `JavaTest.java`.

```
public class JavaTest
{
    public static void main(String args[])
    {
        System.out.println("Hello, World!");
    }
}
```

Refer to http://java.sun.com *for installation instructions and latest downloads.*

With this file in the `bin` folder of the Java development environment, you can now compile the file.

Command-line compiling of Java code is similar to compiling C++ code. Navigate to the `bin` folder at the command prompt and type in the following (see Figure 15-13).

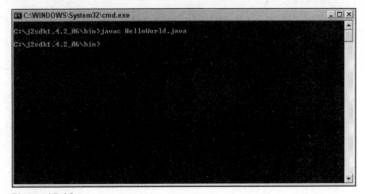

Figure 15-13

```
javac HelloWorld.java
```

The Java code will be compiled silently, and the Java equivalent of an executable created. This will be called `HelloWorld.class`, as shown in Figure 15-14.

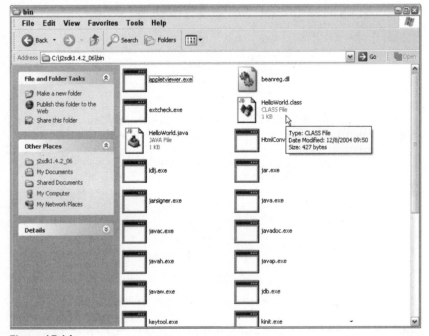

Figure 15-14

Compiled Java code is called bytecode. Java bytecode is supposed to be platform-independent, which means that it can be run on any system on which the Java runtime environment (known as the JVM or Java Virtual Machine) can be loaded.

Java compiled code isn't standalone code and requires that the Java runtime environment be loaded onto the machines running it. This isn't a big deal generally because the use of Java is widespread, but if any of your users are running Windows XP, then they might need to visit the Java site (http://java.sun.com) and download the latest Java Virtual Machine.

Let's run the code. To run the code, type in the following at the command prompt (see Figure 15-15).

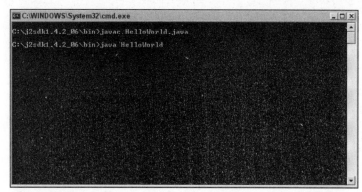

Figure 15-15

```
java HelloWorld
```

The Hello World application will now run, and the message displayed on-screen is shown in Figure 15-16.

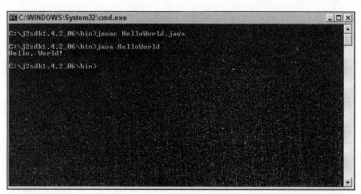

Figure 15-16

Java class files are small. In this case, the source code for this was 151 bytes (bytes, not kilobytes), equivalent to 151 characters of text (some of which are whitespace used in the formatting of the layout of the source file), while the final output class file is only 427 bytes. This small size makes Java code quite fast and also makes it ideal for use on the Internet, where the size of a file you need to send someone is a critical factor.

However, it has to be said that backing up this file and making everything work behind the scenes is the whole of the Java Virtual Machine, which in itself isn't small (the system requirement of Java under Windows calls for 125 MB of free disk space to install the Java Virtual Machine, and the final package itself uses about 10 MB).

It you take a look at the output of the Java compiler (see Figure 15-17), you'll find that the actual byte-code output when looked at in text format is surprisingly similar to the original code. You can make out the output strings, source file names, and commands within the code.

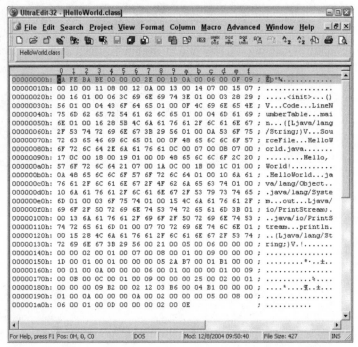

Figure 15-17

Benefits of Compiling

We've spent some time now looking at the compiling process and how different compilers handle the source code to create the final executable. But why bother to compile code in the first place? Why isn't all code processed as plain text at runtime like script is?

Let's take a look at why compiling code is important.

Protection of Intellectual Property

One of the main differences between compiled code and code used in scripting languages is that script code is stored as plain text. For the programmer this isn't a problem; in fact, it can be an advantage because the file you run and the file that you are inputting the source code into is the same file. You are working with one file, and when it comes to testing the code there is no compile stage to go through.

However, the other side of this argument is that the code that everyone else sees is the code that you wrote. As long as someone understands the language, there is nothing stopping that person from copying it, altering it, taking the best parts, and integrating it into his or her project.

Compiling code offers you, as the programmer, security from prying eyes and the rapid cutting-and-pasting ability of others. Compiling the code converts it from plain text into machine code (see Figure 15-18), which means that it's protected from being read and understood by others. This is because the compile process is one-way and can't be undone (or reverse engineered), which means that without the source code your application can't be taken back to the code it was written in, and this stops others from changing your code and stealing your ideas.

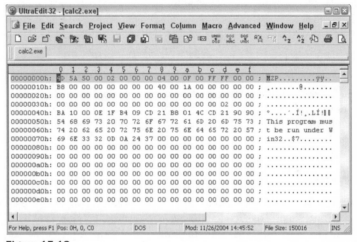

Figure 15-18

Speed

Another reason why compiling (or more accurately, using a language that needs compiling) is important is that compiled code is run by the computer a lot faster than interpreted code.

The main reason behind this improved performance is that compiled code has already been converted to machine code before it is needed, which means that precious time is saved and the applications can begin loading instantly.

Another reason why compiled code is faster than its interpreted code counterpart is that before the interpreted code can be run, the interpreter has to be run and loaded into memory, again taking time, as shown in Figure 15-19.

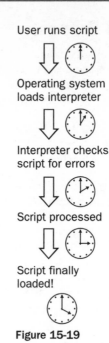

User runs script

Operating system
loads interpreter

Interpreter checks
script for errors

Script processed

Script finally
loaded!

Figure 15-19

Other speed benefits come from the fact that the compiler can optimize the code for particular operating systems, CPUs, or computers that the code is destined to be run on. This optimization can provide considerable improvements in performance, but these features are usually only present in commercial (and therefore paid-for) compilers.

Increased Functionality

Because most interpreted code is script code, which was initially designed for use on the Internet via Web browsers, the functionality of such languages is reduced as compared to a fully fledged language such as C++. There are many functions that are limited or missing from such code:

❑   Ability to create an advanced interface

❑   File handling

❑   Access to peripheral devices

❑   Ability to be integrated into the operating system

❑   Advanced memory and CPU resource handling

❑   Advanced graphics handling

Security

Because people don't have the ability to alter the code of a compiled program directly, there is less scope for others to come along and make alterations to the code. Why would someone want to make alterations to a program? There are a variety of reasons nowadays:

❑ Steal information

❑ Cause damage

❑ Steal system resources (such as Internet bandwidth)

Plain-text, uncompiled code is all open to such abuse and should not be used for applications that have significant access to a system.

Debugging

Another great reason to compile code is that the compiling process finds a lot of bugs and errors in your code. With interpreted code you have to run the code to check it, but this isn't as thorough a debug as that carried out by a compiler.

Alternatives to Compiled Code

Suppose that you want to use a scripting language for a job but you want a little more protection from others peering at your code and stealing your ideas (or even altering the code). Here are a few tricks that you can use to make your code less friendly to others.

Make Code Hard to Follow

Why make your code easy for others to read? Seems counterproductive if you don't want others to read your code.

Here are a few tips to make your code harder for others to read.

Obscure Variable Names

During development you can use names that are easy to follow to make coding easier, but this will make things easier for others reading your code. Before you release your code into circulation, you could change the variables that you've used to make them more obscure and harder to follow by others. The find and replace feature present in most text editors is ideal for this process.

Even small changes to the code make it harder to follow. Compare:

```
Dim subtotal, salestax, ordertotal
salestax = 5
subtotal = 199
ordertotal = ((subtotal / 100) * salestax) + subtotal
MsgBox("Order total is: $" & ordertotal)
```

And this:

```
Dim xxyyxx, chhhcch, yyffyffy
chhhcch = 5
xxyyxx = 199
yyffyffy = ((xxyyxx / 100) * chhhcch) + xxyyxx
MsgBox("Order total is: $" & yyffyffy)
```

Make sure that you keep a copy of the original code in case you want to carry out changes to it or make alterations in the future—no point making things hard on yourself!

Whitespace

The whitespace in code can make it easier to follow because the layout adds visual structure to the meaning of the code. Making alterations to this whitespace can make code harder to follow.

However, removing whitespace that the code contains isn't the most effective thing you can do (because we are used to reading from the left-hand edge of the page). In fact, the most effective thing you can do is add extra space and carriage returns to the code. Compare:

```
Dim subtotal, salestax, ordertotal
salestax = 5
subtotal = 199
ordertotal = ((subtotal / 100) * salestax) + subtotal
MsgBox("Order total is: $" & ordertotal)
```

with:

```
                 Dim subtotal, salestax, ordertotal
        salestax = 5
                         subtotal = 199


         ordertotal = ((subtotal / 100) * salestax) + subtotal
                MsgBox("Order total is: $" & ordertotal)
```

Combine this technique with the previous one and you get a really effective way to protect your code:

```
        Dim xxyyxx, chhhcch, yyffyffy
                                    chhhcch = 5
    xxyyxx = 199


            yyffyffy = ((xxyyxx / 100) * chhhcch) + xxyyxx
                MsgBox("Order total is: $" & yyffyffy)
```

This does add extra load to the code because each character, even whitespace characters, means an extra byte in the code, but as long as you don't overuse this method it shouldn't add a significant number of bytes to the code (1,000 whitespace characters equals 1 KB).

Script Encoding

The great thing about using the Microsoft Windows operating system is that there are a lot of cool tools that you can download and use from the Microsoft Web site. One of these tools is called the Microsoft Script Encoder.

This application takes code written using VBScript or JScript (Microsoft's version of JavaScript) and encodes it to make it pretty much impossible for another person to read, but it can still be understood by the Windows operating system.

The application is a Script Encoder. It encodes the script as opposed to encrypting it. Encryption is different to encoding, but the difference is subtle. With both you take a file and change its format, but with encryption the file is unusable until it is decrypted. Encoding changes the file from the point of view of a human reader, but the script engine can still understand what the file does. If the file were encrypted, the contents would not be accessible to any person or applications without the appropriate password or passphrase.

The Microsoft Script Encoder installation file is available free from Microsoft as a small download (it is about 130 KB) from `www.microsoft.com/scripting`.

The Microsoft Script Encoder is available for the following languages:

- ❑ English
- ❑ Chinese (Traditional)
- ❑ German
- ❑ Korean

Installing the Microsoft Script Encoder is easy. Locate the download (the English language version is called `sce10en.exe`, while the Chinese version is called `sce10cht.exe`; the German version, `sce10de.exe`; and the Korean version, `sce10ko.exe`). Double-click it and follow the prompts.

The default installation location for the command-line application and the help files is `C:\Program Files\Windows Script Encoder`.

As well as installing the command-line application and the help file, the installation application also modifies the Windows registry so that the system recognizes `.vbe` and `.jse` files (VBScript Encoded Script files and JScript Encoded Script files, respectively).

Installation of the Microsoft Script Encoder is not required for running encoded script files. Only the programmer needs to install the encoder.

The Microsoft Script Encoder is a command-line utility and doesn't come with a Windows interface. This means that it's not as easy to use as a GUI application. However, it's not particularly difficult to use.

The Microsoft Script Encoder doesn't do any encoding itself but rather uses the scripting runtime module file (called `scrrun.dll`) already present in Windows to do the encoding for it. This is the file that interprets and runs VBScript and JavaScript already, and all the Script Encoder executable does is provide a command-line mechanism for carrying out the encoding.

Because the installation program doesn't add the path to the encoder to the PATH system environment variable, it isn't available from every folder in a command prompt window. To ensure that using the Microsoft Script Encoder is smooth and trouble-free, we recommend you do one of the following:

- ❑ Add the path to the Microsoft Script Encoder (the default path is `C:\Program Files\Windows Script Encoder`) to the PATH system variable (consult your system manual or help files on how to do this).

❑　Copy the Microsoft Script Encoder executable (`screnc.exe`) to the folder you will be using for script encoding.

❑　Copy all of the scripts you want to encode to the folder used by the Microsoft Script Encoder.

For clarity and simplicity, you will copy all the scripts that you'll be encoding to the folder used by the Microsoft Script Encoder. This is the easiest way to use the encoder.

The easiest way to familiarize yourself with the syntax of the Microsoft Script Encoder is to begin using it. Open a command prompt window and navigate to `C:\Program Files\Windows Script Encoder`. Once there, type the following:

```
screnc /?
```

This will make the application list the help for the application. This can be a very useful reference when you are in a hurry! The output is shown in Figure 15-20.

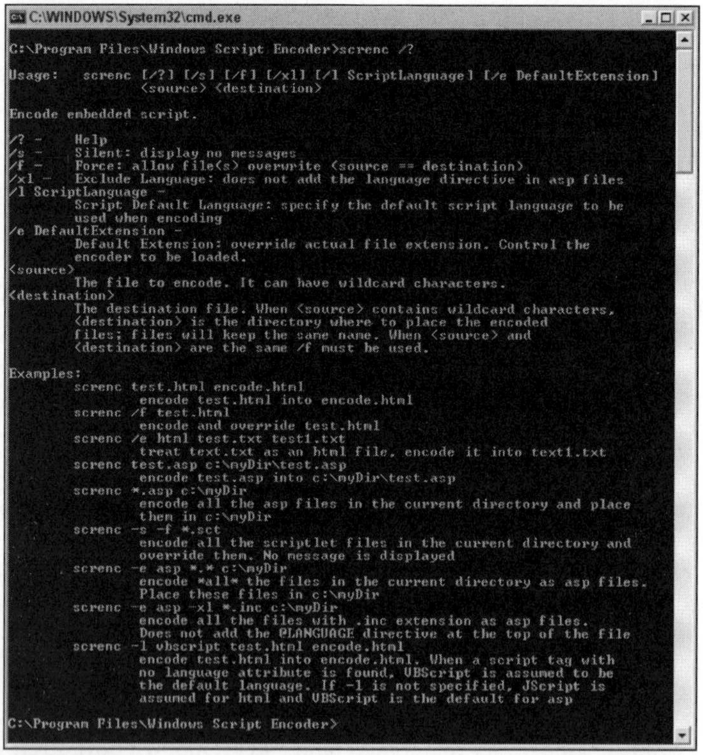

Figure 15-20

The basic syntax for the Microsoft Script Encoder is:

```
screnc inputfile outputfile
```

❏ **inputfile.** Required. This is the name of the input file to be encoded, and it can include any necessary path information relative to the current directory.

❏ **outputfile.** Required. This is the name of the output file to be produced, and it can include any necessary path information relative to the current directory.

What follows are a few examples of the use of the Microsoft Script Encoder, each accompanied by a brief explanation of the results:

To encode the input file `unencoded.htm` and produce an output file called `encoded.htm`, use:

```
screnc unencoded.vbs encoded.vbe
```

So, for example, let's say that we have a VBScript file that contains the following code:

```
' Adrian Kingsley-Hughes
' 02 Dec 2004
' This script prompts the user for his or her name.
' It incorporates various greetings depending on input by the user.
'
' Added alternative greeting
' Changed variable names to make them more readable

Dim PartingGreeting
Dim VisitorName

VisitorName = PromptUserName

If VisitorName <> "" Then
    PartingGreeting = "Hello, " & VisitorName & ". Nice to have met you."


Else
    PartingGreeting = "I'm glad to have met you, but I wish I knew your name."
End If

MsgBox PartingGreeting


Function PromptUserName

    ' This Function prompts the user for his or her name.
    ' It incorporates various greetings depending on input by the user.
    Dim YourName
    Dim Greeting

    YourName = InputBox("Hello! What is your name?")

    If YourName = "" Then
        Greeting = "OK. You don't want to tell me your name."
    Else
```

```
        Greeting = "Hello, " & YourName & ", great to meet you."
    End If

    MsgBox Greeting

    PromptUserName = YourName

End Function
```

If you saved this file as unencoded.vbs and ran the command given above to encode it into a file called encoded encoded.vbe this file would contain the following:

```
#@~^eQQAAA==v,b[MkmxPLPnrxT/s+HOu;Tt+k@#@&EP
F~6mDPy!T&@#@&EPPtbdPkm.raYP2.K:2Yk~Dtn,Ek+D,0K.PDtnkMPUCs+R@#@&B,qY,rUmKDaW.lOnkP-
lMrW!/~LM++Or        odP9na+U9k
oPKx,rxaEOP(X~O4+P!d+MR@#@&v~@#@&B,b[Nn[,lsY□.xmYr-□Po.n□YrxT@#@&B~;tmxo□N,-
lMkC4^+~Um:+k~YKP:mVnPDt□:~:G.□P.+m[l(Vn~@#@&@#@&9b:~nm.DkUTMM++Dk
L@#@&fr:,.rdbYWMHls+@#@&@#@&.b/bYGDHCs+~',KDK:20`/+.Hm:nP@#@&@#@&(6Pjk/bYK.1m:nP@!@
*~ErPK4nx@#@&P,~~nmDDkUo!.□+OkLP{PEu□VVGS,J~[,#b/rDWM1ls+,'PrR~1bmn~DWP4C\□P:□O~XKE
cJ@#@&~@#@&@#@&2^d+@#@&~~,PnC.DkUoV.□+ObxTP',J&v:,os19POG,tl7nPs+Y,zGEBP(EOP(~Skdt,
(P0xnA,XW;.,xC:□
r@#@&Ax9Pq6@#@&@#@&t/LAK6~KmDYbUoVD+□OrxT@#@&@#@&@#@&@#@&s;xlOkKx~KMW:20`/nDgCs+@#@
&@#@&PP,PE~K4kdPwEU^DkW ~wMW:aOdPDt□P;/n.,0GD,Ot□k.~1:n
@#@&~P,~EP(DPbxmKDaGDmYn/,\C.bWEk~oM++DrUokP9+2+U[bxLPKUPbx2;DP4z~DtnP!d□D
@#@&,PP,fbhPIW;Dglhn,@#@&,~P,fks~!D□+DkUo@#@&@#@&~P,~5KE.Hm:+~x,qUw!O~WavJ_+V^We~Pq
tCY,kd~HWEM~xm:+QEb@#@&@#@&P~P-(6PeW!.1m:n~{PJE~:tnx@#@&,P~,P,PPVD□nYbxLP{PE6nRP,eW
!PNKUvY,hmxOPOG,YnV^~:□PzG!DPUCs+
J@#@&,P~,2^/+@#@&,~P,P~P,M.n□YkLP{PJ_nsVK~,J~[~eKE.1mh+,[~EBPo.nmY~YK~s+nDPHWEcJ@#@
&P,P~2
N~(6@#@&@#@&P,PPtdLAK6,M.+nObxL@#@&@#@&,P~~hDWh2Djd+MHm:n,',5W!DgC:□@#@&@#@&2U[,sE^
YbWxh0UBAA==^#~@
```

You can control which part of the script is encoded by using script markers from within the code:

```
'**Start Encode**
```

Note that this marker begins with the VBScript comment tag — don't leave this out!

This allows you to encode only part of the script:

```
' Adrian Kingsley-Hughes
' 02 Dec 2004
' This script prompts the user for his or her name.
' It incorporates various greetings depending on input by the user.
'
' Added alternative greeting
' Changed variable names to make them more readable

Dim PartingGreeting
Dim VisitorName

VisitorName = PromptUserName
```

```
'**Start
Encode**#@~^IAMAAA==@#@&qW,.b/kDWMHls+~@!@*PEE,Kt☐U@#@&PP,~KlMYbxLM.n☐YrxT~',Jun^VW
S~rP'PjrkkOKDgl:☐PL~JcPHk1+~OKPtm-
+,:+D~zW!Rr@#@&P@#@&@#@&3Vkn@#@&P~~,nl.ObxLMMn☐Yro,'PrqEhPTVCN,YG~41\☐~:☐YPHG;~,4!Y
~q~Ab/4P&~3+A~HWE.~lh+cE@#@&3N,q0@#@&@#@&Hko$WXPKCMYkLMM++DrUo@#@&@#@&@#@&@#@&wEUmD
rWPK.K:wOik+.1mh☐@#@&@#@&,PP,B,Ptb/~s!x^ObWx,2DK:wDd~Y4+,Ed+.~6W.PD4+bD~Um:+
@#@&P~P,v,qO,kmWMwK.1D+dP71.rKE/,LD☐+YbUL/,N☐wnx[ro~W~kw;O,4X~O4+~EknMR@#@&P,PPGks~
5KE.1m:n~@#@&P,~PGk:,!.+☐YbxL@#@&@#@&P~P,eW!DHCs+Px~&x2ED$K6crC☐VVK",~☐41OPb/~zKED,
Uls+grb@#@&@#@&,P~P(W,5GEMHls+~x,JJ~P4+U@#@&~,P~,P,PMM+☐Oko~',J6FcPPIGE,NWvOPSlY~YG
~D+sV,h+,XG;MPxCh☐RE@#@&~,P~AVk+@#@&P,~P,P~PVDnnDkxT~',JC☐ssWBPrP'PeG!DH1snPLPES,oD
nCDPOW,h☐+O,XKERr@#@&~P,P3x9P(W@#@&@#@&~P,PHkL$WXPVDn+Or
o@#@&@#@&P,P~KMW:2O`/nDgCs+~{PIWEM1mh+@#@&@#@&Ax[~wEx1OkKxyNoAAA==^#~@
```

This allows you to do something that is quite interesting — add a copyright notice to your code that users can't change it because if they do change it, then the code picks up on it.

```
Dim strCopyright
strCopyright = "This script is copyright to me, 2004!"
'**Start Encode**
If strCopyright = "This script is copyright to me, 2004!" Then
    MsgBox "Copyright notice is unaltered. Script cleared to continue ..."
    MsgBox "Script  continues ..."
  Else
    MsgBox "Copyright notice is altered!!! Script halted!"
  End If
```

The line of code that checks that the copyright notice is unaltered will be encoded and checked when the script is run, and it can pick up on changes made here — a handy way to make sure that copyright notices remain unchanged!

Encoded Scripts — Dos and Don'ts

Before and after encoding there are a few dos and don'ts you should follow to ensure trouble-free scripts after encoding:

Dos

❑ Do keep a plain-text, unencoded, backup of the script.

❑ Take care that you use the .vbe file extension for encoded VBScript files and .jse for encoded JScript files.

❑ Do remove comments prior to encoding — after encoding they are useless and can add a significant bulk to the script.

❑ Do test the script before and after it is encoded to make sure that it works.

Don'ts

❑ Don't make any changes to the script once it's encoded.

❑ Don't leave testing and debugging until the script is encoded!

❑ Don't expect script encoding to offer 100 percent code security. There are ways that the determined script snooper can get around it (which I'm not covering here!).

Summary

In this chapter, you've seen the benefits of compiling code and how different compilers can create different output files for the same source code even though the programming language used is the same. You've also seen how some compilers are faster than others and how two compilers output executable files with significantly different file sizes.

You have also seen how different programming languages result in different executables — some of which are standalone, while others require runtime libraries in order to work.

You've also taken a look at ways you can help to make plain text script harder for code snoops to read, as well as looking at how you can use the Microsoft Script Encoder to encode your script to help protect it from those who would borrow your code.

Distributing Your Project

It's been a long road, but finally you're done. The project was conceived, the plan of action drawn up, the code written, tested, compiled, debugged, fixed, and recompiled. You have your project.

But what next? What do you do now?

This chapter examines the options open to you for distributing your project to others so that others can benefit from what you did.

> *Here's a final note on rights to distribute your applications. Remember to check the license agreement of any compilers that you've used to make sure what your rights are when it comes to distribution. Some license agreements might allow you to distribute code without restriction, while others prohibit "commercial" releases (that is, it prohibits you from selling what you've created).*
>
> *Check and stay legal!*

Types of Distribution

It's now time to think about distribution of your project. The main choice you have to make is decide on the best way to get your project to those that might be interested in it.

There are two types of distribution realistically open to you, and both are discussed in detail in the following sections:

- ❑ Physical distribution
- ❑ Virtual distribution

Physical Distribution

Physical distribution was, until recently, the main way that all software was distributed. Physical distribution involves copying your project onto a data media of one type or another and distributing the media to those interested in your project (as depicted in Figure 16-1).

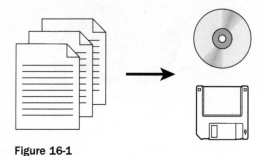

Figure 16-1

There are a number of different media that you can easily make use of to distribute your project:

❑ Floppy disk

❑ CD

❑ DVD

Each of these media types has advantages and disadvantages.

Floppy Disk

The floppy disk, shown in Figure 16-2, used to be the staple media for project distribution.

There are a number of advantages and disadvantages to using floppy disks.

Advantages

❑ **Cheap.** A floppy disk costs cents and is cheap and widely available.

❑ **Widespread availability of disks.** Disks are easily bought from PC stores, office supplies, and even many general stores. They can be bought in large bulk quantities.

❑ **Reuse.** Disks can be reused easily, but the disk can also be locked to prevent overwriting through the use of the lock tab on the rear (shown in Figure 16-3).

❑ **Easily personalized.** Floppy disks can be easily and quickly personalized by printing out labels for attachment to the disks. These labels can be bought in bulk and printed on most home printers.

❑ **Most PCs have floppy drives.** Floppy drives are common in most PC systems (a typical drive is shown in Figure 16-4).

Figure 16-2

Figure 16-3

Figure 16-4

Disadvantages

❏ **Capacity.** The capacity of a floppy disk is relatively poor — 1.44 MB. This generally means that all but the smallest and simplest of projects require more than one floppy disk to hold the files. The low capacity means the end user will probably need to juggle multiple disks.

❏ **Slow to fill.** A floppy disk can take to 2 to 3 minutes to fill with data. If the disk needs to the formatted before it can be used, then the time to create one disk can be as much as 5 minutes. That's 5 minutes for less than 11/2 MB!

❏ **Slow to read.** Reading floppy disks and copying data off them is a slow process too, requiring many minutes.

❏ **Unreliable.** Floppy disks are prone to damage from dirt, dust, heat, magnetic fields, user accidents, and much more.

❏ **Overwriting.** Floppy disks can be overwritten accidentally by the end user and are susceptible to damage from viruses.

❏ **Floppy drives.** While many systems have floppy drives, some don't, and systems without floppy droves (especially laptops) are becoming more and more common.

CDs

Over the last 10 years, CDs (compact discs) has replaced the floppy disks for most software distribution purposes (shown in Figure 16-5).

Figure 16-5

Advantages

❏ **Capacity.** CDs have an enormous capacity — up to 700 MB. This is equivalent to over 480 floppy disks!

❏ **Cheap.** CDs cost pennies and are available in bulk quantities.

❏ **Reliability.** CDs are very robust and can survive long-term harsh use.

❏ **Proliferation of CD drives.** Many PCs have CD drives, giving CD distribution broad appeal.

❏ **Labeling.** There are several systems available that let you personalize and label CDs easily using a home printer.

❏ **Overwriting.** CDs cannot be overwritten by the end user, making them resistant to accidental overwriting and virus damage.

❏ **Easy to create.** It's quick, easy, and cheap to create CDs, with the easy availability of CD burner drives, burning software, and writable discs. Figure 16.6 shows the Disc Creation Wizard in the CD/DVD recording software Nero (for more information visit www.nero.com).

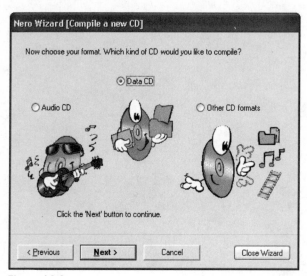

Figure 16-6

❏ **Fast to create.** A CD can be burned on a modern CD burner driver in minutes and duplication is quick and easy.

❏ **Speedy for the end user.** A CD is quick to read, and the data can be copied off it quickly.

Disadvantages

❏ **Capacity.** Just as capacity can be an advantage, it can be a disadvantage — writing a small file to a disc that will hold 700 MB is wasteful.

❏ **Variable quality.** CDs can be of variable quality, and some brands are better than others. Some brands can also be problematic with certain CD drives. Test several different brands and pick the best for you. A lot of information can be found at www.cdfreaks.com.

❑   **Labeling.** Labeling of a CD is a slower job than labeling a floppy disk because of the fact that you have to get the label properly centered. Many gadgets and devices exist to help you do this accurately.

For one range of labeling products, see www.neato.com.

❑   **Cost.** While discs are cheap, jewel cases and labeling materials can add significantly to the cost of using CDs.

❑   **Certain weaknesses.** CDs, while being quite robust, are susceptible to certain kinds of damage, especially spiral scratches and damage to the reflective label side of the disc (as shown in Figure 16-7).

Figure 16-7

DVD

DVDs (the acronym stands for *digital versatile disc*, and not, as is commonly believed, digital video disc) are the latest disc media to hit the market. Like other media, they too have advantages and disadvantages. A typical disc is shown in Figure 16-8.

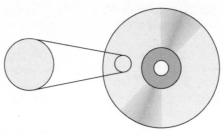

Figure 16-8

Advantages

❑ **Capacity.** DVD discs offer tremendous capacity — 4.7 GB, which equates to over six and a half CDs, or a whopping 3,250 floppy disks!

❑ **Speed.** You can burn data onto a DVD faster than on a CD.

Disadvantages

❑ **Cost.** While the cost per megabyte of DVD is low, the overall cost of discs is higher than that of CDs, which makes then unsuitable if you don't need their massive storage capacity. Remember too that you need to factor in the cost of cases for the DVDs, as well as labeling.

❑ **Capacity.** As with CDs, you will probably be reluctant to want to put small amounts of data on a DVD — a handy rule of thumb is to reserve DVD discs for when you need more capacity than offered by two CDs (1.4 GB).

❑ **Vulnerable to damage.** Like CDs, DVDs are vulnerable to damage, especially on the label side.

❑ **Drive availability.** Remember that not all systems will have DVD drives — especially laptop systems or systems older than 3 to 4 years.

Burning Discs

Burning discs (both CDs and DVDs) is both quick and easy. All you need to start up your own studio is:

❑ A suitable CD/DVD burner (writable drive)

❑ Software

❑ Discs

❑ Labeling gear (optional)

CD/DVD Burner

This is the drive that you will use to create your CDs/DVDs. There are many names that these drives go by, the two most common being:

❑ CD/DVD writers

❑ CD/DVD burners

You can choose between a drive that can create CDs, DVDs, or both. If you are buying a new drive, it is probably best that you get a drive that can create both CDs and DVDs.

Externally these drives look just like any other CD or DVD drive, but they are different in that they contain a laser capable of altering the color of the dye that is embedded in the disc.

Before burning, the disc is a uniform color. After burning, the laser has burned the digital data onto the surface of the disc, altering the dye and giving the reading lasers something to pick up on. See Figure 16-9.

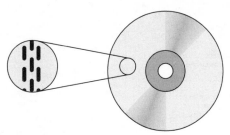

Figure 16-9

CD and DVD burners are capable of reading discs too.

Different drives can burn discs at different speeds. If a drive burns data onto a disc at the same speed that a standard drive reads the data off the disc (a rate of nearly 9 MB per minute) then the drive would be known as one speed, or 1x.

The read speed is equivalent to the speed that an audio CD is played in a CD player. A 700 MB CD can hold 80 minutes of audio.

1x speed drives would be very slow and would take 80 minutes to burn a disc — very slow and cumbersome indeed! To overcome this, faster and faster drives have been released and nowadays you can get a drive that write discs at 52x, or 52 speed, reducing burn time down to about 2 minutes.

Rewritable CDs (CDs that can be written to and erased many times) have to be burned at a lower speed.

Generally, drive specifications are given as something like 52x 32x 52x, which means 52 speed write for standard discs, 32 speed write for rewritable discs, and a CD read speed of 52.

DVD drives don't burn at the same speed. A good DVD burner burns at maybe 8x or 16x, which means that a full DVD can be burned in 8 and 16 minutes, respectively.

These speeds are relative to the standard read speed of a DVD drive – about 1.5 MB per second.

There are other things to look for on "burner" drives. One such feature helps prevent wasted discs through the interruption of the data flow to the disc. This feature is known by various names that include *buffer underrun protection* and *Burnproof*. This feature is available on most higher-quality drives (which generally only cost a few dollars more than cheap drives), but it repays you in saved time and a reduction in spoilt discs.

Chapter 16

Burning Software

Once you have the hardware, it's time to think about the software. There are literally hundreds of software packages available that can be used to create and burn CDs but the best at producing professional results at a low price is Nero by Ahead Software, as shown in Figure 16-10.

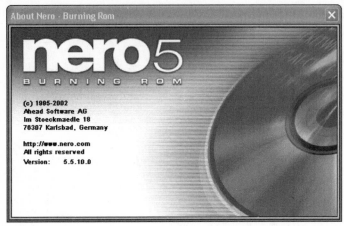

Figure 16-10

Nero makes creating CDs and DVDs easy! The process is as follows:

1. Choose the type of disc that you want to create (as shown in Figure 16-11). Here we can only create CDs (because there is no DVD burner on the system).

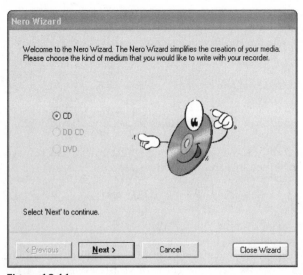

Figure 16-11

2. Next, choose what you want to do. In Figure 16-12 I have chosen to compile a new CD.

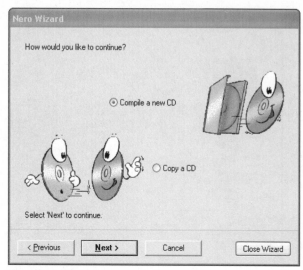

Figure 16-12

3. Choose the CD type. You want to create a standard data CD, as shown in Figure 16-13.

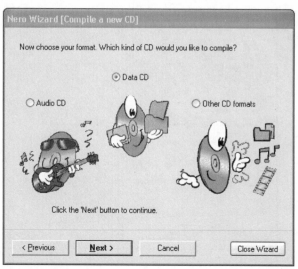

Figure 16-13

4. Choose whether to create a new CD or continue with an existing CD (see Figure 16-14). You will choose to create a new CD.

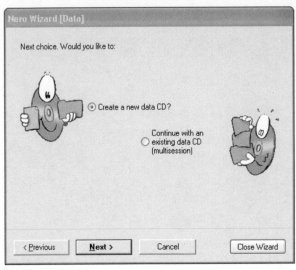

Figure 16-14

5.   Click Finish. This doesn't finish the process; instead it configures the settings of the CD/DVD being burned (see Figure 16-15).

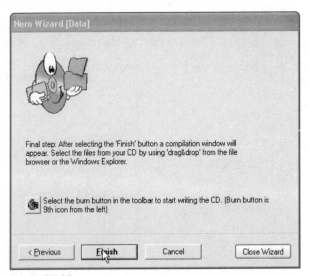

Figure 16-15

6.   Now you are ready to add the files that you want copied to the CD. In the right-hand pane of Nero, navigate to the folder that contains the file or files that you want copied to the CD (see Figure 16.16).

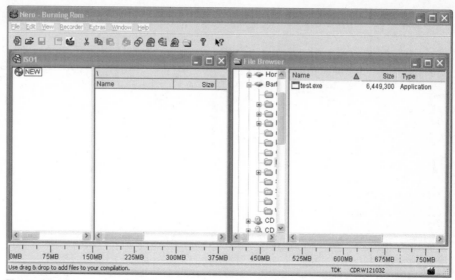

Figure 16-16

7. Drag the files and folders that you want to copy from the right-hand pane to the left-hand panel, as shown in Figure 16-17.

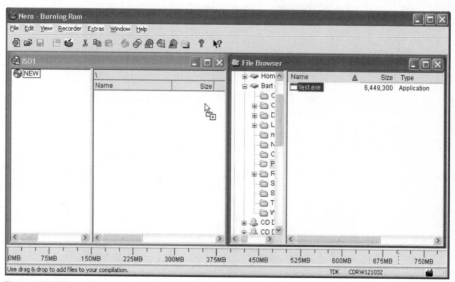

Figure 16-17

8. Once you have copied the files, you need to make sure that you have a blank CD in the burner drive and then click the Burn CD icon shown in Figure 16.18.

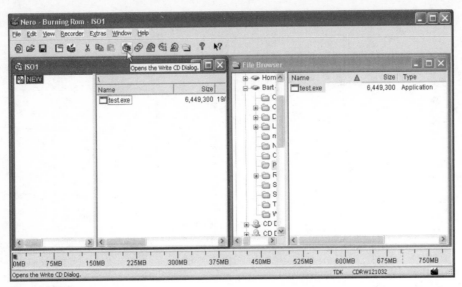

Figure 16-18

9. Once you've clicked on the Burn CD icon, a confirmation dialog box will be displayed that asks you to confirm what's to be done next and the speed of burning. This is shown in Figure 16-19.

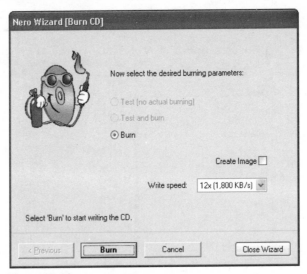

Figure 16-19

10. The disc will now be burned, and once the disc is completed (see Figure 16-21), it will be ejected.

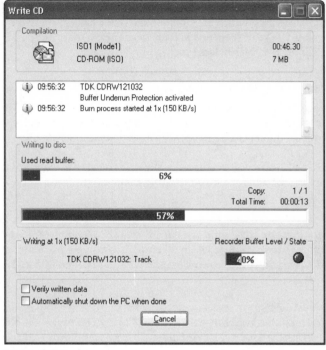

Figure 16-20

11. The process is done, and you can go ahead and label the disc as needed and place it in a case for protection.

CD/DVDs

CDs or DVDs are a key component in the software distribution. There are hundreds of different discs available, but they generally fall into three categories:

- ❑ Cheap discs
- ❑ Fast discs
- ❑ Rerecordable discs

Cheap Discs

Cheap discs are just that—bulk-buy cheap CD or DVD discs. These can be good, but they can also be a false economy because you can get a high number of failures when using them. The other problem is that they are less tolerant of damage and exposure to environmental factors (especially sunlight).

The other problem with cheap discs is that they are normally only rated as low-speed discs, which means that you end up having to burn them at a lower speed than the drive is rated for to reduce errors and dud discs.

Fast Discs

Fast discs are high-quality discs, which are suited to the faster drives. These are more expensive and higher quality. The ability to burn them at a higher speed means that you spend less time on the actual burning, so you can do more copies in less time.

Rerecordable Discs

Rerecordable discs are much more expensive than standard "use once" discs. They are good if you're making backups for yourself or are passing software to someone who will give you the disc back, but are not so good for distribution because people can alter them and delete them.

The other drawback is that rerecordable discs are slower to burn than standard discs. This means that there is little sense in using them for software distribution.

Labeling

It's not a requirement that you label your discs in any way; however, unlabeled discs look unprofessional and can easily get lost or confused with other discs. If you are planning on creating many discs for distribution, consider investing in a labeler. Using labels will make your discs look professional and stand out.

Don't label discs with anything other than labels designed for discs. Sticking anything on a CD or DVD not designed for it can damage the disc and also unbalance the weight distribution of the disc, which means it will be very noisy in the drive and possibly damage it.

Also, another risk of using incorrect labels is that they can come off in the drive and damage it.

Packaging

You have many choices when it comes to packaging your physical distribution package:

❑ Simple packaging

❑ Customized packaging

❑ Elaborate packaging

Simple Packaging

Simple packaging is the minimum that you can get away with to protect the CD and provide basic information to the end user. A simple label and CD sleeve that goes into the jewel case or plastic sleeve is basic but adequate packaging. Refer to Figure 16-21.

What you put on the label and sleeve is up to you but the minimum should be:

❑ Program name

❑ Version number

❑ Author contact (Web address, e-mail address)

❑ Basic copyright information

❑ Type of disc (CD or DVD)

❑ Basic setup or installation instructions

Widget 1.02
Adrian Kingsley-Hughes
www.kingsley-hughes.com
(c) 2004

To install click on
"Start" then "Run"
then type "d:\setup"
and click OK.

Figure 16-21

Customized Packaging

Customized packaging means making more effort with the packaging. This can mean logos and graphics and perhaps a user manual or separate installation instructions.

Remember that these all add more complexity and cost to the project, and if you make changes to your application you may need to alter the packaging, so don't print out more than you think you'll need.

Elaborate Packaging

This means becoming even more elaborate and getting boxes and covers made. This usually adds a significant amount to the cost unless you are dealing with high volumes and is not suited to small- or even medium-scale distributions.

Virtual Distribution

As you can probably guess, virtual distribution involves using the Internet as a distribution medium for your project. Before the Internet became mainstream, physical distribution was the only option available to most people, but even back then pioneering programmers were harnessing the power of electronic distribution by uploading their software to BBs, or bulletin boards, for others to download. Things are much more elaborate now and as always, there are pros and cons to using the Internet as a software distribution system.

Pros of Virtual Distribution

There are a huge number of benefits to virtual software distribution:

❑ **Cheap.** Very cheap, for that matter. You don't need CD burners, discs, labeling gear, or to bother with sleeves and stuff. All you need is an Internet connection and somewhere to upload the software to.

❑ **Available 24/7.** Anyone wanting your software can have it quickly and easily. No need to wait for the product to be delivered through the mail.

❑ **Speed.** There are a lot of speed benefits — speed of updating the product, no need to bother with burning CDs or DVDs, speed of making new version available. The Internet is all about speed, and it is the fastest way to make software and projects available.

❑ **Massive audience.** There's no bigger audience to tap into!

❑ **Direct communication with the public.** A Web site lets you to talk directly to your users and potential users in a way that no other medium allows you to.

Cons of Virtual Distribution

Before you use the Internet as a medium for distributing your software, there are a few things you need to bear in mind.

❑ **Unauthorized distribution.** There is no doubt that the Internet has encouraged the unauthorized distribution of software and unless you want to get clever or invest a lot of money in special software, it is hard to protect against it (and even then it's virtually impossible to make anything that guarantees protection).

❑ **No access to non-Internet customers.** The problem with using the Internet as a means to distribute software is that you cannot tap into the small but significant unwired market.

❑ **News travels fast.** One thing that you need to be careful of with the Internet is that if you release a version of a software project that has a problem with it, that news could travel around very fast.

❑ **Be prepared to be reviewed.** One thing that netizens like to do is review stuff, and if your product gains recognition you will see it reviewed in places. Take the negative with the positive, and use the feedback to improve on the product.

❑ **Support.** Software can be a victim of its own success, and you may get a wider audience than you anticipated. More users mean that you have to provide more support, and that can be a huge drain on your time and resources. Factor in support for any commercial product you release.

Considerations for Virtual Distribution

Before you take the plunge into any form of distribution, but Internet distribution in particular, here are a few things for you to consider.

Do not rush what you do. Take your time and look at how other people handle distributing products on the Internet.

Free versus Commercial?

Are you planning to make your software freely available on the Internet for others to download and use or will people have to pay for the software? There are many ways that you can take payment for software, or you can operate a donation system.

Taking payment isn't tricky, and there are a number of sites that can help you. Here are a few:

- ❑ www.paypal.com
- ❑ www.download.com
- ❑ www.handango.com
- ❑ www.tucows.com
- ❑ www.winplanet.com
- ❑ www.shareware.com

Either way, another area you need to think about is licensing of your software. A software license can be simple or complex. With a commercial product you are probably better off and safer if you seek legal advice because laws vary from state to state and country to country. If you are going to release your software freely, then you can protect is using the GNU General Public License.

Copies of the GNU General Public License can be found at www.fsf.org/licenses/gpl.html.

Remember that distributing software for free under the GNU Public License does not mean that you, as the author, lose copyright over the software. You retain copyright and also the ability to later charge for the software. Under the Berne Convention, everything written is automatically copyrighted from whenever it is put in fixed form by the person or company that put it into that form. So, you don't actually have to do anything to claim copyright on what you write, as long as nobody else can claim to own your work.

Registering the copyright in the United States is a very good idea. For more information on how to do this and what it means visit www.copyright.gov. *Fees start from as little as $30 for basic registrations.*

If you are interested in distributing free software along with the source code, then a great place on the Web for this is www.sourceforge.net. Here you can organize the code, applications, bug reports, and reviews.

Full-Time Job versus Hobby

Are you programming and releasing software as a hobby or do you see it as a new full-time job? This depends on how much effort and commitment you want to put into promoting software and, ultimately, selling.

My advice would be to tread carefully, take your time and do a lot of research. Just as it takes time to learn to program, it takes time to learn how to promote and sell products via the Internet. Be careful not to enter a legal minefield, and take each step only after you have done your research and, if you feel the need, have sought legal advice.

Legal advice can be very expensive — bear this in mind before seeking it, especially if you think that the return you will make is low.

Supported versus Unsupported

Most successful products will need some element of support because no matter how good the program and your programming (even if it is flawless) are, some people will have trouble with your work simply because of conflicts with hardware or other software on their system.

On one hand, if the software is free, you can decide not to provide any support — the key phrases in the software licenses are "own risk" and "as is." On the other hand, if the software has a good following, you could set up a forum or venue where other users can support those in trouble. This formula has worked well for many software developers.

If the software is a commercial application or if you decide to offer support for a free application, here are some of the options open to you.

Detailed FAQ

You could decide to make available a list of detailed FAQs (frequently asked questions) that cover problems you can foresee with the application. You can add to this as problems make themselves apparent to you.

A good, comprehensive list of FAQs can be used to augment other support methods and free you from fielding the same questions over and over (although you will never be able to make everyone read the FAQs before asking you for an answer to a question covered!).

E-mail Support

Providing support by e-mail is one method open to you. People e-mail you their questions, and you reply to them.

If you choose this method, make sure that you list the basic information you need from users in their first e-mail (otherwise, you will be forced into exchanging a number of e-mails just to get the basic information).

Some basic information you might need could be:

❑ The product

❑ Product version

❑ Operating system

❑ Other software installed

❑ Hardware (CPU, RAM, and so on)

If you choose to support a product by e-mail, make sure that you have a specific e-mail account set up for support e-mails. The last thing you want is your personal e-mail account filled up with support stuff! By having a separate account, you can choose to deal with the support issues when you want to.

Forum/Web Support

Nowadays, it seems that pretty much everyone has a Web site and a forum — so why not use this method to support your product?

- ❏ Web and forum support has several key advantages over other support methods:

  - ❏ The users with a problem can post their questions at any time, and you can post your replies when you want to.

  - ❏ Your answer to one person might help others with the same problem.

  - ❏ Other users of the forum might help new users who have a problem.

  - ❏ It keeps your support open, makes you seem approachable, and shows that you take problems seriously and deal with problems.

Telephone Support

Be very careful about doing this — telephone support can take up all your time. This is OK for big companies that have enough sales to warrant hiring support staff.

Summary

In this chapter, you've looked at the final stage of many software projects — the distribution of the product or application.

You've looked at both physical and virtual distribution schemes and examined the pros and cons of each in some detail. You've also looked at the cost differences associated with both methods of distribution.

The bottom line is that which one you choose depends on a number of factors, such as what the audience cost is and what scale of the distribution you plan. The answers to questions such as these help shape the right choice for your needs.

You've also looked at the support mechanisms that you might like to offer and examined the costs and pros and cons of each and even whether you might not need to provide any support whatsoever for your projects.

What you choose to do depends of what your plans are—if you've come up with a small app that solves a problem for you, and you want others to benefit from it, then the route you take is going to be very different from that taken by someone who has spent months working on a large-scale project that they hope will make them some money. Choose carefully based on your needs and your plans.

Glossary

This appendix is a glossary of the important programming terms, most of which have been used in the book. Some have not and have been included out of completeness.

Don't try to memorize the glossary by heart or worry that you can remember everything listed here — take your time. The more you program and practice, the better you will get, and you'll find that over time the terms will start to stick.

Feel free to make notes in the margins and to add your own terms to the glossary.

Term	Description
Address	The term for a memory location.
Algorithm	The precise definition of computational steps.
Argument	A value passed to a function.
Array	A contagious sequence of linked elements of the same type.
ASCII	The American Standard Code for Information Interchange is a standard 7-bit code used for character representation.
ASP	Active Server Pages. A server-side Web language developed by Microsoft. It primarily uses VBScript.
Assignment operator	An operator used to assign a value to a variable. These vary from programming language to programming language.
Backdoor	A means of access to a program that bypasses all the security.
Backup	A copy kept of important files in case of loss, accidental over-writing, or corruption, or a copy kept for archival purposes.

Table continued on following page

Term	Description
Beta test	The testing of a program to discover any missed bugs. Beta testing is best carried out by nonprogrammers who aren't familiar with how the program should be used.
Binary	A number system that uses only the digits 1 and 0 (called bits).
Bits	The 0s and 1s that make up the binary number system.
Block comment	A comment block is a block of text defined as comments for humans to read rather than instructions for the computer to process. In C++ and JavaScript, a comment block is defined by beginning it with /* and ending it with */.
Boolean (or Bool)	A built-in Boolean type. It can have the values of true (1) or false (0).
Boot up	The process of starting a PC.
Bug	A common programming term used to describe an error that occurs.
Byte	8 bits.
C	A programming language.
C++	The follow-on to the C language. C++ is a general-purpose programming language that is in widespread use. C++ is considered to be a very powerful and versatile programming language.
Call	A term used to describe the running of one function from another. The function is said to have been "called."
CD-ROM	Compact disc-read-only memory.
CD RW	Compact disc-read/write.
Comment	Text inserted into the source code that isn't for the benefit of the computer but designed as notes for the programmer to read later or for other programmers who might later read the source code. Comments are designed to make the actual code easier to read.
Compiler	A program that coverts source code into machine-readable code.
Concatenate	The joining of two or more test strings together to make one string.
Constant	A literal. It can be though of as a variable that doesn't change.
Curly braces	{ and } that are used extensively in C++, Java, and JavaScript. These are used to define blocks of code within the source code.
Cursor	The pointer on a computer screen.
Database	A database is a collection of information that is organized so that it can easily be accessed, managed, and updated.
Debug	The process of removing bugs from code.

Term	Description
Demo	The name given to a trial of a program or software application. Usually demos are time limited of have reduced functionality.
Donateware	A program that is free to use but for which the author asks for donations if you like the program.
DVD	Digital versatile disc.
End user	The person who use applications developed by the programmer. End users generally have no knowledge of the inner workings of the application. These are the people you need to bear in mind while developing your application.
Equality operator	Equality operators are used to test whether one value is equal to another value. In C++ the == operator is used. If you have two variables (x and y) and both are set to the value 7 then $x == y$ would result be true.
Error	Something unexpected. Indicates either a fault with the code or unexpected input or output.
Escape character	The character \ (also called backslash). This is used as the initial character in representations of characters that cannot be represented by a single ASCII character — for example, newline (\n) and horizontal tab (\t).
Exception	Another term for error.
Executable	A complete program that can be run.
False	A Boolean value. Usually represented by 0. Declaring in code that 1 + 1 = 3 would be an example of a false statement.
Field	A text area that may require some input (such as text or numbers).
File	A sequence of bytes or words that holds information in a computer. Files are usually stored on the hard drive or external drives or storage.
Floppy disk	Removable storage medium in the form of magnetic media housed in a rigid plastic case measuring 3.5 square inches.
Function	A grouped sequence of programming statements.
Gigabyte	1,073,741,824 bytes.
Grammar	The description of the syntax of a language.
Hard drive (hard disk)	Long-term storage in a PC. Data saved to the hard drive will be available after the PC has been switched off then back on again.
Help file	A file that contains information about using an application.

Table continued on following page

Term	Description
Hexadecimal	A base 16 number system. Instead of using 10 digits, it uses 16 (0 to 9 and A, B, C, D, E, and F).
HTML	Hypertext Markup Language. The language used to create Web pages.
Hungarian notation	A coding convention that, among other things, describes how to encode data type information into variable names, making the code easier to follow.
I/O	Input/output.
If statement	A statement that selects between two alternatives based on a condition.
Inequality operator	Inequality operators are used to test whether one value is not equal to another value. In C++ the ! = operator is used. If you have two variables (x and y) and both are set to the value 7 then x != y would be false.
Input	Data entered into an application (usually through the keyboard).
Interpreted code	Code that doesn't need compiling, instead it is translated as required into machine-readable code using an interpreter.
Interpreter	An application that takes source code (generally script code) and converts this into machine-readable code when required. JavaScript is an example of a language that uses an interpreter.
JavaScript	An interpreted programming or script language from Netscape.
Kilobyte	1,024 bytes.
Linux	An operating system based on Unix, usually free.
Liteware	A program that is made available where some of the features are disabled until you pay for the program.
Machine code	Code written entirely in binary (0s and 1s). This is the code that the computer understands.
Markup	A sequence of characters or symbols in a text file that indicates how that file should be displayed and interpreted.
Megabyte	1,048,576 bytes.
Null	Zero, 0, nothing.
Nybble	4 bytes.
Open source	A program with source code that is made available for use or modification as users or other developers see fit. This differs from most commercial applications, where the source code is kept secret.
Operating system	The program that, after being initially loaded into the computer's memory, manages all the other programs on a computer.

Term	Description
Operator	Conventional notation for built-in operation, such as +, , -, *, and /.
Output	Data sent out of an application. This can be to the screen, a file, or a printer.
Parameter	A variable declared in a function representing an argument.
PHP	Hypertext Preprocessor. This is used as an alternative to Microsoft's ASP (Active Server pages) to generate Web pages on the server that are sent to the user's browser for display.
Plain text	Another name for unformatted alphanumeric text.
Platform	Another name for the system that runs an application. Different operating systems and computers are classed as different platforms.
Postcardware	Freeware that requires the user only to send a postcard to the author of the software.
Procedure	Another name for a function. This is a set of programming statements grouped together for running.
Programming	The science (although some would call it art) of writing instructions that a computer can understand.
Pseudocode	A detailed but readable description of what a computer program or particular algorithm does. This is expressed in a formally styled natural language rather than in a programming language.
RAM	Random access memory. The temporary memory of a PC used to hold programs and data while in use. Data here is deleted when the system is shut down.
Runtime	When a program is running.
Script language	An interpreted language. Not compiled.
Setup	The common term used to describe the process of installing software on a computer.
Shareware	A program distributed on the Internet or on discs. Payment is required to use the program, although there may be a trial period available.
Software	A collection of programs.
Source code	The code typed by the programmer. This is usually in plain-text form.
Source file	The file that contains the code. This code will need compiling or interpreting to work.

Table continued on following page

Term	Description
Statement	The basic unit in a function. Statements control the flow of the execution.
Statement delimiter	A character or set of characters used to indicate the end of a statement of code. JavaScript and C++ both use ; (although its use in JavaScript is optional).
String	A sequence of characters.
Switch statement	A statement that selects from a list of alternatives based on the value of an integer.
Syntax	A set of rules that can be compared to spelling and grammar for a spoken/written language that describes how the source code of a program should be written so that it can be run without errors.
Text	A human-readable sequence of characters.
Text editor	A program for viewing, editing, and creating plain-text files. The text in these files is not formatted in any way and is simply a sequence of characters, spaces, and carriage returns.
True	A Boolean value. Usually represented by 1. Declaring in code that 1 + 1 = 2 would be an example of a true statement.
Undefined	A variable that holds no value.
Value	The value of a variable is the data that it holds.
Variable	A named object. It is generally regarded as a named portion of memory used to hold a value.
VBScript	An interpreted language that is loosely based on Visual Basic. It is the language normally used for ASP.
Version	A number (or numbers) associated with code or a program that indicates its age. The later the version number, the newer the code or program.
Visual Basic	A programming language by Microsoft that is similar to BASIC.
Visual C++	Microsoft's implementation of the C++ language.
While statement	A loop statement that continues while a condition is satisfied.
Whitespace	Characters that are represented only by the space they take up on a page or screen. The most common examples are space ( ), newline (\n), and tab (\t).
Widget	A term used to describe a discreet object, an object that doesn't have a name or something that you've forgotten the name of.
Zero	Another term used for null.

Web Resources

The Web has become a huge resource for pretty much everything—the idea of having a library in every home is virtually a reality. However, the problem is that there is no librarian to guide you through it and maintain a certain level of quality in the material made available.

This appendix lists my favorite sites on the Internet that are associated with programming in some way. They are grouped into categories but they are listed within those categories in no particular order.

Enjoy!

Most of the freeware licenses for products listed in this appendix only allow for noncommercial use of the product. Please check the license details carefully and if you are in any doubt as to whether you are using the product legally, consult with the makers or the authors of the software.

Programming Tools

Site	Description
www.ultraedit.com	Shareware This is one of the best text editors available. It offers a whole raft of features that a programmer will find useful, including: Line numbering Support for massive files (over 4 GB!) Multiple undo 100,000-word spell checker Syntax highlighting

Table continued on following page

Site	Description
`www.ultraedit.com` *(continued)*	Comprehensive macro support
	Built-in FTP client
	Project/workspace support
	Hex editor
	Powerful find/replace
	Also available is a new application called UltraCompare. This tool is the ultimate in file compare tools and can work with;
	Text files
	Binary files
	Folders
	UltraCompare also comes equipped with powerful merge and file management capabilities.
`www.textpad.com`	Shareware
	Textpad is a powerful and fully featured text editor. It has support for massive files and offers spell checker.
`www.crimsoneditor.com`	Freeware
	A powerful and professional source editor for Windows. Small and fast but not lacking in features.
	Crimson Editor offers the following features:
	Syntax highlighting for HTML, C++, Java, and so on
	Spell checker
	Multiple undo/redo
	Macro facility
`www.jedit.org`	Freeware
	A powerful text editor that has the advantage of working on multiple operating systems:
	Mac OS X
	OS/2
	Unix
	VMS
	Windows

Site	Description
	Some of the features it offers include:
	Built-in macro language
	Extra features that can be added via downloadable plug-ins
	Syntax highlighting for more than 80 languages
	Support for a huge range of character encodings

Java Tools

Site	Description
www.borland.com/ products/downloads/ download_jbuilder.html	Freeware (JBuilder Foundation)
	A powerful Java IDE/Compiler. Easy to use and quick.
	JBuilder Foundation will run on the following operating systems:
	Windows
	Solaris
	Linux
www.jcreator.com	Freeware (Lite version)
	A Java IDE that is packed with advanced features such as:
	Project templates
	Project management
	Automatic code completion
	Syntax highlighting
	Debugger
	Runs on the following operating systems:
	Windows XP
	Windows 2000
	Windows ME
	Windows 9x

Table continued on following page

Site	Description
www.netbeans.org	Freeware Netbeans is a fast, easy-to-use and fully featured Java development environment, which will run on most operating systems. Can be used to create Java applications, Web services, and mobile applications.
java.sun.com/j2se/	Freeware This is a link to the free Sun Java development kit. As well as offering a powerful development environment, it also provides a fast and easy-to-use compiler. The site also contains a wide array of documentation and code examples. This site is well worth visiting and bookmarking.
www10.software.ibm.com/ developerworks/ opensource/jikes/	Freeware This is a Java compiler made available by IBM. It has support for a wide variety of operating systems: Windows Solaris Sparc Linux OS/2 AIX
hsqldb.sourceforge.net/	Freeware A free open-source SQL database engine created solely in Java.

Java Sites

Site	Description
java.sun.com	The main Web resource for all things Java, by the creators of the language.
www.javaworld.com	Java news, links, code, resources, forums, and lots more!

Site	Description
www.javalobby.org	An online resource for Java users everywhere.
www.blackdown.org/java-linux.html	Resource for Linux users wanting to get into Java.
www.mindview.net/Books/TIJ	*Thinking in Java* A free electronic book all about Java programming.

C++ Tools

Site	Description
upp.sourceforge.net	Freeware Ultimate++ is different from other C++ development environments because it is a Windows/Linux development environment. The idea is that working in an environment that is compliant with bother operating systems reduces development costs. Ultimate++ consists of: Source editor Package management system Debugger Layout designer Image designer Language editor
www.bloodshed.net/devcpp.html	Freeware Fully featured integrated development environment (IDE) for the C/C++ programming language. The IDE features include: Code completion Debugger Syntax highlighting Tool manager Print support

Table continued on following page

Site	Description
`www.bloodshed.net/devcpp.html` *(continued)*	Powerful find and replace Listing of functions
`www.borland.com/products/` `downloads/download_cbuilder.html`	Freeware (compiler only) A basic, but fully featured command-line compiler. No frills, but a fast compiler. Includes free debugging tools.
`www.cs.virginia.edu/~lcc-win32`	Freeware All you need to get started programming with C: Code generator Integrated development environment Comprehensive documentation and user manuals
`sunset.backbone.olemiss.edu/` `~bobcook/eC`	Freeware A C++ compiler with a difference — this one was designed especially for use in high schools and junior colleges.
`www.digitalmars.com`	Freeware C and C++ compiler. Suitable for: Win32 Win16 DOS DOS32 Everything you need to build C++ applications. Lots of source code and documentation included.

C++ Sites

Site	Description
`www.cprogramming.com`	An excellent C++ tutorial site.
`www.glenmccl.com/tutor.htm`	Another superb tutorial.
`devcentral.iticentral.com/` `articles/C++/default.php`	A site packed with tutorials covering advanced.C++ concepts.

Site	Description
`bdn.borland.com/cpp/`	The Borland C++ community.
`www.developerfusion.com/forums/forum-26`	DeveloperFusion C++ forum.
`www.cuj.com`	C/C++ User's Journal Web site.

BASIC Tools

Site	Description
`www.basic4gl.net`	Freeware Free BASIC programming language for the Windows operating system. This is easy-to-learn and easy-to-use and can be used to create games, 3-D demos, and utilities.
`www.maxreason.com/software/xbasic/xbasic.html`	Freeware Advanced BASIC compiler with a powerful graphical interface development tool. This tool was formerly a commercial product but is now freeware. This programming tool creates source code suitable for: Windows Linux Unix
`www.basicguru.com/rapidq/`	Freeware Rapid-Q is a cross-platform BASIC programming language capable of generating GUI and console applications. It directly supports: MySQL DirectX Direct3D Sockets

Table continued on following page

Site	Description
	Some COM
	Component/object programming
	And much more!
www.nicholson.com/rhn/basic/	Freeware
	Small but versatile. Can be used with many old BASIC program with little or no modification.
	Versions available for:
	Windows
	Mac OS
	Linux
	Sun OS
	SGI
www.yabasic.de	Freeware
	YABasic (Yet Another Basic) is a console mode interpretor.
	Small download that runs on Windows operating systems.
www.libertybasic.com	Shareware
	BASIC for Windows and OS/2.
	Can be used to create games, business applications, utilities, and much more.
www.freebyte.com/ programming/compilers/ envelop.html	Freeware
	Simple, yet powerful BASIC programming tool. Quick and easy to use.

BASIC Sites

Site	Description
www.qb4all.com	Everything for those wanting to get started programming in Quick Basic.
www.programmersheaven.com/zone6	Programmer's Heaven BASIC site.
www.codepedia.com/1/ BeginnersGuideToBasic	Beginner's guide to BASIC.

Web Scripting Languages

Site	Description
asp2php.naken.cc	Freeware ASP (Active Server Pages) to PHP (PHP: Hypertext Preprocessor). Quick, easy, and quite reliable.
www.php.net	Powerful, yet easy to learn Web scripting language. This language has become very popular and offers serious competition to Microsoft's ASP.
www.perl.org	Another powerful Web scripting language.
www.zope.org	Zope is an open-source application server for building content management systems, intranets, portals, and custom applications.

CD Burning

Site	Description
www.nero.com	Shareware The premier CD creation tool. Nero offers a wide range of features: Support for a massive range of CD recorders Support for BURNProof recorders (to minimize unreadable discs) Support for a wide range of disc types (ISO, VideoCD, AudioCD, Bootable CD, UDF, and so on) Automatic file backup Virtual CD support (run disc images without needing to burn a CD) Support for printing of covers/labels Nero does it all and is everything that you need from CD recording software.
www.roxio.com	Commercial product Powerful CD-burning tools to create many different kinds of CDs quickly and easily.

Compression Tools

Site	Description
www.winzip.com	Shareware
	Winzip is a powerful and easy-to-use compression tool that uses the popular ZIP compression algorithm.
	Winzip features include:
	Quick zipping/unzipping of files and folders
	Allows you to create self-extracting .exe files for running on systems that don't have Winzip or another unzip tool
	Creates simple setup applications
	Support for large files
	AES encryption to keep your data safe
	Internet file support
	Good integration with Windows
	Split file support (handy when you want to break a file up into portions that can be stored on floppy disk, Zip disk or CD
www.winace.com	Shareware
	Another powerful, fully featured compression tool.
	Winace features include:
	Support for a vast array of compression algorithms: ACE, ZIP, LHA, MS-CAB, JAVA JAR
	Can decrypt the following compressed archives: ACE, ZIP, LHA, MS-CAB, RAR, ARC, ARJ, GZip, TAR, ZOO, JAR
	Multilanguage support (using plug-ins available as a separate download)
	Create powerful setup applications (with plugins)
	Supports CD and floppy disk spanning
	Can create self-extracting archives
	Password protection
	Can repair damaged .zip and ACE files
	Drag-and-drop support
	Quick viewer for common file types
	Archive optimization

Site	Description
www.pkzip.com	Shareware The original compression tool. The site offers a variety of different tools that have different features. Compression Security Antivirus integration Good operating system support: Windows, DOS, VM, VSE, Unix, iSeries, zSeries
www.pb-sys.com	Freeware TaskZip is a handy backup tool for those who do not want to buy a more fully featured tool. TaskZip is packed with features and easy to use.
www.ultimatezip.com	Shareware A cheap, but very functional and competent compression tool. It looks and feels like Windows Explorer, which makes it easy to use. Features include: Support for: ZIP, RAR, ACE, BH, CAB, JAR, LHA (LZH), GZIP, TAR, BZIP2, ARC, ARJ, XXE, UUE formats Supports large .zip files (greater than 4 GB) Supports AES encryption (256-bit encryption) Supports disk spanning and file splitting Backup feature ZIP repair feature
www.7-zip.org	Freeware (donations accepted and license needed for support) 7-Zip is a file archive tool with highest compression ratio. Features include: Very high compression ration using proprietary compression algorithm (called 7z) Self-extracting capability (with 7z algorithm) Fully integrates with the Windows interface

Table continued on following page

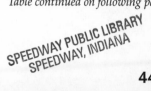

Site	Description
www.stuffit.com	Shareware Powerful compression tool. Began life as a Mac tool but now supports a variety of operating systems. Features include: Creates archives, compressed and encoded files Allows you to browse through content File search facility Built-in FTP and e-mail facility

Miscellaneous Tools

Site	Description
www.freebyte.com/hjinstall	HJ-Install is a freeware installer that runs on: Windows 95 Windows 98 Windows ME Windows NT 4.0 Windows 2000 Windows XP It can be used to create many types of installation programs: Internet-distributed CD-Rom/DVD Single-floppy-disk Multi-floppy-disk Network installations The program can create install directories, copy files into them, create program groups and items, copy whole directory structures, and interact with the end user. HJ-Install is small and adds on 138 KB to the final package, thus saving space and download time.

Site	Description
`www.gregorybraun.com/IconEx.html`	Shareware Icon Extractor is a small utility that loads and displays all the icon resources found in any file and allows you to select icons to be saved as individual ICO files. You can also copy selected icons directly to the Windows Clipboard, from which they can be pasted into documents or other graphics applications for editing.
`www.icongrabber.com-http.com`	Shareware Icon Grabber is a 32-bit utility that is designed to scan the directories and drives on your computer and extract all icons it finds inside of all .exe, .dll, .scr, .ocx, .ico, and .icl files. Icons of everything you see on your desktop or in the Start menu can be located and extracted with Icon Grabber.
`www.mirekw.com/winfreeware/mwsnap.html`	Freeware MWSnap is a small, yet powerful Windows program for capturing images from selected parts of the screen.
`www.progency.com/other.html#screenrip32`	Freeware ScreenRip32 is a freeware screen capture utility that lets you capture areas of the screen with a variety of methods
`www.axialis.com/axcursors/`	Shareware Axialis AX-Cursors 4.5 is a powerful and easy-to-use cursor-editing and -managing program that is ideal for retouching, creating, archiving, and distributing cursors.

Miscellaneous Sites

Site	Description
www.kingsley-hughes.com	Author's Web site. Lots of programming information, hints, tips, and tricks.
msdn.microsoft.com	The Microsoft Developer Network—a huge resource for developers of all kinds. This information used to be only available on subscription but is now available to all on the Internet.
www.w3schools.com	Tutorials for all thing Web-related: HTML XHTML XML CSS JavaScript VBScript SQL ASP PHP And much more. An excellent site that is worth bookmarking and visiting often.
www.dcs.ed.ac.uk/home/mxr/gfx/utils-hi.html	Masses of information on graphics file formats. Site includes: Programming code FAQs Links
http://www.chami.com/tips	Masses of programming tips for a variety of programming languages. An excellent site!
www.webopedia.com/quick_ref/fileextensions.asp	Data formats and file extensions.
condor.stcloudstate.edu/help/faqs/fileformats.html	Massive list of file formats.
www.filext.com	Search engine for file extensions. FileExt will find the type of file a file extension represents and/or the program using that file type.

Index